Writing Motherhood

TAPPING INTO YOUR CREATIVITY AS A MOTHER AND A WRITER

LISA GARRIGUES

Scribner
NEW YORK LONDON TORONTO SYDNEY

SCRIBNER

1230 Avenue of the Americas
New York, NY 10020

For information about special discounts for bulk purchases,
please contact Simon & Schuster Special Sales:
1-800-456-6798 or business@simonandschuster.com.

Designed by Kyoko Watanabe
Text set in Minion

Manufactured in the United States of America

1   3   5   7   9   10   8   6   4   2

Library of Congress Control Number: 2006052935

ISBN-13: 978-0-7432-9737-0
ISBN-10: 0-7432-9737-7

The names and identifying characteristics of some individuals have been changed.

Page 319 constitutes an extension of the copyright page.

To Natalie Goldberg,
who told me to
keep filling notebooks.

And to Deborah Chiel,
who made sure
that I did.

Contents

List of Writing Mother's Helpers   xi
Foreword: Rocks in the River   xiii

INTRODUCTION:
THE BIRTH OF *WRITING MOTHERHOOD*   1

    ↬ My First Writing Mothers   5
    ↬ My Story: How I Came to Teach *Writing
       Motherhood*   9
    ↬ Your Story: What You Will Take from *Writing
       Motherhood*   14

PART ONE:
THE 7 BUILDING BLOCKS OF *WRITING MOTHERHOOD*   19

    ↬ The Mother's Notebook   21
    ↬ The Mother Pages   27
    ↬ The ABC's of *Writing Motherhood*   32
    ↬ A Holistic Writing Schedule   38
    ↬ A Room of Your Own   43
    ↬ The Time Out   50
    ↬ The Playdate   56

PART TWO:
BECOMING A WRITING MOTHER   63

In the Beginning—Taking Your First Steps   65
1. Throw Away the Rules   67
2. A Disclaimer and a Dedication   72
3. Moments of Motherhood: The Extremes,
   Routines, and In-Betweens   78
4. Very (Nearly) Pregnant   86
5. Birth Stories and Other Beginnings   90
6. Baby Names   100
7. First Words and Other Firsts   106
8. Family Album: From Baby Pictures to
   Photo Stories   114
9. The Essential Question: *Why?*   120

In the Middle—Finding Your Balance   133
10. One Day in the Life of a Mother   135
11. Bedtime Stories   143
12. Body Language   149
13. Copycats   156
14. Left Out   160
15. Dump Truck   166
16. Fathers (or Marriage after Motherhood)   169
17. Improvising Motherhood   175
18. Mothering Our Mothers   180

Beyond Motherhood—Holding On and Letting Go   189
19. Portrait of Myself as a Writing Mother   193
20. The Things We Carry   202
21. Push Me, Pull You   211
22. Love Letters   216
23. Closed Doors   223
24. Backflips   228
25. Making Scents of Womanhood   231

26. Good Enough   239
27. Then and Now   244

PART THREE:
WRITING MOTHERHOOD FOR LIFE   249

Coming out of the Notebook   253
 ❧ A Sabbatical: Playing Hooky   255
 ❧ The Game of Dibble: Rereading Your
   Mother's Notebook   258
 ❧ Revision: Re*seeing* Your Mother Pages   262
 ❧ Ways to Share Your Mother Pages:
   Going Public   269

Connections and Collaborations—
Finding Other Writing Mothers   275
 ❧ How to Start and Run a Group of
   Writing Mothers   277
 ❧ Ways to Connect in Cyberspace   289
 ❧ Games Writers Play   295

Afterword: Your Mother's Notebook Will
   Keep You Afloat   303
Appendix I—No End to Writing Starts:
   A List to Keep You Going   305
Appendix II—A Writing Mother's Library:
   Recommended Reading   309
Acknowledgments   315

List of Writing Mother's Helpers

Guidelines for Buying Your First Mother's Notebook   25

13 Reasons to Write Your Mother Pages by Hand   30

5 Characteristics of a Holistic Writing Schedule   41

Writing on the Run: Public Places to Write   47

24 Ways to Spend Your Time Out   54

12 Ways to Spend Your Play Date   60

Like Mother, Like Writer   84

Sometimes You Can't Say It Without Sounding Sappy   96

Unforgettable First Lines   112

Why Writers Write   126

Every Day Is Mother's Day: A History of the Holiday   141

Learn to Listen   147

Let Your Body Talk   154

The Rhythm of Writing   178

How Writers Write about Their Mothers   186

Me, Myself, and I   200

The Weight of Words   209

Writing from Opposite Ends of the Story   214

Unsent Letters   221

Writing with Your Nose: A Collection of Mother Scents   237

Then and Now: Places to Revisit   247

Rereading Your Mother's Notebook: How to Play the
    Game of Dibble   260

8 Reasons to Revise Your Writing   264

New Visions of Revision: From First Draft to Final
    Copy in 10 Easy Steps   265
5 Ways to Respond to Readalouds   273
8 Reasons to Join a Group of Writing Mothers   285
6 Pitfalls of Writing Groups—and How to Avoid Them   286
Sample Mission Statement for a Group of Writing
    Mothers   288

Foreword

ROCKS IN THE RIVER

One New Year's morning, I made a list of all the reasons I could not keep my resolution to write an article for a national education journal:

1. *The deadline for submission was January 15, which left me only thirteen days, provided I was willing to pay $13.65 to send the manuscript overnight by Express Mail.*
2. *I was contracted to teach a new writing course beginning January 9, and I had not yet developed the curriculum.*
3. *I was scheduled to take a three-hour exam for state certification in teaching on January 11, and I had only just begun to study.*
4. *I had registered for an all-day workshop in storytelling at the 92nd Street Y on January 12, and the fee was nonrefundable.*
5. *My husband was out of work, and I feared he would ask me a question every time I sat down to write: Where is the newspaper? Where is the butter? Where are the car keys?*
6. *Even if I did attempt to write at home, my obsolete Power Macintosh would not permit me to save the*

article to a PC-formated disk, which was among
the submission requirements.

7. —

    As I sat poised to pen the next reason I could not write the article, I remembered a story I had read in Georgia Heard's memoir, *Writing Toward Home,* about a rafting trip her friend had taken one July down the Rio Grande in Taos, New Mexico. The water was low, but the guide instructed the group not to try to avoid the many rocks in the river. Much to their surprise, every time the raft bumped into a rock, it gently bounced off it, glided backward, then drifted on downstream with the current. Heard has since applied the rafting lesson to writing: "The obstacles I face—lack of time, too many projects at once—as well as the obstacles all writers face—rejection, criticism, doubts and insecurities, unfinished poems and stories—are impossible to avoid and can be valuable teachers. I can gather strength from them. They are inevitable parts of a writer's life." The poet went so far as to mount the slogan like a bumper sticker on her writing chair: *Don't try to avoid the rocks.*

    I suddenly recognized my reasons as rocks in a river, so I crumpled up the list, borrowed a laptop, and arranged to spend my days writing in my parents' home since they were in Florida for the winter. On the morning of January 2, with my children back in school, I packed a bag lunch, a thermos of Peet's Holiday Blend coffee, and a crate of reference books and drove forty minutes north on the Palisades Parkway to Exit 12. The driveway was impassable from unplowed snow that had crusted over after an all-night, freezing rain. It was cold in the house, even after I thumbed the old thermostat to seventy-eight degrees. By ten o'clock, I was typing with gloves on my hands, an alpaca throw over my shoulders, and my father's extralarge L.L. Bean long-underwear bottoms on top of my jeans. I decided to check the furnace. The light switch to the basement did not work, so I toed my way down in the dark, groping for the string that dangled from the bare bulb above the hot-water heater at the bottom of the stairs. I never found it; my foot hit water three steps above the concrete floor. I spent the remainder of the day conferring with plumbers, huddling in front of the oven, and taking frigid stabs at the keypad in spite of the deafening drone of the water pump and the squeaky march of rubber boots up and down the stairs.

Eleven days later, I submitted my manuscript, and six months after that it was published in *English Journal*, the nation's premier magazine for English educators. The following year, my article was selected winner of a prestigious writing award. To this day, I cannot help but think that of the thousands of people who have read the article, not one knows the story of how it came to be written—or nearly *not* written. Nor does anyone know the lesson I learned in writing it. If you let the obstacles in your life—dishes, diapers, dirty laundry, just plain doubt—mount one on top of the other, you will create a hurdle so high that you will never be able to clear it. If instead you learn to maneuver around the obstacles, bumping into some, bouncing off others, like a raft navigating a river, sooner or later you will get where you want to go. In the process, you will become more agile, more resilient, more resolute.

When I sat down to begin work on *Writing Motherhood,* my brother was battling terminal cancer, my mother was orbiting Alzheimer's, my sister was calling hospice and home care, my husband was starting a new business, my children were entering adolescence, and my country was at war. None of it stopped me. I was approaching another stretch of the river. Perhaps the rocks were bigger, the white water rougher, but I knew that if I kept on course, I would eventually reach my destination.

Introduction

THE BIRTH OF *WRITING MOTHERHOOD*

The day I left the maternity ward at New York Hospital and came home to my apartment on Eighty-fifth Street and West End Avenue, I drew down the blinds, crawled into bed, and hid under the covers with my newborn baby. We stayed there for two weeks. The overhead light was too bright, the street noise too loud, and the kitchen smells from neighboring apartments too strong. Shadowy figures came and went, walking on tiptoe, talking in whispers, as I sat propped up on pillows, my newborn at my breast, a La Leche coach at my side. I could not breast-feed my baby, much less change a diaper the size of a cocktail napkin or clip fingernails that curled under like cellophane. The last time I had felt so disoriented and alienated was the day I turned twenty-one and landed in New Delhi, India. The doctors called my condition postpartum depression. I knew better. I was in culture shock.

No matter how prepared we think we are—how well informed or widely read—becoming a mother is like landing in a foreign country. Only after we disembark do we discover that motherhood is a geographical place with its own language, customs, rituals, and taboos. The terrain is dizzyingly rugged in some places, deadeningly monotonous in others. The weather is unpredictable year-round. No sooner do you adjust to one climate than the temperature changes: Your angelic baby hits the terrible twos. Your talkative preteen turns into a mute or a monster. Like me, lots of mothers—especially new mothers who have recently traded in briefcases for bottles, high heels for house slippers, and pagers for nursery monitors—typically experience feelings of isolation, loneliness, and exile. Most of us acclimatize with time, but then we realize with a gulp that there is no going back. We are lifelong citizens of this other country.

Even before I became a professional writer, I had always turned to writing for help in navigating my life. As a teenager, I kept diaries with yin-yangs and peace signs on the covers. Late at night, burrowed under the blankets, I wrote about my crush on a boy who never so much as looked at me from behind his blue eyes, blond curls, and bubble-gum cheeks that ballooned when he played the tuba. Around the time I left home for college, I stopped keeping diaries and began writing journals. Bored with the self-pitying stuff of adolescence, I filled my journals with reflections on books I read, foods I ate, people I met. After college, when I landed a job as an editorial assistant in midtown Manhattan, I stopped writing for myself altogether. During all the years I spewed out manuals, newsletters, and magazines for corporations, museums, and universities, I never wrote one page for or about me.

Then I became a mother.

I don't know what prompted me (it might have been desperation), but soon after my first child was born I began my first writer's notebook, which sounded more grown-up to me than the diaries and journals I had kept in my teens and early twenties. In the beginning, I wrote in fits and starts, with weeks, sometimes months, between entries. But in time, I managed to make writing a daily practice, and I practiced writing the only way I knew how—the same way I had practiced cello as a teenager, by starting with whole bows on open strings. No matter how hard I tried to do "real" writing, however, my life as a mother bled onto the pages of my writer's notebook. Interspersed among exercises on dialogue and scene and setting appeared recommendations for child care, tips for gaining admission to preschool, notes from teacher conferences, a recipe for dinosaur nuggets, sketches of Halloween costumes, bits of backseat conversation overheard on the way to baseball practice. Soon I found myself writing in my notebook in doctors' offices, at bus stops, on hayrides, in toy stores, on the swing set, in the bleachers. Without my willing it, my writer's notebook became a Mother's Notebook, a receptacle for all the notes and stories, all the scrap paper and scraps of my frenzied days as a mother who writes and a writer who mothers. For nearly eighteen years, my Mother's Notebook has been my passport to motherhood, and my pen the needle on the compass that points my way.

From before my children started preschool until now as they look ahead to college, I have written almost every day because, at every step along the way, there is so much to sort through and so much to say. In the pages of my Mother's Notebook, I have written about the moments I will never forget and the moments I would otherwise never remember. I have written about having too little time and too much to do. I have written about pockets and closets and toy chests, and about all the things I have saved or lost. I have written about names and nicknames, busyness and boredom, grief and gratitude and guilt. I have written about planning ahead, and about improvising along the way. I have written about holding on and letting go. I have written about my children's missteps and my own mistakes, and about forgiveness. I have written about mothering *my* mother, and about longing for the woman she once was. I have written about seeing myself in a magnifying mirror because motherhood exposes every blemish and scar. I have written about the softening of my body, especially my heart, and the sharpening of my vision, because once I became a mother, I saw things I didn't see before. Scribbled in black on white, the pages of my Mother's Notebook illuminate what it means to be a mother in all its colors and complexities and contradictions. And as I keep on writing, I hear the echoes of mothers everywhere—across the canyons of race and place and time—singing the universal song of motherhood.

INSPIRATIONS

How could I have spent so much time thinking about the birth process, and so little envisioning what might lie beyond it? Perhaps, deep down, I realized that there was no preparing for the experience of motherhood itself, or for the irrevocable transformation that would occur as my son was delivered out of my body and into my arms. (KATRINA KENISON)

I had crossed over to a strange new world, a world where another person's life literally depended on me . . . and this sense of being in a strange land was all the more jarring since, of course, I hadn't left home. (ANDREA BUCHANAN)

Writing can be a crucial skill, like cartography. Everybody lives in the middle of a landscape. Writing can provide a map. (PHYLLIS THEROUX)

My First Writing Mothers

The first time I taught *Writing Motherhood*, in the fall of 2000, I thought the course would draw from a homogenous cross section of suburbia—mostly young, stay-at-home mothers of babies and toddlers. I was wrong. My first Writing Mothers ranged in age from twenty-five to fifty-five, with children from four months to twenty-seven years old. Some mothers had as many as four or five children; a few had one child; one mother was pregnant. There were biological mothers, adoptive mothers, stepmothers, even a grandmother. Two women had been remarried, one was on the brink of divorce, another was single. Most of the women no longer worked outside the home, but several worked part-time. They included a waitress, a rabbi, a certified public accountant, a graphic designer, a hairstylist, a midwife, a physical therapist, a painter, two teachers, an attorney, and a geriatric social worker. In short, these twelve women represented *every* mother.

The writing experience of my first Writing Mothers was as varied as their professions. Lynn contributed a monthly food column to a parenting newsletter. Nancy prepared weekly sermons for the synagogue. Inge wrote poetry for special occasions. Denise had tried her hand at children's stories. Rebecca wrote letters to friends. Susan kept a journal. Elaine kept her dream of being a novelist hidden in the desk drawer among the yellowing pages of a completed manuscript. Cindy had not written since she was an English major in college. Robin had never gone to college, discouraged by her experience as a struggling student in high school.

So what brought together these twelve women from such disparate backgrounds? On the first day of class, I asked students to share their expectations for the course—what they hoped to gain from *Writing Motherhood*. Here's what they said:

EXPECTATIONS

- to know where to start—I'm overwhelmed by it all!
- to get organized—I have piles of notebooks and letters and journals.
- to become less afraid of writing.
- to reconnect with my premotherhood self.
- to tap back into my creative side.
- to find myself—I miss *me*!
- to reengage my brain.
- to resurrect a sense of *self* during this selfless time.
- to remember my children's childhood—photos and videos don't capture the essence.
- to bring more wisdom to parenting.
- to feel better about myself as a mother.
- to connect with other mothers.

I then asked students to express their fears—the demons that had almost prevented them from signing up for the course. We shared these aloud, too:

FEARS

- I'm a lousy writer.
- I'm too rusty.
- I will have nothing to put down on paper.
- what I write will be trite or sentimental.
- being stuck.

- discovering I don't have the time—or the talent—to do this.
- being too tired to pick up a pen.
- I can't be a mommy and a woman with my own interests.
- my son will hate the child care and will scream until I come to get him.
- I will unearth deep, humbling secrets about myself.
- I'm emotional—I cry easily when exploring or sharing something personal.
- being judged.

What became apparent is that this seemingly dissimilar group of women shared many of the same expectations and fears of writing about motherhood. They wanted to write, but they doubted that they had anything meaningful to say. They wanted to capture their experience of motherhood on paper, but they didn't know how to begin or how to keep going. They wanted to find an avenue for personal growth, but they feared what they might discover along the way. They wanted to set aside sacred time for themselves, but they didn't know if they could juggle writing and parenting. They wanted to join a community of mothers, but they were afraid of being judged by their peers. Whatever their differences, these twelve women came to class with two commonalities: they were mothers, and they wanted to write about motherhood. And by coming to class, they had taken the first step toward overcoming the fears that had long kept them silent and alone.

My first Writing Mothers arrived feeling physically exhausted and emotionally spent—in some cases "brain-dead," their imagination and creativity anesthetized by the rigors and routines of daily life. In just eight weeks of writing, they discovered that motherhood need not be an impediment to creativity. On the contrary, it can be a limitless source for story—a mother lode, if you will. As my students began to fill the pages of their Mother's Notebook, I helped them mine their days for material to write about. Turning dross into gold, they found their stories in a glass of

spilled milk, a bout of the stomach flu, a bad report card. Motherhood, they discovered, can be a woman's most inspiring muse.

Long after the course had ended, my first Writing Mothers
continued to meet in one another's homes once a month. I sometimes joined the group—for birthday celebrations, for naming
ceremonies, or simply to witness the magic that happens when
women come together to share their stories. Year after year, these
mothers supported one another through miscarriages and births,
illnesses and deaths, job changes and geographical moves, divorces
and remarriages. Through it all, they wrote about potty training
and homework hassles, thumb sucking and nail biting, sleepless-
ness and sexlessness, raging fevers and rage, holiday concerts and
playground fights, the first day of kindergarten and the last day
of high school. To this day, these mothers hold on to their pens
the way rodeo riders hang on to their reins; no matter how rough
the ride, they land on their feet.

INSPIRATIONS

Writing Motherhood *has given me the confidence to pursue
something for myself, even now as a mother with a full plate.*

*I write things in my Mother's Notebook I didn't even know I
was feeling!*

*I've found that I actually have thoughts, no matter how
trivial, that are worth writing about. I've also found that my
thoughts flow more freely than I ever dreamed possible.*

Writing Motherhood *has made me realize that my writing
is really OK. It has pushed me to continue writing.*

(IN THE WORDS OF WRITING MOTHERS)

My Story:
How I Came to Teach
Writing Motherhood

I remember the exact moment I decided to teach writing. *Date:* August 9, 2000. *Time:* 4:15 p.m. mountain time. *Location:* Naiset Meadow, Mount Assiniboine Provincial Park, British Columbia, Canada. *Longitude:* 50° N. *Elevation:* 7,400 feet. It was toward the end of a strenuous day's hike that straddled the Continental Divide at Wonder Pass and dropped steeply down to Mount Assiniboine Lodge, a backcountry inn built in 1928 by the Canadian Pacific Railway and accessible today only by helicopter, on horseback, or on foot. Walking along the desolate, windswept pass, out of breath and in a cold sweat, I asked myself the same question I had asked as a teenager every time I walked onto the stage with my cello: *Who talked me into this?*

The last of the stragglers in my hiking party were nearly out of sight, so I scurried down a five-hundred-foot vertical drop in clumsy jumps, digging my heels into the loose scree to punctuate my fall. The trail leveled out at the tree line, where I paused in a stand of lodgepole pines to shake the gravel and dust from my boots and pockets. Through the needled shade, I beheld Naiset Meadow, a profusion of colors and textures backlit by the late-day sun. Beyond the meadow rose the craggy promontory of Mount Assiniboine, its shoulders cloaked in blue-green glaciers that sat in troughs like dirty Styrofoam or old freezer ice. No longer wanting to hurry after the others, I meandered through the meadow, fingering the midsummer wildflowers. Intoxicated, I felt like Dorothy in the poppy fields, except that she fell asleep whereas I woke up.

Early that morning, I had finished reading *Writing Down the Bones* by Natalie Goldberg, who had dedicated the book to her "students past, present, and future." Fourteen years after the best seller was first published, I felt as if the author were speaking directly to me. In the book, Goldberg listed a number of tricks to motivate oneself to write. Some were obvious: *Go to your writing desk first thing in the morning.* Some seemed childish: *Promise yourself a cookie once you've written for the allotted time.* One surprised me: *Teach a writing class.* Goldberg herself had not been writing for long before she began to teach writing. She had followed the advice of Baba Hari Dass, an Indian yogi, who said, "Teach in order to learn."

This idea was a revelation to me. I grew up forty miles northwest of New York City in a cooperative community called Skyview Acres. Founded in the 1940s by a group of pacifists seeking a harmonious environment in which to raise their fledgling families, Skyview strived to be democratic and inclusive, yet the community fostered a kind of intellectual elitism. Success in Skyview was measured not in dollars or material possessions but rather in academic credentials and artistic achievements. The more letters after your name, the wider a swath you cut in the community.

Like other first-generation Skyviewers, I have spent much of my adult life hanging degrees on the wall the way my son collects sports trophies on his shelf. And like his trophies, my degrees gather dust. Long after I have earned them, I persist in seeing myself as the novice. Goldberg's suggestion that I could teach writing before acquiring what I believed were the requisite credentials was not only radical, it was liberating. Besides, at seven thousand feet, inspired by big beauty, big ideas, and big aspirations, I felt sure that any height was within reach. There among the wildflowers in Naiset Meadow—with months and years to go before I would earn certification as a teacher and recognition as a writer—I decided it was time to teach writing.

The day I came home to New Jersey, before I could change my mind, I met with the director of the Ridgewood Library, Nancy Greene, and offered to lead a weekly writing workshop. What better place to write, I argued, than at a round oak table with books at your back, eager writers at your elbows, and the musty smell of bound paper under your nose! Nancy agreed. In the two-mile ride home from the library, however, I sank beneath the steering wheel. *Me, teach? Maybe I could call in sick. Maybe I could move. Maybe . . .*

The telephone was ringing as I jiggled the key in my kitchen door. Grabbing the handset, I was certain that Nancy, too, was having second thoughts. But the voice was not Nancy's.

"May I speak to Lisa Garrigues?" a woman said.

"Speaking," I said.

"My name is Dee Waddington. I'm the director of Women's Studies at the YWCA of Bergen County. I just got off the phone with Nancy Greene. She suggested I call you."

I waited.

"I'm looking for someone to teach a writing class on short notice," Dee went on.

My first impulse was to hang up. Instead, I managed to ask, in a voice thin and breakable like porcelain, "When do you need her?"

"Tomorrow," she said.

I arrived at the Y the next day feeling like an impostor—like a child playing grown-up or, worse, a substitute standing in for the real teacher. Other than telling me that the students were mothers who wanted to write, Dee had offered no more direction on how to teach the class than did my great-aunt Lena divulge her recipe for chicken soup: A pinch of this and a pinch of that was all she said. Bleary-eyed from lack of sleep, I could barely read the eight-page lesson plan I had stayed up all night preparing. But through the fog I noticed that my students were as nervous as I was. They felt as unqualified to be writers as I felt to be their writing teacher. I relaxed.

In the weeks ahead, I invented exercises that became a part of our shared experience, and I coined words that became a part of our common vocabulary. I discovered that teaching is not a performance so much as it is an improvisation: you make things up as you go. Since that first class of *Writing Motherhood,* I have grown into the role of teacher the way a child grows into a pair of shoes purchased a half size too big. In other words, I became a teacher by teaching just as one becomes a writer by writing and a mother by mothering. There is no other way. Descartes would not be offended, I hope, if we were to rephrase his famous line: *I do, therefore I am.*

This book is, in part, a story of growing up and into a role I claimed for myself. But it is also a story of taking a first step—any step, no matter how small. The world-famous mythologist Joseph Campbell believed that if you follow your heart, doors will open where before there were none. When high in the Canadian Rockies I decided it was time for me to begin teaching writing, I could not have guessed which doors would open. I could not have predicted that the director of the YWCA, frantic for a writing teacher, would have telephoned the director of the Ridgewood Library the moment I had left her office. Was that coincidence? Carl Jung would call it *synchronicity.* A priest might call it *fate;* a romantic, *serendipity;* a skeptic, *luck.* However you choose to explain this phenomenon, know that one step always leads to the next. This is how mountains are scaled, deserts are crossed, and whole journeys are made.

INSPIRATIONS

> *The grace to be a beginner is always the best prayer for an artist. The beginner's humility and openness lead to*

exploration. Exploration leads to accomplishment. All of it begins at the beginning, with the first small and scary step. (JULIA CAMERON)

Whatever we learn to do, we learn by actually doing it. People come to be builders, for instance, by building, and harp players by playing the harp. In the same way, by doing just acts, we come to be just. By doing self-controlled acts, we come to be self-controlled, and by doing brave acts, we come to be brave. (ARISTOTLE)

Your Story:
What You Will Take from
Writing Motherhood

Congratulations! You just took your first step. You opened this book. Now your journey begins.

The metaphor is a good one, for if you think of *Writing Motherhood* as a journey, you will know how to use this book, the same way you would use a Fodor's guide to Italy—for information, inspiration, and direction. Just as a travel guide offers tips for packing, sightseeing, lodging, and dining from coast to coast, so *Writing Motherhood* charts your voyage through the Mother's Notebook from cover to cover. Pocket it, palm it, highlight passages, dog-ear pages, stash it in your car, carry it in your purse—don't just read the book; *use* it. If you make *Writing Motherhood* yours, it will take you places you have never dreamed of going.

Before you start out, you may want to skim the book to get the lay of the land. Part One introduces the 7 Building Blocks of *Writing Motherhood.* Here you will discover how to start and fill your first Mother's Notebook—two Mother Pages at a time. You will also learn how to use the ABC's of *Writing Motherhood,* how to find the time and space to write, and how to incorporate two nonwriting activities: the Time Out and the Playdate.

You will then embark on a three-stage journey through *Writing Motherhood,* as mapped out in Part Two of the book:

- "In the Beginning—Taking Your First Steps" explores some of the issues that surface when we first become mothers and writers.
- "In the Middle—Finding Your Balance" traces the shadowy line we straddle in middle age, when we find ourselves wedged between growing children and aging parents.
- "Beyond Motherhood—Holding On and Letting Go" examines the fears, questions, and possibilities that arise when we begin to redefine ourselves independently of our children.

Part Two follows the chronology of raising our children from birth to adulthood, but motherhood does not follow a straight path. As mothers, we spiral back year after year to the same issues and emotions viewed from a different perspective. So whether your children are newborn or full grown, whether you are raising toddlers at twenty or at fifty, whether your parents are agile or aged, you will find inspiration and relevance throughout the book.

Every chapter of *Writing Motherhood* begins with a story from my life or my classroom, and each ends with an invitation to explore the subject in your Mother's Notebook. (Notice how the word *invitation* is so much more enticing than the words *homework* or *assignment* or even *exercise*.) Daily Invitations range from drafting a help-wanted ad to writing a letter you don't intend to send, from charting extreme moments of motherhood to creating a scent box, from telling a birth story to writing a photo story. Many of the chapters include sidebars, or Writing Mother's Helpers, offering tips to help you hone your writing skills. I have also included a number of sample Mother Pages by my students to serve as models for your own writing. Some of the samples have been reprinted raw out of the notebook; a few have been revised following the 10 Easy Steps of revision in Part Three. Finally, you will find throughout the book inspirational quotes by well-known writers and mothers, my way of inviting you to join a literary dialogue that spans historical time periods and geographical borders, gender and genre.

Give yourself plenty of time to proceed through each chapter. If you read one chapter on Monday, say, then take the rest of the week to complete the writing Invitations. As you read, I will remind you again and again to put down the book and pick up a pen. Although *Writing Motherhood* is your guide, writing is the vehicle that will take you where you want to go.

You may be wondering how you will find the time to write when some days you can barely manage to take a shower or walk the dog. Each chapter of *Writing Motherhood* can be read in as few as five minutes, and the daily Invitations can be completed in fifteen. Even so, some days you will succeed in writing nothing more than a grocery list. That's okay. As mothers well know, there will always be phone calls and fevers and lost lunches, so just do the best that you can. Make *Writing Motherhood* a guilt-free zone.

Because I hope you will continue writing long after you finish the book, I conclude *Writing Motherhood* with suggestions for coming out of the notebook and connecting with other Writing Mothers. In Part Three, you will discover lots of ways to share your Mother Pages, both in person and online. To start, you may choose to journey solo, but in time I encourage you to invite other Writing Mothers to be your traveling companions.

As you set out on your journey, let me be your guide. More than a teacher, I see myself as a writer and a mother on my own voyage. Periodically, I welcome passengers on board. Sometimes they paddle or help steer; other times they sit back and let me point out the sights. Then, around the next bend, they disembark and continue on their own way. I invite you now to climb on board and travel with me through the first stretch of *Writing Motherhood*.

INSPIRATIONS

Motherhood is a roughed-out roadway with the tours and detours each and every family takes in order to survive. The roadway is littered with missing school shoes and forgotten school assignments; . . . with broken swing sets, fenderless bikes, and a thousand Matchbox cars; damp hair and sticky fingers; with tears and hugs and kisses; and many broken hearts. That is why every mother needs to feel free to navigate that roadway on her own terms. (EILEEN McCAFFERTY)

Writing is not easy. It is a journey over rugged terrain of saguaro and prickly pear and then, with any luck, into valleys of still water and lush green. (GEORGIA HEARD)

The scariest moment is always just before you start. After that, things can only get better. (STEPHEN KING)

PART ONE

The 7 Building Blocks of *Writing Motherhood*

Just as your child builds a tower with wooden blocks of different sizes and shapes, so you will need an assortment of "building blocks" to reconstruct— and deconstruct—moments of motherhood on paper. There are 7 Building Blocks of *Writing Motherhood*. The biggest, the one on which all the other blocks are stacked, is the Mother's Notebook. Next come the Mother Pages and the ABC's, the scaffolding you will need in order to write day in and day out. The Holistic Writing Schedule and a Room of Your Own will help you carve out the time and the space to write. Finally come two nonwriting Building Blocks: the Time Out and the Playdate. These are not embellishments; they are essential supports to you as a Writing Mother.

As you begin using the 7 Building Blocks of *Writing Mother-hood*, think of your child at play. Building with blocks is both educational and entertaining, both art and architecture. It takes ingenuity and faith, planning ahead and plunging forward. It can be fun or frustrating. Some towers become skyscrapers; others topple down. Whatever happens, you will always have a set of blocks with which to begin building again. So let's roll up our sleeves, get down on our knees, and pull out your crate of Building Blocks.

Building Block #1
The Mother's Notebook

Everyone tells you how quickly your children will grow up. You nod indulgently, thinking you know better, until one morning you awake to discover that your infant is out of diapers, your toddler is in middle school, and your firstborn is shaving. In the race against time, you scramble to document your children's lives—in scrapbooks, in photo albums, on video. But as you flip through the highlights of birthday parties, baseball games, and ballet recitals, you can't help but feel that something is missing: *your* experience, *your* story, *your* voice.

The Mother's Notebook is the foundation of *Writing Motherhood*. In some ways, it is a tool to document our children's lives. In its pages, we can record our children's first words, favorite games, best friends, fractured bones, what they want to be when they grow up. We can preserve (in prose if not with paste) birth announcements, party invitations, ticket stubs, favorite recipes, report cards. We can capture scraps of conversation, misspoken words, quirky mannerisms. More important than telling our children's stories, however, the Mother's Notebook allows us to tell our own stories. But it is much more than a *product*—a document that records our experiences as mothers. It is also a *process*—a means of understanding who we are as mothers. Barbara Kingsolver once wrote, "I can hardly count the ways that being a mother has broadened my writing. . . . As difficult as it is, sometimes, to find a way to be a writer while taking care of children, I think it would be harder to be a writer who has never known what it means to care for a child." You, too, will discover that *Writing Motherhood* works both ways: Just as mothering gives us material for writing, so writing gives us tools for mothering.

Think of your Mother's Notebook as an open space for contemplation, reflection, and meandering. Sure, your Mother's Notebook will become your most sacred place for writing. But sacred does not mean spotless. Let it be messy. Don't fret if the pages get splattered with coffee or baby formula or finger paint. Let it be experimental. Push yourself to try those writing Invitations you especially resist. Let it be colorful. Feel free to paste in scribbled Post-its, newspaper clippings, e-mails—bits and pieces of your days that might otherwise end up in the trash. Let it be collaborative. Copy down conversations, quotes, endearing expressions that would undoubtedly evaporate with the years. And let it be practical. Use the pages to plan parties, weigh decisions, reconcile disappointments, vent anger, ask questions, rehearse answers. Your children's voices will echo across the pages of your Mother's Notebook, but always remember that this space is not so much about *them* as it is about *you*. The Mother's Notebook, finally, is where we can write down *our* experience in *our* voice—where we can write in between the lines of experience, where there are shadows and silences and white spaces.

Students often ask me to explain the difference between writing in a Mother's Notebook and writing in a journal or diary. The two have many similarities, of course. Both encourage self-exploration and self-expression, and both bring about self-discovery and healing, sometimes catharsis. But there are important differences, too. Journal writing begins and ends with the self, so we rarely go beyond recording our innermost thoughts and feelings in the pages of a journal or diary. For most journal writers, the goal is to feel better. On the other hand, while the Mother's Notebook may begin with the self, it eventually leads us out into the world.

Since we are writing each day in response to a preassigned topic—
what I call a *writing start*—the writing is both more focused and
more directed. In the pages of our notebook, we find our voice
and tell our stories at the same time that we hone our craft. The
goal is to make our way as writers and mothers. I like to think
of the Mother's Notebook as the first cousin to the writer's
notebook—this is where we take ourselves and our writing seriously. So even if your Mother Pages occasionally digress into
myopic self-absorption, as they probably will, don't confuse your
Mother's Notebook with its poor relative, the diary. And always
remember that you are not journaling. You are writing.

The following Writing Mother's Helper will guide you in
choosing your first Mother's Notebook. Over the years, my students have used marble composition notebooks, single-subject
school spirals, three-ring binders, field journals, artist's sketch-
books, teenage diaries, travel logs, museum daybooks. Some are
decorated with polka dots or impressionist paintings on the covers; others offer poetic inspirations inside. I cannot seem to part
with the Spartan simplicity of the notebook of my choice: black-
covered, hard-backed, spiral-bound, wide-ruled, measuring seven
by ten inches—small enough to fit in my purse but large enough
to hold one moment of motherhood on each page. Whatever you
choose, get in the habit of carrying your notebook around with
you. You never know when or where you will be able to snatch fifteen minutes to write—in your car, at the Laundromat, before bed.

The purchase of your first Mother's Notebook is significant:
It represents the beginning of something new, an increased commitment to writing and a willingness to step out into the
unknown. It deserves your time and attention. But don't take so
long to select your notebook that you never get down to writing.
The act of writing is far more important than the ritual of finding the perfect notebook. Besides, before you know it, you'll be
out looking for a second notebook, and then a third.

INSPIRATIONS

My best teacher of writing was my journal. . . . In hard-backed composition notebooks I gave unfettered rein to my thinking. Journal writing became woven into the ritual of my day. I often wrote after school when my toddler daughter napped. Sometimes I wrote late at night when she was abed and my wife had not yet returned from the afternoon shift at the hospital. Sometimes I wrote in the morning, a cup of coffee within easy reach. (TOM ROMANO)

A writer's notebook is the receptacle for ideas and trying out words and images. A place for making notes to yourself. (JUDY REEVES)

My notebook is a constant weight in my already-too-heavy black bag as I try to find a few minutes to write over scrambled eggs and coffee at a Queens diner or in the cramped seat of a plane heading to Arizona. Its presence always reminds me I'm a writer, and it helps me live a considered life that doesn't spin by focused only on groceries, dinner, and car repairs. A notebook is a fertilizer for my writing, not just a record of daily events. It's a place to dream, to explore, to play. It's a companion. (GEORGIA HEARD)

WRITING MOTHER'S HELPER

Guidelines for Buying Your First Mother's Notebook

Make a ritual of buying your first Mother's Notebook. Set aside a morning or afternoon to visit your favorite stationery, book, or art supply store. Large retailers offer a wide assortment of notebooks to choose from, but smaller stores sometimes carry imported, handmade, or other specialty items you won't find elsewhere. In choosing a notebook, consider the following:

Size. William Carlos Williams wrote some of his most famous poems on a small pad for prescriptions (he was a medical doctor by trade), but you will most likely want more space on which to write your Mother Pages. Lots of factors will determine the optimal size for you: your penmanship, aesthetic sensibility, writing habits as well as the dimensions of your purse or bag. Writer's notebooks range from four by six to nine by twelve inches, with thicknesses varying according to the number of pages. Experiment until you find the size that suits you best.

Weight. Taken together, a notebook's size, backing, binding, and pages all add up to its weight. As mothers, we already shoulder more weight than is comfortable for most of us, so beware of notebooks that are too heavy. You don't want to have to leave yours at home.

Backing. Notebook covers, like book jackets, can be juvenile or sophisticated, whimsical or scholarly, colorful or plain. Manufacturers back notebooks in a variety of materials: leather, cardboard, plastic, even denim or cloth. Aside from aesthetics, be sure to consider the sturdiness of the backing. Softcovers, though sometimes lighter, can be flimsy, whereas hardcovers are usually stable enough to let you write on your lap.

Binding. Bound books are beautiful, but they can be unwieldy and weighty, not just in pounds but also in expectations. When we write in a bound book, especially one with a leather cover and gold edges, we feel the pressure to write well. Spirals, on the other hand, are familiar and friendly. Because they open back onto themselves, you can comfortably write in tight spaces. Also, you can hook a pen inside the coil so that you are never without a writing implement. Just resist the temptation to rip out pages you don't like.

Pages. Look for a notebook with eighty to one hundred pages. Any longer and you won't have the satisfaction of reaching the last page in a reasonable length of time. You will have a choice of blank pages or lined, college-ruled, or wide-spaced; if the lines are too narrowly spaced, your hand may cramp, so feel free to skip every other line. Consider also the weight of the paper. If the pages are too thin, your pen will bleed through, making it impossible to write on both sides of the page.

Building Block #2
The Mother Pages

If the Mother's Notebook is the foundation of *Writing Mother-hood,* then the Mother Pages are the walls that hold you up. They give you structure and security and a sense of safety. They are the blueprints of your life as a Writing Mother. In the movie *Center Stage,* a seasoned ballet mistress turns to a disaffected student, places her hand on the ballet barre, and says, "The smart dancers know where to look when things get rough: *here.* No matter what happened in class, in performance, last week, five minutes ago, if you can come back here, you'll be home." Remember that. Whatever arises in your life as a Writing Mother, you can always come home to the Mother Pages.

The Mother Pages constitute your daily writing. Begin with two pages, enough to write down one moment of motherhood. More important than how much or how long you write is how regularly you write. Don't worry about how well you write, either. For now, just commit to putting pen to paper, two pages every day. Some days you may write more; other days you will not write at all. Over time, your Mother Pages will add up.

You will need just fifteen minutes to write your Mother Pages. Try timing yourself. If your notebook is oversize, you may need to write only a page and a half; if your notebook is pocket-size, you will need to write more. It doesn't really matter whether you give yourself a page requirement or a time limit, just as it doesn't matter whether a runner sets out to jog for three miles or thirty minutes. Writers, like runners, find both effective. In my experience, writing to a time limit prompts me to speedwrite, helping me outrun my inner critic, while writing to a page count encourages me to freewrite, letting me fall into the rhythm of my breath as I find my own pace. You decide what works for you. But whether you write for two pages or fifteen minutes, once you begin, try not to stop until you reach the finish line.

When you first open your Mother's Notebook, you may be snow-blinded by the blank page. Most writers are. *What do I write about? How do I begin? Where do I start?* You begin with a *writing start*—a word or phrase intended to do just that, to get you started writing. More dynamic than a topic and more inviting than a prompt, writing starts come in many forms. It may be a directive (*write about closed doors*), a phrase (*mothering your mother*), or a word (*bedtime*). It may be a line from a book or a song (*What my mother never told me*), a traffic sign (*Do Not Enter*), or a three-dimensional prop, such as a baby blanket or picture book, any object that holds a story or memory. Most chapters of *Writing Motherhood* include suggestions for writing starts, and the book ends with a list of ninety-nine to keep you going day after day. But over time you will begin to generate your own ideas for things to write about. Keep a list in the back of your notebook and add to it whenever you think of a writing start. In this way, you will always have a place to begin.

Every time you sit down to write your Mother Pages, jot down a writing start and start writing. Do not pause to ponder the prompt or plan what you will write. Do not stop to edit along the way. Writing starts are meant to be open-ended. There is no right answer. Ten different people responding to the same writing start will generate ten different writings. Just pick up the string of the first image that comes to mind and fly it like a kite. If the wind changes direction, let your writing change direction. If the wind dies down, rewrite the writing start and fly another kite. Keep in mind that a writing start is not an essay assignment; you do not have to stay on topic. Nor will you be graded. A writing start is a place to begin, a starting line. By the time you finish two Mother Pages, you will be amazed by where you end up.

A writing start gives us a set of footprints to follow onto a blank page. Here is another trick I use to jump-start my writing. I don't remember his name (it might have been Hemingway), but he was a wise writer who ended each writing session mid-sentence so that he would not have to start at the beginning each time. I never end my Mother Pages at the bottom of a page. I always let my writing track onto a new page, if only for a line or two. The next day, I skip a few lines, record the date, and resume writing. Instead of feeling adrift each time I sit down to write my Mother Pages, I am fortified by the knowledge that I have already traveled a distance as I continue on my journey through *Writing Motherhood.*

Beginning students invariably ask me why, with the convenience of computers, I insist that we write our Mother Pages by hand. This is what I tell them. Two years ago, at my dear friend Dana's fortieth birthday celebration, I stood in line to have my palm read. An inveterate skeptic, I discredited the palm reader because she was stereotypically dressed in a madras skirt, bangle bracelets, and hoop earrings. And because I was afraid of what she might tell me. I kept moving to the back of the line until there was no one left to go but me. The woman took my dominant hand, the right one, in hers and studied it, tracing the lines and creases with her index finger. Twice she started to say something, then stopped. Finally she said, "You are a writer?" It was more a statement than a question. I got goose bumps. *How could she know? Did somebody tell her?*

Afterward, I went straight to the bathroom and examined my hands under the vanity light. I realized that you don't need to be a palm reader to know that I am a writer. I have a writer's hands—strong muscles, raised veins, short nails, ink smudges, a callus on the middle finger. From all these years of writing by hand, my hands have become an extension of my writer self. They tell the world who I am.

In yoga, we hold our palms together in front of our heart center because the language of the hands is connected to the language of the heart. Lovers know this when they grope for each other's hand in the dark. Mothers know this when they reach for a child's hand at a busy intersection. Writers know this when they feel the beat of their pulse in their fingers while they write. As you will see in the Writing Mother's Helper that follows, this is why it is so important to write your Mother Pages by hand: Our hands are hardwired to our hearts.

INSPIRATIONS

The page, the page, that eternal blankness . . . that page will teach you to write. (ANNIE DILLARD)

The typewriter separated me from a deeper intimacy with poetry, and my hand brought me closer to that intimacy again. (PABLO NERUDA)

WRITING MOTHER'S HELPER

13 Reasons to Write Your Mother Pages by Hand

The time will probably come when you will be ready to venture out of your notebook, so don't box up your computer and send it back. Even so, I recommend that you always write your Mother Pages by hand. As one of my teachers once said, "Just because we have cars doesn't mean we no longer walk." Here are thirteen reasons to keep your writing hand strong:

1. Writing requires physical effort; holding a pen connects your hand to your arm to your body. It awakens your muscle memory.
2. Writing is a creative act; artists work with their hands. Moving a pen across the page is like moving a paintbrush across a canvas.
3. Writing is a craft; craftspeople work with their hands. Scribbling, doodling, jotting down, crossing out—when we write by hand, we are carpenters at work.
4. Words that are handwritten have the familiarity of things that are handmade.
5. When we write by hand, we develop writer's hands, not carpal tunnel syndrome.
6. Penmanship reveals personality. Do you notice how your penmanship changes with your moods, your energy, the time of day?
7. When we write by hand, we fall into the natural rhythm of our breath. And with breath comes inspiration (the word *inspiration* derives from the Latin verb *spiro,* which means "to breathe").
8. Writing by hand creates continuity, connecting this writing to other writings—times in your life when you may have kept a diary or written letters.
9. Writing by hand connects you to the generations of writers who came before you, to their handwritten notebooks and manuscripts. Interestingly, the Latin derivation of *manuscript* is "to write (*scribo*) by hand (*man*)."
10. Writing in a notebook takes the pressure off; we understand that the writing is rough, the pages in draft form. We feel free to explore and experiment.
11. Writing by hand is more fluid and less percussive than tapping a keyboard. It is like the difference between barefooted modern dance and steel-soled tap dance.
12. You do not need electrical power or battery life to write by hand.
13. No matter how sophisticated a laptop may be, a notebook is both more portable and more reliable, not to mention more affordable.

Building Block #3
The ABC's of Writing Motherhood

The ABC's of *Writing Motherhood* will ease you into the daily practice of writing your Mother Pages. More important than showing you how to get started, however, they will empower you to keep going. Paste a copy of the ABC's into your Mother's Notebook.

AWAKEN TO THE MOMENTS OF MOTHERHOOD. Both the extremes and the routines—the highs, the lows, and the in-betweens—are rich in material for writing. Don't worry about getting it all down or even getting it right. Just try to express some truth about what it means to bear and care for your children on a given day, at a given moment.

BE A WRITING MOTHER. Mothers don't wake up every morning and decide whether to feed their children breakfast. Nor do writers wait around for inspiration or the desire to begin writing. When it is time to write, write. The more you do it, the easier it becomes. Ideally, this is something you do every day for *you*.

CHOOSE YOUR TOOLS. Writing Mothers need two tools: a Mother's Notebook and a pen. You may later want to transcribe select pages onto a computer, but the notebook is both more portable and more personal. Get in the habit of taking your Mother's Notebook and pen wherever you go. You never know when you will find fifteen minutes to write.

DATE YOUR MOTHER PAGES. You do not need to begin writing at the top of a new page every day, but be sure to date each entry. You may also want to note the time and place. Simply skip a few lines after your last entry, jot down today's date on the far right margin, and begin writing. Dating your Mother Pages allows you to locate material you may later want to revisit.

EASE INTO IT. More important than how long—or how much—you write is how regularly you write. Begin with short stretches—two pages (approximately fifteen minutes) each day. In just two Mother Pages, you can easily capture one moment of motherhood.

FORGET THE RULES. Rules encourage us to think of writing as correct or incorrect, right or wrong, good or bad. When you write your Mother Pages, forget about punctuation, grammar, spelling, accuracy, logic. You can do the housekeeping later. For now, just write.

GENERATE A LIST OF WRITING STARTS. Writing starts are intended to get you started writing. They come in many forms: a directive (*write about bedtime*), a phrase (*on the day you were born . . .*), a word (*hand-me-downs*). Begin a list of writing starts in the back of your notebook. Then, whenever you sit down to write, just copy down a writing start and start writing.

HAVE FAITH. It takes courage and confidence to be a mother today, especially when we feel anything but courageous and confident as we send our children out into the world. And it takes equal amounts of courage and confidence to write about motherhood when no other experience in our lives will dredge up more fear and doubt. Trust that you have something to say and the means to say it.

IGNORE THE CRITIC. Every time you sit down to write, you may hear the voices of your mother, your brother, or your sixth-grade English teacher telling you that you can't write. These are the voices of your self-critic. Ignore them. Silencing these voices is the first step toward liberating your own.

JOT DOWN A WRITING START AND START WRITING. Pick up the string of the first image that comes to mind and fly it like a kite. If the wind changes direction, let your writing change direction. If the wind dies down, rewrite the writing start and fly another kite. There is no right answer. Ten writers responding to the same writing start will come up with ten different writings.

KEEP YOUR FEET ON THE GROUND. When you fly a kite, you must keep both feet firmly on the ground. Do not get carried away by big ideas or abstract thoughts because you will quickly lose your footing. Focus instead on small details and concrete words to keep you grounded. The opposing forces of the wind in your kite and your feet on the ground will produce the necessary tension in your writing.

LET YOUR WRITING GO. Writing starts are not essay assignments. You do not have to stay on topic. Do not pause to ponder the prompt or plan what you will write. Do not stop to edit or rewrite. Let the writing go where it wants. And as you follow along, you should try to let go, too—of expectations, inhibitions, and judgments.

MEET OTHER WRITING MOTHERS. Both writing and mothering are lonely occupations. At first, you may be content to go it alone, but in time you will probably crave the companionship of other Writing Mothers. For just as mothers need mothers, so writers need writers.

NEVER LET WRITING BECOME ANOTHER CHORE ON YOUR LIST. Most mothers already feel overworked and under-appreciated, so don't let writing become a responsibility. You write because you *want*—or *need*—to write, not because you *have* to write. Remember that *Writing Motherhood* is a guilt-free zone.

OWN YOUR STORIES. Like other forms of personal narrative, *Writing Motherhood* asks you to write from the text of your own life. Your days—and nights—could fill pages. Claim your stories and write them down.

PRACTICE PATIENCE. Push yourself to pick up a pen and write every day. But know that practice alone is not enough to make you a better writer. You must also practice patience. You have a lifetime to write about your life.

QUESTION FREELY. At the core of all great writing is a question: *Where did I come from? Why am I here? Where am I going?* Use your Mother Pages to explore the big questions that arise as your children grow up and you grow older. The questions are often more interesting and illuminating than the answers.

READ LIKE A WRITER. Other than writing itself, reading is the best way to learn how to write. Train yourself to read like a writer. Pay attention to *how* an author writes, not only *what* she writes. Record your observations in your Mother's Notebook. When you read for craft, not just for story, you take on authors as models and mentors.

SAVE YOUR MOTHER'S NOTEBOOKS. When you come to the end of a notebook, give it a number and jot down the dates on the cover so you can easily reference pages later on (e.g., "Notebook #1, December 2005–July 2006"). Display your notebooks on a bookshelf or, for privacy, store them in a box. Together, they will track your journey through *Writing Motherhood*.

TELL THE TRUTH. Write your Mother Pages as if no one will read them. You do not need to be polite or apologetic, nor do you need to consider the ethics of writing about real people. In the pages of your Mother's Notebook, be bold and honest. Tell the truth. But understand that *your* truth is necessarily different from anyone else's truth, and that your perspective today may no longer hold true tomorrow.

USE YOUR IMAGINATION. Don't get bogged down by details you can't recall: the color of the dress, the name of the restaurant, the flavor of ice cream. Feel free to reinvent the story of your life. You may find that fiction sometimes gets you closer to the truth than fact.

VENTURE OUT OF THE NOTEBOOK. Although it may seem scary at first, you must eventually come out of the notebook or your pages will grow mildewed like a basement that has neither light nor air. There are lots of ways to come out of the notebook, from reading aloud your Mother Pages to starting a group of Writing Mothers.

WRITE TO DISCOVER, NOT TO BE DISCOVERED. Of all the reasons to write, public recognition, while admittedly gratifying, is often short-lived, not to mention unlikely. Reassess your reasons for writing from time to time. You will be more inclined to continue writing if your goal is to understand yourself, not to impress others.

X-OUT DOUBT. Crossing out lines and ripping out pages are manifestations of self-doubt and can, in extreme cases, lead to writer's block. Let your notebook be a practice in self-acceptance. Your Mother Pages include *all* your writing—good and bad, inspired and boring. Don't X-out anything except doubt.

Y ELL LESS, WRITE MORE. You will be less irritable and more patient as a mother on the days you write, even if some days your pages sound more like whining than writing. Give yourself permission to vent on paper, to question and complain, rant and rave. Your Mother Pages don't have to be poetry; they don't even have to be good prose.

Z OOM IN ON YOUR LIFE. Writers, like photographers, examine the world as if through a magnifying lens, seeing things that may seem invisible to the naked eye. When you write your Mother Pages, go for the close-up, not the panoramic view. Zoom in on your subject with a magnifying lens and write down exactly what you see. As you write, you will begin to see things you didn't see before.

Building Block #4
A Holistic Writing Schedule

Stephen King, for fear of coming across as a workaholic dweeb (his words), once told an interviewer that he writes every day except Christmas, the Fourth of July, and his birthday. That was a lie, he later admitted. The truth is that when he is working on a book, he writes every day, *including* Christmas, the Fourth of July, and his birthday. Because I believe it is better to confess than to cover up our idiosyncrasies and idiocies, I want to tell you about the small spiral notebook I recently found in a storage box among yellowing sheet music, crumbling rosin, and cello strings gone slack with age. Dated 1975, the summer between my junior and senior year of high school, when I was studying cello at the Manhattan School of Music, the notebook records my daily practice schedule. Here is page one:

Monday, June 30

9AM—10AM	bowing exercises
10:00—11:00	vibrato practice
11:00—11:45	Kol Nidrei
11:45—12:15	thumb position
12:15—2:00	lunch break
2:00—4:00	Bach Suite D Minor
4:00 on	enjoyment playing
TOTAL	6 hours

The subsequent pages of the notebook show that I practiced four hours on Tuesday, four and a half on Wednesday, and five and a half on Thursday. Although I practiced only two hours on Friday (hey, it was the Fourth of July), I made up for the lapse with seven hours on Saturday. Before you decide that I am saintly, know this: By the time I turned twenty, I had packed away my cello and I have hardly played it since. You can carve a schedule out of a life, but you can't carve a life out of a schedule.

Still, I get fidgety when I hear that Stephen King does not rise from his worktable until he has hammered out two thousand words, or that Tim O'Brien writes for nine-hour stretches seven days a week. I tell myself that they are men. I grow panicky when I hear that Eudora Welty used to write from 9 a.m. until 5 p.m., and Annie Dillard from 5 p.m. until midnight. I tell myself that they were not mothers in those days. (Annie Dillard later had a daughter, after which, I imagine, she reformed her writing habits.) But then I remember that there are lots of writers—Mary Higgins Clark, E. L. Konigsburg, and Barbara Kingsolver among them— who somehow manage to birth babies and books, sometimes in the same year.

These Writing Mothers follow what I call a *holistic* writing schedule—one that allows for children and parents, sickness and setbacks, fitness and friendship, breakups, breakdowns, and just plain breaks. They write before their children wake up in the morning or after they have gone to bed at night. They write when their kids are at school or next door on a playdate. They write before the orthodontist or after the pediatrician. They write when the babysitter arrives or when their husband comes home. They write in notebooks, on napkins, on laptops—in coffee shops, at the public library, in a car or closet. In short, mothers write whenever, wherever, however, they can.

A holistic writing schedule takes into account your *whole* life. As described in the following Writing Mother's Helper, it is flexible and forgiving, capable of compassion and compromise. But it is still a schedule. Just because I could not sustain my daily practice routine as a young cellist does not mean that schedules don't work. They do. In fact, most of us would never get the writing done without one. As Annie Dillard says in her book *The Writing Life,* "How we spend our days is, of course, how we spend our lives. What we do with this hour, and that one, is what we are doing. A schedule defends from chaos and whim. It is a net for catching days."

So if you feel as though the days are slipping by and you are not getting the writing done, try this: Take out your calendar before the start of each week, say, on Sunday evening, and block out time for writing. You may prefer to write at the same time every day—first thing in the morning or last thing before bed. Or you may want to schedule your writing around other commitments. Remember, all you need is enough time to fill two Mother Pages, about fifteen minutes, but don't be surprised if some days your writing stretches to thirty minutes or more. And don't forget to set aside a day off now and then. Today's busy moms must schedule *un*scheduled time, too.

A schedule takes the discipline and the doubt out of writing. You don't have to decide each day when you will write or if you will write; you just write at the appointed time. There it is on your calendar, before work, after yoga class, or during your son's piano lesson. Writing will eventually become a part of your daily routine—something you do without deliberation or forethought, like washing your hands, brushing your teeth, or feeding your children breakfast. In the meantime, use your calendar to help you catch the days.

INSPIRATIONS

Getting the writing done day in and day out is what separates the writer from the hope-to-be writer. (DONALD MURRAY)

Writers write. But one of the big challenges is finding and defending time to do the writing. Any craftsperson knows that a regular work schedule makes for consistent production. (BILL ROORBACH)

Things I must do every day become routine. I don't have to think about making time for them anymore, I just do them. Once I've made the time for writing, I can be free to think about my ideas and not about how I'm ever going to find time to write them down. (GEORGIA HEARD)

WRITING MOTHER'S HELPER

5 Characteristics of a Holistic Writing Schedule

The word *schedule* may conjure up images of school and work, so focus instead on the word *holistic*. A *holistic* writing schedule takes into account your *whole* life. Think of it as a friend, not a foe. Its purpose is to support you, not to make you feel guilty. Make sure your writing schedule has these five characteristics:

1. **Nonnegotiable.** Use your schedule as a defense against all the distractions and temptations that arise in the course of the day. When it is time to write, write. Don't let anyone—or anything—talk you out of it.
2. **Individual.** Just as parents argue over whether to feed their babies by the clock or on demand, writers disagree about the ideal writing schedule. Some writers write at approximately the same time every day; others vary the time. Experiment until you find a schedule that works for you.
3. **Reasonable.** When you schedule your writing time for the week, be realistic. If you are committed to an all-day field trip

on Wednesday, consider giving yourself the day off. Set goals you can reach.

4. **Resilient.** If one day the walls close in and your writing time is squeezed out—your secretary quits, the car won't start, a child is home sick with the flu—be flexible. Take your child to the doctor and write in the waiting room, or skip it altogether.

5. **Compassionate.** Applaud yourself for the days you write, and forgive yourself for the days you don't write. Be as compassionate toward yourself as you are toward your children.

Building Block #5
A Room of Your Own

Back in 1928, Virginia Woolf advocated that women need a room of their own in order to write. More than three-quarters of a century later, many of us are still struggling to find a space separate from our realm of work and from our domain as mother, wife, and housekeeper. Maybe you live, as I did when my children were little, in a one-bedroom apartment that you subdivided with shoji screens so as to create a home office or nursery. Perhaps your five-year-old still sleeps in your bed, your college-age child has moved back home, or your mother-in-law is visiting. You can't get the bathroom to yourself for fifteen minutes, much less find a room of your own in which to write!

A room of your own need not be a room. It can be a corner or a closet, a folding table or a comfortable armchair. One of my students writes in the passenger seat of her Dodge Caravan; another, at the vanity in her master bath, the one room in the house with a door that locks. If for now you can manage to write only at the kitchen counter, on the living room couch, or at work, try to find some way of distinguishing the space as a place for writing, even with something as simple as a book of poetry or a jar of favorite pens. Over time, as your practice deepens, you will most likely find a way to claim a writing space that is truly yours. Not only will this demonstrate your increased commitment to write, but others will be more likely to honor your intention as well.

Here are some suggestions to help you build "a room of your own":

- **CREATE A SACRED SPACE FOR WRITING.** Look around your house or apartment for a spot you can call your own. When I heard that an author I admire once wrote in a toolshed, I considered converting my children's playhouse in the backyard into a writing studio. But there were too many spiders, and besides, there was no heat. Instead, I took over our formal dining room; we're not formal, and we don't dine. Out went the table and chairs, in came a desk and bookshelf. On one wall, a butler's door swings into the kitchen, and on the other, an open doorway leads to the foyer. I keep meaning to install screens or curtains to seal off the space. For now, I write when my family is asleep or out of the house.

- **CONSIDER A ROOM WITH A VIEW.** Annie Dillard, distracted by a softball game outside her study, one day lowered the venetian blinds and taped a pen drawing of the view from the window to the flattened slats. This way, she said, "imagination can meet memory in the dark." As a young cellist, I, too, sequestered myself in the four walls of a windowless, soundproof practice room, oblivious to Vietnam, Watergate, and the Beatles. Now I prefer to write in a room with a view. I like to look out the window, to notice when the trees are in bud, when the leaves turn red and yellow, when the branches are barren against the cold blue sky. I like to watch the rain pelt the pavement and the shadows darken the page because I am reminded that my writing exists in the real world. You decide whether it will be a distraction or an inspiration to write in a room with a view.

- **GIVE IT A NAME.** Writers use different names to refer to their writing spaces: a study, studio, library, den. I used to call mine an office. The term is not romantic, I admit, but that was where I would go to work. I now prefer to think of it as my writing room,

a name I borrowed from the title of a workshop I teach. Partici-
pants know that, if no place else, they will get the writing done
there—in "the writing room." Whatever you call your writing
space, when you give it a name, you claim it as your own.

- **STAKE OUT YOUR TERRITORY.** Make sure that everyone knows
  this is your sacred space—not to be shared or tampered with.
  Your family will not resent your proprietorship. They will respect
  your sincerity.

- **FURNISH THE ROOM.** To get started, you need only your notebook and pen. In time, you may want to add a lamp, a paper-
  weight, a computer and printer, a dictionary and thesaurus, as
  well as other books that inspire or inform you (see Appendix II
  for a list of books I recommend). You may choose to decorate the
  space with textiles, collectibles, and candles, or you may want to
  keep it clear of clutter. Let the room reflect your personality and
  work style. Do you like everything in its place? Or do you prefer
  a little disorder—yesterday's coffee mug on the desk, piles of
  books on the floor, one shoe kicked in the corner? How you furnish the room is up to you. This is *your* space.

- **GET TO WORK.** Don't let interior decoration become a form of
  procrastination. You don't need to paint the walls and refinish
  the floors before you start writing. All you need to do is close the
  door—metaphorically if not literally—and open your Mother's
  Notebook.

Sometimes, no matter how well-constructed our room may be,
its walls cannot withstand the seismic intrusions of family life. On
September 11, 2001, my husband narrowly escaped the terrorist
attack on the World Trade Center in New York City. When he lost
his place of work, I lost my space to write. For ten years before that
indelible day, I had written in the quiet of my home, scribbling in

notebooks at the kitchen counter and writing on my computer in the dining-room-turned-home-office. In the months after 9/11, Mark, like so many other men and women traumatized by the event, could not bear to commute to a temporary trading floor in Long Island City. He felt he had no choice but to take a sabbatical. Every weekday morning when my children went to school, he stayed home. He sat on the stool where I had once sat writing. His newspaper covered the counter where my Mother's Notebook had once lain. Whenever I wrote at my desk, I smelled shaving cream, felt the fall of footsteps, overheard telephone talk. The color of his life bled into mine, muddying things. With my room no longer my own, I grabbed my notebook and fled.

On and off for two years, I wrote at a corner table in Starbucks, at a booth in the Tom Sawyer Diner, in an armchair at Barnes & Noble, on a park bench at Vets Field. One month I drove each day to a different branch of the Bergen County Public Library system, choosing destinations for their exotic names, such as Bogota, Lodi, and Weehawken. Instead of being frustrated by the changing scenery, I used the surroundings as material for writing: the trashy titles of young-adult novels on library shelves, the noisy arrival of gum-chewing girls at the table next to mine. My writing became boisterous and rebellious.

Now, with my husband back to work, I write mostly at home in my writing room. Occasionally, I send myself out the door in search of a public place to write, if only to keep the pulse of my writing strong. But I am reassured by the knowledge that I can always return to a "room of my own."

INSPIRATIONS

You can read anywhere, almost, but when it comes to writing, library carrels, park benches, and rented flats should be courts of last resort—Truman Capote said he did his best work in motel rooms, but he is an exception; most of us do our best in a place of our own. (STEPHEN KING)

Find a place you can return to unheeded. A place that won't be discovered and tampered with. Make an altar for yourself. Leave it empty to help you invoke a sense of simplicity, or put a picture of someone you love: a teacher, a mentor, your godchild, anyone who is a guaranteed heart opener. Add a candle, or a whole bunch. (NANCY SLONIM ARONIE)

Over the years I've had my table in the corners of my various bedrooms, in the front of a one-room cabin, in the loft of a barn, at picnic tables in campsites, in the mushroomy basement of an insanely busy house in Martha's Vineyard. I've looked out windows at alleyways and river valleys, brick walls, backyards, playgrounds, forests. But always I had a particular place to sit when it came time to write, a recognizable place, even if temporary, and always it's been the same place: my office. (BILL ROORBACH)

WRITING MOTHER'S HELPER

Writing on the Run: Public Places to Write

In the spirit of Ernest Hemingway and the other legendary writers who frequented the Paris cafés in the 1920s, writers today, with notebook or laptop, seek refuge in coffeehouses, in bookstores, in public parks. One of my students is a regular at Starbucks. A writing friend spends her days at the New York Public Library. When the walls of your room close in and you need to get out, try writing in these public places. But be sure to choose a place where you won't run into someone you know. Nothing will derail your intention to write more quickly than an unexpected encounter with a friend or an acquaintance.

Cafés and coffeehouses. You can find a Starbucks on almost every corner in major metropolitan areas, but independently owned coffeehouses can be found in most small towns, especially those near college campuses. For the cost of a caffe latte, you can sit and write for hours.

Restaurants and diners. As long as you go off-hours, you can usually sit in family-style restaurants and diners as long as you like without having to order much. Just leave a decent tip. Booths offer the most privacy and space, but counters can be lively.

Public libraries. In most public libraries there prevails a reverential quiet: no food, no phone, no conversation. Be sure to explore the different spaces. Many libraries have a young-adult room, a silent-study room, and a reading room, as well as the usual assortment of carrels, tables, and chairs placed in and around the circulation stacks. If you have access to a college campus, check out the libraries there—not the cavernous research libraries frequented by rowdy undergraduates, but preferably the small collections housed in graduate departments.

Bookstores. Many bookstores, especially those in cities or near universities, offer designated reading areas for book lovers. Some even have cafés where you can read and write. You may feel obliged to buy a book now and then, but consider the purchase as financial and moral support for a fellow writer!

Out of doors. Think of Henry David Thoreau's *Walden* and you'll understand the inspiration that comes from writing in nature. Begin with the space just outside your home or apartment: a balcony, backyard, or front porch. Then check out the public parks, picnic areas, and playgrounds in your community. Or take a drive to a nearby bird sanctuary, nature preserve, or historic site. Lakes and seashores make ideal writing destinations off-season. And don't forget walking paths and hiking trails, where you can stop to write along the way.

On the road. Jack Kerouac memorialized his cross-country adventures in the classic Beat book *On the Road,* but people have written travelogues since the time of Homer's *Odyssey.* I do some of my best writing when I'm traveling—on airplanes, at bus stops, at ferry crossings, in front of monuments, in hotel rooms. But you don't have to go abroad to write on the road. As long as you have your Mother's Notebook in hand and fifteen minutes to spare, you can write in your car before school pickup, on the train home from work, on the drive back after dropping your son or daughter at sleepaway camp.

Building Block #6
The Time Out

I am sitting down now for the fourth time to rewrite this chapter. The first draft was titled "The Wellness Fund." I was recovering from an illness at the time and figured we mothers better take care of ourselves *before* we get sick, not after. The second draft prompted my editor to hand me a self-help book and suggest, ever so gently, that I read it and try again. The third draft was potholed with quotes and references. The fourth draft lacked sincerity.

"I'm not convinced," my editor said.

Duh! How can I write convincingly about advice I myself rarely follow? How can I tell you, my readers, to take a Time Out when I do everything short of hypnosis to talk myself out of one?

"Do you know what you need?" my editor said the day she rejected the fourth draft. "You need a Time Out."

"What I need is to get this chapter written," I said. My family was away for the weekend, skiing at Windham, and I was determined to make use of every minute.

"No," she insisted. "You need a Time Out."

On my way home from the meeting, against my better judgment, I found myself parked outside the Riverside Square Mall in Hackensack. I rationalized that I needed to return a gift to Williams-Sonoma; it would take just a minute. But once inside I wandered the wide corridors and ended up somehow in Bloomingdale's. The entire store was on sale! Three hours later, I emerged with a pair of all-weather boots, an alpaca coat, and cashmere-lined leather gloves—all 40 percent off, less another 15 percent because I had been suckered into opening a Bloomie's charge account. Giddy, I called my editor from the car. "I took a Time Out!"

Of all the mothers I know, only one nurtures herself regularly with shopping sprees, spa treatments, Pilates classes, morning walks, afternoon naps, and nights out with the girls. The rest of us spend all our reserves on everyone else until we have nothing left for ourselves. However busy we may be, most of us could surely manage to carve out a half hour of free time every day. Many of us have a few extra dollars in the bank. So what prevents us mothers from setting aside time, energy, and funds for our own self-care?

As if in answer to this question, Alice Domar, a psychologist and expert in women's health, coauthored a book with Henry Dreher titled *Self-Nurture: Learning to Care for Yourself as Effectively as You Care for Everyone Else.* In the book, she says, "Our families and our culture have (sometimes unwittingly) conditioned women to be self-denying, caretaking, appeasing, and people-pleasing. The simple but devastating message we're brought up to believe is that if we nurture ourselves we are being selfish." So bent are we on not being selfish that far too many of us have become self*less*—burying ourselves beneath a mountain of motherhood so that nobody knows we are there. Until one day we snap. We scream. We get sick. We run away.

I know because it happened to me. One Sunday morning, in the middle of doing the breakfast dishes, sorting the white laundry from the dark, fielding telephone calls, wrestling with my son over homework, shaking my daughter out of bed, and finalizing the invitation list for my husband's fiftieth birthday party, I suddenly grabbed my keys, jumped into the car, and sped away. Still in my sweats, I had no idea where I was heading. All I knew was that I wanted out: of my house, my town, my life. For the first time as a mother, I understood what propelled the protagonist of

Anne Tyler's novel *Ladder of Years* to set out one day for a walk down the beach and never come back, leaving her family and her life behind. She remembers no premeditation. She offers no explanation. Just gone. Do not think that I am condoning this behavior; I am confessing it.

Like most truants, I did nothing special during my few hours of freedom. I drove on autopilot to my parents' house, took a two-hour nap, downed a burger in a greasy diner, stopped at a girlfriend's for a glass of wine. But when I returned home twelve hours later, I felt at once reckless and renewed.

Because mothers cannot make a habit of running away, you might consider giving yourself a regular Time Out—so many minutes, and sometimes dollars as well, to spend on yourself every day, away from the kids, out of the house, on your own. With none of the negative connotations but all of the restorative benefits of the "time-out" parents give children when they are overwrought and undisciplined, this Time Out is not about punishment but about replenishment. It is not about restraining but about restoring. It is not about taking away but about giving back.

How you spend your daily Time Out is up to you. The choices will vary from day to day, and from person to person. Check out the following Writing Mother's Helper for ideas. I find it useful to keep a list in my Mother's Notebook of those activities that restore and sustain me. *A visit to the acupuncturist. A manicure or massage. A catnap in the afternoon. A bubble bath before bed. A Tuesday-night movie.* Neither writing nor therapy is on my list. They count as work. Nor is exercise; for me, going to the gym falls in the category of *should,* not *could.* When you think of ways to spend your Time Out, try to think about indulgence, not diligence—and certainly not duty.

The Time Out does not have to cost money (like my outing to Bloomingdale's), nor does it need to take much time (like the day I ran away). Even a mini Time Out, the domestic equivalent of the corporate coffee break, can be enough to recharge you. And you don't always have to go out. Fifteen minutes of day-dreaming in the quiet of your kitchen will sometimes suffice. On those inevitable do-nothing days, try chanting the words of Jon Kabat-Zinn, author of *Everyday Blessings: The Inner Work of Mindful Parenting,* who said, "Don't just do something, sit there!" Whether you take fifteen minutes or one hour, stay home or go out, do something or do nothing, I recommend that you spend your Time Out alone, since solitude is the antidote to family life. On occasion, you may crave the companionship of a friend, if only for a cup of coffee. Go ahead. What's most important is that every day you take time out from housekeeping and caregiving, motherhood and work, errands and ego. This time is about you caring for *you*—your health, your spirit, your creativity, your dreams.

Of all the Building Blocks of *Writing Motherhood,* you may struggle the most with the Time Out. I know I do. Time is a finite commodity for every woman (and man), but especially for mothers, who typically feel that our time is no longer our own. Every minute is accounted for, every second stolen by someone or something, a steady outpouring, so that some days we feel as though it is not just time that is slipping away but we ourselves, wearing thin and wearing out. Even if you manage to take a Time Out just once every third day, this is the one way I know how to slow the slippage, to turn the hourglass upside down if only for fifteen or twenty minutes.

If you are still not convinced about the essential goodness of the daily Time Out, then ask yourself these two touchstone questions posed in the book *Self-Nurture*: "By endlessly giving and doing, are you depleting yourself?" and "When you are physically and spiritually exhausted, are you the best mother you can be?" If your answer to the first question is yes, and if your answer to the second question is no, then you need—and deserve—the daily Time Out.

INSPIRATIONS

> *Make sure every day that you care for yourself in at least one*
> *way that will give you pleasure and stimulate one of your*
> *senses.* (HESTER HILL SCHNIPPER)

> *Take a little sabbath every day.* (NANCY SLONIM ARONIE)

> *Self-nurture is about much more than treating ourselves*
> *to a nice movie or pleasant massage once in a while. It is*
> *about reclaiming our right to pleasure and wholeness,*
> *and it requires us to make strong statements to loved ones*
> *about our limits, boundaries, and needs.*
> (ALICE DOMAR AND HENRY DREHER)

WRITING MOTHER'S HELPER

24 Ways to Spend Your Time Out

You do not need to be well-to-do to treat yourself well. Here are some cost-effective and time-efficient ways to spend your Time Out. Some days you may give yourself an hour; other days, only fifteen minutes. Be sure to do one thing every day just for you.

1. Go to a bookstore and browse.
2. Window-shop.
3. Take a walk in the woods.
4. Read *People* magazine cover to cover.
5. Go bird-watching.
6. Read a romance novel in the middle of the afternoon.
7. Write a letter to an old friend.
8. Gather wildflowers or autumn leaves.

9. Go for a bicycle ride.
10. Treat yourself to a classical concert.
11. Fly a kite.
12. Take a yoga class.
13. Have your makeup done.
14. Buy new mascara.
15. Listen to music you loved as a teenager.
16. Rent *Gone With the Wind* or another epic and watch it in one sitting.
17. Play "Chopsticks" on the piano.
18. Reread a book you cherished at age ten or twelve or twenty-one.
19. Meditate for fifteen minutes.
20. Browse at a flea market or garage sale.
21. Check out the open houses in your neighborhood.
22. Listen to affirmation tapes.
23. Bake brownies—the way you like them.
24. Do nothing for twenty minutes.

Building Block #7
The Playdate

One of the great ironies of modern motherhood, one that is rarely talked about, is that mothers are at once so utterly lacking in privacy and so desperate for companionship. With young children pulling on our skirts and older children stepping on our toes, we are rarely alone, yet we often feel so lonely.

For as long as women have been birthing children, mothers have come together for cooperation, comradeship, and comfort. In previous centuries, the gatherings typically centered around domestic work, such as quilting, laundry, and harvesting. Community was a natural part of every woman's daily life. No longer. Women today cook, wash, and work alone in their own home, the way toddlers sit side by side in parallel play. There is no overlap, no intersection, sometimes no communication.

Not surprisingly, the past few years have seen a proliferation of special-interest and support groups for women. Is there anyone you know who *doesn't* belong to a book club, for instance? Beyond Oprah, though, groups come in every size and shape: garden clubs, college clubs, social-service organizations, knitting circles, newcomers groups, not to mention the myriad of support groups for every issue from infertility to single parenting. The existence of so many groups, I think, is not a sign that we have succeeded in re-creating community so much as it is a symptom of the deep isolation women continue to feel.

When our children are young, mothers naturally come together.

We sit on a park bench or at the kitchen table, sipping coffee and swapping stories while we watch our toddlers play. As our children grow older and more independent, however, mothers become increasingly isolated. A giant *Keep Out!* sign seems to appear wherever we go. Our children begin to play behind closed doors (a healthy step toward establishing boundaries). The schools that once depended on our volunteer work now shut their doors to us, too (appropriately so). We drop our kids at curbside for activities we once did in tandem (no more "Mommy and Me"). As we disengage from the minute-to-minute watch of our children, many of us disconnect from other mothers as well, our relationships reduced to quick phone calls to arrange car pools and sleepovers. Sometimes we go for weeks without seeing another mother face-to-face.

About the time my friends and I stopped arranging playdates for our children, we began arranging Playdates for ourselves. Once a month, Lynne, Kathleen, Dana, and I devote a full school day to play. Our playground is New York City. Some days we tour an exhibit at the Museum of Modern Art or the Metropolitan. Other days we explore a neighborhood, such as Little Italy, Chinatown, or the Lower East Side. Our outings always end with lunch at a restaurant none of us has been to before. The only rule of the day is that we cannot talk about our children: This is about girls going out, not mothers en masse.

Because it is so easy to become marooned in motherhood, I invite Writing Mothers to set aside one day each month for a Playdate with friends. You don't need a full day to play; a morning or afternoon will do. If your children are in school and you don't work outside the home, schedule your Playdate during school hours. Otherwise, consider a weekday evening or a weekend day, whenever you can arrange for child care. Try to set aside the same day each month, such as the third Thursday or the first Monday, and block out the day on your calendar. You may want to spend the Playdate with the same favorite few friends; why not call it a *playgroup*? Or you may prefer to see different friends each month. Whatever you decide, make sure to keep your playgroup small—no more bodies than there are seats in your car.

In planning your Playdate, let *play* be the operative word. This day is not about personal development, intellectual stimulation, or spiritual evolution. It is about adventure, discovery, and escape. It is about having fun. For guidance, think of what your children do (or did) for playdates. Trust me, Sally and Johnny are not looking for enlightenment or learning in the sandbox. They are just having a good time together. You'll know you're on the right track if, in the course of the day, you find yourself laughing and smiling a lot. You'll know you're on the right track if you return home giddy, bursting with stories that suddenly sound silly in the retelling. You'll know you're on the right track if you bring back a purchase that, in the white light of your kitchen, seems a bit frivolous or extravagant or absurd. You'll know you're on the right track if you come home happy to roll up your sleeves and do the dinner dishes. You'll know you're on the right track if the day after your Playdate you find yourself flipping through books or surfing the Web in search of ideas for your next Playdate.

Which brings me to another point. The Playdate is about play, so don't make it work. Unless you're the travel-agent type (I'm not), don't agonize over the arrangements. Here are some tips to help you keep the Playdate from becoming work:

- **PLAN AHEAD.** Don't leave the planning to the last minute. Schedule next month's outing while you're on this month's Playdate, or begin the year with a planning session to brainstorm ideas and set down dates.

- **SHARE THE RESPONSIBILITY.** Assign a different person each month to be responsible for logistics (inquiries, reservations, ticket purchases). Also, let someone else drive (or arrange for transportation) each time.

- **CREATE A FOCUS.** Limitless choices can be overwhelming. In planning your Playdates, narrow the options. Consider choosing a "theme" for your playgroup, such as culture, comedy, or outdoor adventure. The Writing Mother's Helper that follows offers lots of ideas for a focus.

- **MAKE USE OF RESOURCES.** Take advantage of the research experts have done for you. If yours is a restaurant club, check out a book like *Zagat.* If you are interested in taking day trips, stop by your local bookstore for a guide. Other resources include town newspapers (which typically print a weekly calendar of events), popular magazines (which often include food and cultural reviews), and Web sites (the chamber of commerce is a good place to begin). And don't overlook college campuses, which often host a variety of interesting events.

In her book *Self-Nurture,* Alice Domar urges women, especially mothers, not only to take time for themselves (what I call the Time Out) but also to make time for friends (what I call the Playdate). One complements the other. If the Time Out is about solitude, the Playdate is about socializing. If the Time Out is about selfhood, the Playdate is about friendship. If the Time Out is about getting quiet, the Playdate is about being boisterous. If the Time Out is about recharging, the Playdate is about recreation. Above all, if the Time Out is about reclaiming your inner self, the Playdate is about resurrecting your child self—you know, the part of you that still loves to make snow angels and host pajama parties.

INSPIRATIONS

> *A little fun can go a long way toward making your work feel more like play. We forget that the imagination-at-play is at the heart of all good work.* (JULIA CAMERON)

While parents, spouses, and children may represent the hub of our support systems, friends and siblings are the spokes that hold the wheel together. When we strengthen these spokes, we can keep traveling in good health and high spirits for a long and hardy lifetime. (ALICE DOMAR AND HENRY DREHER)

WRITING MOTHER'S HELPER

12 Ways to Spend Your Playdate

Here are some playful ideas for Playdates. You may want to choose a theme for your playgroup, from the ones listed below, or you may prefer to sample a variety of activities over time. Either way, let *play* be the operative word.

1. **Restaurant club**—Sample a new restaurant every month.
2. **Movie review**—See a new movie, ideally in a different theater each time.
3. **Spa day**—Visit a new spa or try a different spa service every month.
4. **Culture club**—Tour a museum, go to a play or ballet, see your favorite rock band, visit a jazz club, go to a classical concert.
5. **Day-trippers**—Tour a botanical garden, historical site, crafts fair, any landmark destination within driving distance.
6. **Shopping spree**—Drive to a new mall, shop your city's equivalent of Fifth Avenue or Greenwich Village, buy something frivolous, window-shop.
7. **Tour group**—Be a tourist in your own town, exploring a different neighborhood each month. (Do you have a Little Italy, a Chinatown, a garment district?)
8. **Comedy hour**—Nothing makes for more fun than a good laugh. See a slapstick movie or get tickets to a stand-up comedy routine.

9. **Outdoor adventure**—Go mountain biking, skiing, hiking, boating, ice-skating.
10. **Antique freaks**—Make the round of garage sales, go to a flea market, drive to a town known for its antique shops.
11. **Child's play**—Go to an amusement park, see an animated film, have a pajama party.
12. **Yogis**—Try a different yoga class or studio each month.

PART TWO

Becoming a Writing Mother

Motherhood, while hardly new, is newly in vogue. Whereas women once spent their pregnancies in confinement, expectant mothers today exercise in gyms, hold public office, and commute to work. Formerly stigmatized as matrons, mothers today are popularized as supermoms, in some cases glamorized as sex symbols. Movie stars are having babies on-screen and off, and models pose pregnant or with newborns on the covers of *Vogue, Glamour,* and *Vanity Fair.* Everywhere we look—on the television, on the newsstand, on the sidewalk—we see an unveiling of motherhood. But motherhood is not a fashion statement, nor is it a fad or a trend or a public show. On the contrary. No other experience in a woman's life is more private and personal and mysterious than that of ushering a child—literally and figuratively—from the womb into the world. No wonder so few of us

mothers see our reflections mirrored in the airbrushed pictures
of motherhood mass-marketed by the media.

In the past few years, real-life mothers have begun speaking
out in their own voices. Newspapers now feature columns by and
about mothers, including Lisa Belkin's witty commentary, published bimonthly in the *New York Times,* on the "collision" (as she
likes to call it) of career and motherhood. Web sites offer forums
for mothers to read and write about any issue from sinus infec-
tions to sexual orientation. And bookstores have created whole
sections for mothers, displaying not only manuals and magazines
on the how-tos of parenting, but also fiction and memoir that
celebrate motherhood, for the first time in history, as a worthy literary subject in its own right.

Mothers are no doubt beginning to hear their personal experiences echoed in these newly published pages. But what about
the mother who wants to record her own stories? I believe that
each of us has our own voice and our own songs to sing. *Writing
Motherhood* invites *every* mother to join the chorus.

AUTHOR'S NOTE

Every chapter in Part Two of Writing Motherhood *may not seem
pertinent to every Writing Mother. If a chapter title does not call out
to you, or if it makes you uncomfortable for any reason, feel free to
skip it. Keep in mind, though, that the subjects we most fiercely avoid
are sometimes the ones we most need to face. You can always come
back to a chapter later, when you are ready.*

In the Beginning—
Taking Your First Steps

It is not surprising that more and more women want to write about motherhood in an era when what it means to be a mother is changing so dramatically. A few years ago, I escorted a class of Writing Mothers to the 92nd Street Y in New York City for a talk titled "Reflections on Motherhood." The guest speakers—all of them writers who have turned their pens to the topic of motherhood—represented almost every prototype of the new mother. There was a stepmother, an adoptive mother, a single mother, a lesbian mother, and a mother of five who was raising her children in a long-standing marriage. For two hours, we listened to these women debate almost every facet of bearing and caring for children: whether we should go to work or stay home, raise children on our own or with a partner, start families before establishing a career or after, take an epidural or deliver our babies drug-free, battle infertility or adopt, breast-feed or bottle-feed, send our children to school or educate them at home, let our toddlers cry themselves to sleep Ferber-style or invite them into our bed. One of my students, a grandmother pushing seventy, leaned over my shoulder and whispered, "When my generation had babies, we didn't think about it; we just did it." No longer. Mothers today think about everything as each of us reinvents and re-creates the role of mother for ourself.

In this section of the book, I will walk you through the first steps of becoming a Writing Mother. Yes, I will invite you to write about the early years—pregnancy and birth, baby names and first words—but my focus here is to help you discard your doubts and instill the confidence you will need in order to write at every stage of parenting. I know that being a beginner is not easy, especially for us mothers who are accustomed to the role of authority. It may help you to know the words of Shunryu Suzuki, author of *Zen Mind, Beginner's Mind,* who says, "In the beginner's mind there are many possibilities; in the expert's, few." Always remember that with beginnings comes the possibility of rebirth.

Inspirations

Never have women had such freedom in electing the circumstance in which we become mothers. We are bearing the children of our husbands, married lovers, and anonymous sperm donors. We are adopting and raising the children of other women. On the other hand, never have our struggles, once our children are born, been so daunting. We no longer step into well-defined, circumscribed roles when we become mothers. (Katrina Kenison and Kathleen Hirsch)

While today's young women know from the start they'll face thorny decisions regarding careers, marriage and children, those of us who married in the 50s anticipated lives similar to our mothers' and grandmothers'. Then we watched with bewilderment as all the rules changed, and the goal posts were moved. (Terry Martin Hekker)

1

THROW AWAY THE RULES

It is the first day of *Writing Motherhood*. Students are seated three to a table, the tables touching at inside corners like squares on a checkerboard so that we face one another seminar-style. One student keeps crossing and uncrossing her legs. Another drinks a Starbucks coffee, her eyeglasses clouding over each time she sips from the sleeved paper cup. A third coughs into her fist as she slides a diaper bag under her chair to make room for a late-comer old enough to be her mother. They exchange nervous smiles. I instruct the class to put away their notebooks and pull out a pen. You can hear the clock tick and the hearts beat as I place a blank sheet of lined paper on the table in front of each participant.

I ask students to list five to ten rules of writing—rules that sit on their shoulder and squawk while they work. At first, they draw a blank. *Rules? I don't remember any.* They fidget. They chew the ends of their pens. They glance at a neighbor's page, but it, too, is blank. They begin to panic. They look for the door. Then, out of the blankness, comes the pinched voice of Mrs. Johnston, their sixth-grade English teacher, with her hooked nose, feathery hair, and gnarled fingers wound around a red marking pen. Now you can hear the scratch of pens on paper as students scribble down the rules, chuckling and groaning and sighing.

- Never begin a sentence with the conjunctions *and, but,* or *because.*
- Never end a sentence with the prepositions *to* or *with.*
- Write in complete sentences—no run-ons, no fragments.
- Don't be repetitive.
- Use descriptive language.
- Avoid adjectives.
- Plan ahead what you will write.
- Let the writing go where it will.
- Messy penmanship reflects disorganization.
- Poor spellers are poor writers.
- Write what you know.
- Write to learn what you don't know.
- Always tell the truth—the reader demands it.
- Never tell the truth—it may come back to haunt you.

Reading the rules out loud makes us laugh. At best, they sound arbitrary; at worst, contradictory. I place a dented metal garbage can in the middle of the room and direct students to crumple up their pages and throw them away. They glance at me questioningly. Their eyes dart from one to the next. They giggle. You would think I had just told a group of seventeen-year-olds to cheat on a test or to speed through a four-way intersection without stopping. "There is a time and a place for rules," I assure the group. "They don't belong here. Not now." Then I repeat, "Go ahead, throw away the rules." One by one, students ball up their papers and toss them in the garbage can. They smile. They stretch. They breathe. Now we are ready to begin writing.

Most of us who were funneled through twelve years of public schooling and standardized testing learned how to write by the rules. My classmates and I plodded through swampy grammar texts that illuminated such murky sights as transitive verbs, appositive fragments, and nominative absolutes. We charted our course from chapter to chapter with worksheets and pop quizzes that separated the writers from the rest. I excelled in grammar because it required repetition, memorization, and regurgitation. I was good at chewing things up and spitting them out again.

Every writer needs to know the nuts and bolts of her craft. For that, I am eternally indebted to my public-school teachers. But the danger is that the nuts and bolts can crucify the imagination. Never once do I remember my teachers exhibiting an emotional response to my writing. There was no apparent interest, no curiosity, no surprise, only a blind effort to expose the mistakes—what educator Constance Weaver calls the "error hunt" in her book *Teaching Grammar in Context.* Every mark made by my pen was subject to the ruthless repair of my teacher's pen. Like the all-in-one tool carpenters use, it had a screwdriver for tightening up the prose, a hammer for nailing down the point, a chisel for gouging out the excess, and a file for smoothing down the edges. Anything creative was marked "ambiguous." Anything poetic was deemed "awkward." The *i*'s were dotted; the *t*'s crossed. It's a wonder the ink in my pen didn't just dry right up.

Whether we are trying to get it right or trying not to get it wrong, this is what happens when we write by the rules. Our imagination is dampened, our creativity constrained, our voice muffled, our style whitewashed. We begin to sound like everyone else, or, worse, we stop sounding at all, silenced by the fear that we can't write.

Ten, twenty, thirty years later, these silenced voices come to my classes. The first thing I tell students is to do away with the school mentality that views writing as correct or incorrect, right or wrong, good or bad. Real writers break the rules, I tell them, and have been breaking the rules for centuries. This is how words are invented, styles defined, trends set, whole genres created. One scholar, Winston Weathers, went so far as to catalog the most common and accepted rule-breakings in a book titled *An Alternate Style: Options in Composition.* Calling to mind the works of such well-known poets and writers as Walt Whitman, Emily

Dickinson, and e. e. cummings, Weathers legitimizes a host of stylistic offenses, including the sentence fragment, the run-on sentence, and invented spellings. Weathers shows us that writers break the rules of standard English because what they have to say breaks boundaries, takes daring, demands innovation. But sometimes writers take liberties simply because of a playful and mischievous love of language, the way a child delights in tongue twisters, spelling *M-i-s-s-i-s-s-i-p-p-i* over and over for the sheer pleasure of getting tangled up. Either way, breaking the rules helps us move from polite constraint and obedient reserve to bold abandon and breathless liberation. Breaking the rules lets us cut loose on paper.

But what about the conventions of the English language? my students still want to know. *What about Strunk and White?* "The hard truth," writes author Rick DiMarinis, "is that there is no system, no set of rules that guarantees able composition or abundant production. There is no magic formula that will make hard work, commitment, inspiration, taste, and good luck unnecessary." Somerset Maugham would probably agree. He once said that there are three rules of writing. Unfortunately, he admitted, nobody knows what they are. The only rule of writing, then, is that there are no rules. We don't learn how to write by learning the rules. We learn how to write by writing. So open your notebook, and let's start writing.

INVITATION

↬ *Throw Away the Rules.* Think of all the rules of writing you have learned in school, from books, or on the job. Some rules may seem indisputable, especially those that govern grammar, spelling, punctuation, and capitalization. Others may reflect personal preferences or stylistic choices. This is your chance to conjure up the nastiest, most small-minded rules that have bugged you since the fourth grade. Take out a blank sheet of paper and begin writing down the rules. Fill up the whole page if you can. Now crumple up the paper and toss it in the garbage. Don't you feel better now that you've thrown away the rules?

INSPIRATIONS

In our family, I try to limit rules. I think that rules themselves indicate some kind of breakdown in the family atmosphere. Rules are imposed by the powerful on the powerless. They are an invitation to rebellion. In an intelligent, humorous, and loving atmosphere, rules are not necessary. (SUSAN CHEEVER)

There's no rule on how it is to write. Sometimes it comes easily and perfectly. Sometimes it is like drilling rock and then blasting it out with charges. (ERNEST HEMINGWAY)

My high school English teacher taught me never to write long sentences, and she might have asked Virginia Woolf to cut her long sentence into shorter ones, told her it was a run-on. But sometimes writers need to break all the rules they were taught in school. (GEORGIA HEARD)

2

A Disclaimer and a Dedication

Almost every time one of my students prepares to read aloud a passage from her Mother's Notebook, she offers some excuse for her writing: *I haven't slept in days. I had root canal. My children were screaming bloody murder when I wrote this.* The inclination to disclaim our writing has become a running joke in my classes, but we can't help ourselves. Apologizing before reading our writing, it seems, is as automatic as clearing our throats before speaking.

Joking aside, I tell students to reserve the first page of their Mother's Notebook for a Disclaimer, an overall apology for their writing. I borrowed the idea from Bill Roorbach, author of *Writing Life Stories,* and I pass it along to you. Title the first page of your notebook "Disclaimer" and write down—in list or paragraph form—every excuse you can think of to explain the lack or lackluster of your writing: *I have no time to write. The sink is piled high with dirty dishes. My son needs help with homework. I'm so tired. I feel fat. My mother-in-law is visiting. Who am I to think I can write? Nobody is interested in what I have to say. It's so boring.*

Get it all down—the excuses, the self-doubts, the self-incriminations. Then, whenever you feel discouraged about your writing, read over your Disclaimer and recognize the sniveling voice of your self-critic for the wimp he (or she) really is. Julia Cameron, creator of *The Artist's Way,* suggests that you give the tyrant, as she calls it, a name and a face. But don't be alarmed if your tyrant is multiheaded, representing a chorus of critics including your father, who constantly corrected your grammar, and your best friend, who was a natural-born poet. By personifying—even ridiculing—our inner critic, we disempower it. *Oh, that's you again,* we say. Then we can get on with the business of writing.

I wrote the following Disclaimer at the start of a notebook in the fall of 2002:

> *I apologize for the rough edges, the misspellings, the ink smudges, the food stains, the blank pages. I apologize for the torn corners, the shredded memories, the false starts, the tangents, the days I don't write and the days I don't write anything worth reading. I apologize for every line that is boring or self-pitying or secondhand. Mostly, I apologize for the time I spend writing and for the time I spend not writing.*

If you were to read a Disclaimer from one of my other notebooks, it would be different, depending on the time of the year, the time of the month, the weather.

Now that you've written your Disclaimer, set aside a second page of your notebook for a Dedication. Begin by asking yourself for *whom* you are writing. Your children? Your mother? Your grandmother? Yourself? The person to whom you dedicate your notebook is not your audience but your inspiration or support. You are not inviting that individual to read your notebook but thanking her or him for being your muse or scaffolding. The opposite of the self-critic who wears you down, this person holds you up as you write. Our children are obvious choices, for they are the inkwell into which we repeatedly dip our pens. So are our mothers. I dedicated my current notebook to my mother, "for all the moments I will never forget and the moments she can no longer remember."

Lots of other people may also support and sustain you as a writer and a mother. You may choose to acknowledge someone you emulate (the mother next door who never gets flustered, never raises her voice); a mentor who believed in you (your fifth-grade teacher who said you should become a writer); a relative you want to immortalize (your great-grandmother whose inky eyes you inherited along with a trunk filled with diaries and letters); a lover, a friend, a fan—anyone who quietly, trustingly, gives you the space to explore yourself on paper. It might even be someone you've never met, perhaps an author whose books you admire, or an abstract idea such as time, which speeds up when we parent and slows down when we write.

Go back to your favorite books and take a look at the dedication and acknowledgment pages. Alice Walker dedicated her published collection of womanist prose, *In Search of Our Mothers' Gardens,* to her daughter Rebecca, who, the author wrote, "saw in me what I considered a scar and redefined it as a world." Susan Cheever dedicated her memoir of parenting, *As Good as I Could Be,* to her children and all the adults who helped her raise them. Editor Claudia O'Keefe, in the dedication to her book *Mother,* wrote this: "To my mom, who wouldn't let me write a goopy dedication." And James McBride, at the start of his memoir, *The Color of Water: A Black Man's Tribute to His White Mother,* wrote this dedication: "I wrote this book for my mother, and her mother, and mothers everywhere." Because you are not writing for publication, however, you do not have to limit your Dedication to a smart one-liner. Allow yourself the space to honor everyone and anyone who comes to mind.

Acknowledging someone—or something—at the start of your Mother's Notebook is a way of expressing gratitude and allowing abundance: *Thank you. Now I have what I need to be a Writing Mother.* And you do. A whole team of coaches and cheerleaders is there to support you. If nothing else, remember that you are walking in the footsteps of all the writers and mothers who came before you. They will light your way.

INVITATIONS

✢ *Write a Disclaimer.* Title the first page of your Mother's Notebook "Disclaimer" and write down, in list or paragraph form, every excuse you can think of to explain why you can't write. Maybe you have poor penmanship or you can't spell or you never took college English. Perhaps your daughter is in bed with mononucleosis or your husband is out of work. The reasons can be external or internal, real or imagined. Once you've written your Disclaimer, you will never again have to excuse your intentions or abilities as a writer.

✢ *Write a Dedication.* Title the second page of your Mother's Notebook "Dedication." This is your chance to acknowledge the people who inspire and support you as a Writing Mother. Over time, the people to whom you dedicate your notebooks may change. That is natural. As our children grow up and we grow older, our support networks realign to meet our changing needs. Know that you can write a different Dedication at the start of your next notebook, or feel free to add to this one as you go.

INSPIRATIONS

For just one day, try listening to the voices in your head. If you keep a rough record of the comments you make to yourself, you'll discover that the vast majority are negative in tone and content. In my experience with women who

*carefully monitor their thoughts, most find that 90 percent
are negative. How many of us wake up in the morning,
look in the mirror, and say, "How stunning!" "Great hair!"
"Fabulous thighs!"* (ALICE DOMAR AND HENRY DREHER)

*In workshops and elsewhere, I am struck by the apology and
justification that infuses so much writing, especially female
writing.* (LYNN LAUBER)

*Our apologies are like a diver's testing the board just before
jumping, or an animal's turning around and around before
lying down. They are a way of preparing the way, preparing
the place, reassuring ourselves, testing our voices before fully
letting go.* (PAT SCHNEIDER)

SAMPLE MOTHER PAGES

Disclaimer
by Susan Loccke

I apologize in advance for the pseudo-intellectual
writing that may appear in this notebook. I want to
express my thoughts, feelings, emotions, and observations in unique and profound ways, but this may
not happen due to these factors:

1. lack of sleep
2. lack of privacy
3. feelings of unworthiness
4. hunger
5. lack of chocolate

6. writer's block
7. lack of talent
8. laziness

I absolve myself of guilt, remorse, castigation, and low self-esteem associated with writing. Even spelling errors!

Dedication
by Alice T. Whittelsey

I dedicate this notebook to my mother for all the ways I am like her in spite of myself, all the ways that I tried for so long to deny. I have come to honor our sameness and acknowledge our differences in a loving spirit, now that the writing process has washed my bitterness away. Last year I wrote obsessively about my childhood, ripping scabs off the past with a vengeance, until suddenly I found myself appreciating my mother, really appreciating her, beyond anything I could have imagined. Mom invested her whole being in motherhood, which for many years felt like a burden to me, but now I am thankful that she was exactly who she was and did what she did to make me who I am.

My mother died this past January. My new-found appreciation enriched for me—and surely for her as well—our last months together. I finally was able to write words for my mother to share and enjoy.

3

Moments of Motherhood: The Extremes, Routines, and In-Betweens

As a child, I was easily overwhelmed. *Overwhelmed* was my father's word (he was a therapist). The feeling was like falling through a black hole. A math test, a term paper, a cello recital—all loomed on my horizon like rain clouds. I suffered from headaches. I endured stomachaches. Sunday nights were sleepless. When my anxiety became unbearable, my father would ask me, "How do you eat an elephant?" By ten, I knew the answer: "One bite at a time."

Motherhood is like an elephant. It is big. It is gray. It lumbers—moving, grazing, growing, aging. So how do we write about motherhood? The same way we would eat an elephant: one bite at a time.

In *Writing Motherhood*, I will invite you each day to capture on paper one moment of motherhood as it unfolds or as you remember it—an expression, a conversation, an interaction, a disappointment, a mannerism, a nightmare, a wish. Rather than feeling overwhelmed by what may seem like the monumental chore of writing about motherhood, you only need to take on the manageable task of writing two Mother Pages each day—one moment at a time. You may begin writing about a moment in the present: your twelve-year-old son sprawled across the bed, whining that his brain hurts from too much homework. That image may lead you to write about a moment in the past: your son crying at the start of first grade, saying he missed spending his afternoons with you. You make a connection because the two moments express the same Peter Pan longing, though they are five years apart—one, at the start of middle school, the other, at the beginning of elementary school. Now you feel compassion instead of annoyance because you, too, mourn the moments that slip away.

When we look back on our own childhoods, most of us do not remember years or days. We remember moments. A scary moment. An embarrassing moment. A sacred moment. A stolen moment. A moment we wish we could do over, either because it was so good or because it was so bad. Virginia Woolf called these memory flashes "moments of being." They are not necessarily sensational or traumatic, but they are usually transformative. We remember them because they changed us in some way. I believe this is what my yoga instructor means when she says, "The moment is our best teacher."

The same is true for motherhood. What makes motherhood memorable is not the vast chronology of raising our children from diapers to adulthood, but rather the moments—big and small, significant and insignificant—that happen every day. Author Katrina Kenison says it best in her book *Mitten Strings for God: Reflections for Mothers in a Hurry*:

> The most precious moments of my family's life are not the ones illuminated by birthday candles, Christmas lights, or amusement park rides, and they cannot be captured on film or tape. The moments I hold most dear are those that arise unbidden in the course of any day—small, evanescent, scarcely worth noticing except for the fact that I am being offered, just for a second, a glimpse into another's soul. If my experience

as a mother has taught me anything, it is to be awake for such moments, to keep life simple enough to allow them to occur, and to appreciate their fleeting beauty: a lip-smacking good-night "guppy kiss"; a spoonful of maple syrup on snow, served to me in bed with great fanfare on a stormy winter morning; a conversation with a tiny speckled salamander discovered, blinking calmly, under a rock.

These are the moments you will write about every day in the pages of your Mother's Notebook. Together, they will reveal, as Kenison suggests, the changing color, the light and shadow, of your days as a mother.

I know you are eager to start writing. Before you begin, I invite you to scroll back through time to reconstruct a representative sampling of memorable moments of motherhood. Don't be con-cerned if your memory, like mine, is poor. I promise that as you complete the Invitations that follow, you will begin to recall moments you had long forgotten. With the understanding that motherhood begins well before the arrival of your newborn and continues long after your eighteen-year-old leaves home, you will create a T-chart, a simple graphic, in the form of the letter *T*, that will allow you to compare the highs and the lows of motherhood. Then, whenever you are at a loss for something to write about, you can circle a moment on your T-chart and write down on two Mother Pages everything you remember—as well as anything you don't remember—about that moment.

Your chart will serve as inspiration for writing for months to come. What's more, it will reveal an important truth about motherhood. If you were to graph the moments listed on your T-chart, you would have a visual representation of the rugged ter-rain of motherhood. There, on graph paper, you would see the ups and downs, the highs and lows. Indeed, if your experiences as a mother are similar to those of my students, your graph would most likely resemble a road map or an electrocardiogram. Not surprising. Of all life's journeys, motherhood is perhaps the one most closely connected to the heart.

INVITATIONS

∻ *Charting Moments of Motherhood.* On a blank page in your Mother's Notebook, construct a T-chart: first draw a vertical line down the center of the page to create two columns, then draw a horizontal line about one inch from the top of the page to form the letter *T*. Label the left column *Highs* and the right column *Lows*. Now make a list of the extreme moments of motherhood, beginning with the earliest high and low you can remember and proceeding chronologically up to the present. To jog your memory, flip through photo albums and scrapbooks, read baby diaries and old letters, rummage through toy chests and closets. Think of births and deaths, firsts and lasts, beginnings and endings, celebrations and milestones, accidents and illnesses, reunions and estrangements, achievements and disappointments. Examples include a landmark birthday, the death of a grandparent, a geographical move, a wedding, a divorce, a hospitalization, a graduation, cutting a first tooth, returning to work, driving to sleepaway camp, a romantic getaway, a bad vacation. Your list does not need to be exhaustive; ten highs and ten lows will do. It only needs to include occasional signposts along your journey through motherhood.

∻ *Interpreting Your T-Chart.* What would your T-chart look like if you were to plot the highs and lows on graph paper? What did you learn about the emotional landscape of motherhood? Why is motherhood characterized by such conflict and contradiction? Why are the highs so high and the lows so low? Did some moments (say, a premature birth) land in both columns of your T-chart? Did you find it easier, as many of us do, to recall the lows than the highs? If possible, encourage friends to complete the exercise so that you may compare charts. Feel free to add to your T-chart and to write from it.

INSPIRATIONS

Every life has its own moments of transition and self-discovery. And it is these emotional and physical milestones that we often write about, again and again. (LYNN LAUBER)

I began to see it as my task to bear witness to the moment, to give voice to the incredible world around and inside me.
(GAYLE BRANDEIS)

Many of the greatest moments we experience are moments we cannot adequately prepare for, the birth of a child, the death of a loved one. (AMY TAN)

You must know that the crux of life exists not in some long period of time but in a single moment.
(REVEREND SUN MYUNG MOON)

SAMPLE MOTHER PAGE

Moments of Motherhood—the Highs and Lows
by Phyllis Rosenthal

HIGHS	LOWS
1. Reena's heartbeat at 8 weeks.	1. Mugged in Brooklyn Heights at 7 months pregnant.
2. A visit from my mother just hours after giving birth.	2. Taking an epidural after 17 hours of unproductive labor.
3. Reena, at 16 months, wears panty hose on her head to give herself long hair.	3. The Neonatal Intensive Care Unit at Mount Sinai Hospital.
4. First trip to the Museum of Natural History.	4. The last summer with my mother.
5. Finding out I am pregnant with Sarah after my mother's death.	5. Sarah's ear infections lead to surgery at 18 months.
6. Sarah's first snowfall.	6. My last school trip as a chaperone for the 5th grade.
7. Reena, age 8, stands up for the class scapegoat.	7. Sarah's emotional breakdown.
8. A moment of glory on the soccer field.	8. Reena falls on the stairwell at Teaneck High and ends up in the ER.
9. American Idol audition.	9. American Idol audition.
10. College acceptance letters.	10. College rejection letters.

WRITING MOTHER'S HELPER

Like Mother, Like Writer

As you begin to fill the pages of your Mother's Notebook, you will discover unexpected parallels between writing and mothering. Whether we are talking about finding our voice, learning to listen, or telling the truth, writing and mothering obviously traverse common ground, but they also carry much of the same emotional freight. The strengths and uncertainties you bring to mothering are most likely the same strengths and uncertainties you bring to writing. If you tend to hold on tightly to your children, you may be reluctant to let go on paper. If you second-guess yourself as a mother, you may doubt yourself as a writer. If humor keeps your household happy, humor may lighten up the pages of your notebook. The good news is that, as a mother, you have already mastered many of the skills you will need as a writer.

COMMON CHARACTERISTICS BETWEEN . . .	MOTHERS . . .	AND WRITERS
Voice	A mother's voice carries authority. When she speaks, children listen. (Notice that the word *authority* derives from the word *author.*)	A writer's voice is individual and distinctive. It is what distinguishes one author from another.
Storytelling	Like tribal elders, mothers hand down our family's stories from one generation to the next.	As society's storytellers, writers retell myths and legends, fairy tales and folklore, from before the time of Homer.
Listening	Mothers must learn to listen if we want our children to talk. In order to listen, we must first be quiet.	Writers are good listeners. We take in the world around us, noticing things other people miss.

COMMON CHARACTERISTICS BETWEEN . . .	MOTHERS . . .	AND WRITERS
Word Choice	No one knows better than a mother the importance of choosing her words carefully . . .	. . . except perhaps the writer, who agonizes over every line.
Tell the Truth	As mothers, we must always tell our children some version of the truth. Only then will we maintain our credibility.	Writers believe that it is our mission to mirror the world, to expose the way things really are, whether in fiction or in nonfiction.
Teach by Example	Mothers know that children do what we do, not what we say. We must set a good example.	Writers subscribe to the age-old adage "Show, don't tell." Don't tell me you're nervous; show me a nervous habit.
Dispel the Myths	From supermom to alpha mom, society perpetuates as many myths about mothering . . .	. . . as we do about writing—myths that sometimes have little to do with reality.
Audience	Mothers play to our children. Whatever their age, our children are both our toughest critics and our biggest fans.	Writers write to an audience. Whether that person is real or imagined, most of us have a reader in mind.
Trust	As mothers, we must trust our ability to make decisions for our children, and we must trust our children to make decisions for themselves.	As writers, we must have faith in our subject matter and in ourselves.

4

Very (Nearly) Pregnant

Mr. Spitz, my ninth-grade English teacher, wrote these two words on the blackboard: *very pregnant.* "Class," he said, "what is wrong with this construction?" Keith, the class clown, blurted out, "Obviously, she forgot the birth control." Then Joel, who wanted to be a writer but became, I am told, a gynecologist instead, raised his hand and said, "Pregnancy cannot be expressed in degrees. Either a woman is pregnant or she is not." Nodding his head, Mr. Spitz held up a copy of Strunk and White's *Elements of Style* and read aloud from page 73: "Avoid the use of qualifiers. *Rather, very, little, pretty*—these are the leeches that infest the pond of prose, sucking the blood of words." Ever since, I have avoided the blood-sucking adverbs for the freshwater worms they are.

You can imagine my surprise, therefore, when Anne Lamott, an author I admire, began her memoir of motherhood, *Operating Instructions,* with this sentence: "I woke up with a start at 4:00 one morning and realized that I was very, very pregnant." Not one but two *verys*, in case Mr. Spitz or Strunk and White were not paying attention. Evidently, pregnancy *is* experienced in degrees and worthy of qualification.

So, too, is what I call *near* pregnancy—the months spent trying to conceive (what one mother dubbed "infertility hell") or waiting to adopt (waiting for the papers to be approved, waiting for a match to be made, waiting for the adoption date to be set).

Like pregnant mothers, women undergoing infertility treatments or adoption protocol endure the physical and emotional weight of waiting for their baby to arrive.

Reflecting on their pregnancies and near pregnancies, Writing Mothers have compared themselves to voodoo dolls, beached whales, pods ready to split open. One very pregnant mother described herself as Buddha without the enlightenment. My mother, on the other hand, remembers pregnancy as the only time in her life when she felt whole. But the concept of wholeness, as she soon found out, is just one letter away from the chasm of emptiness (*whole* as compared with *hole*). After she birthed me, my father refused to have a fourth child, and so my mother spent the next twenty-one years trying to fill the emptiness with food and drink. She never succeeded. Instead, she became overweight and alcoholic.

For me, pregnancy was like a vacation—nine months of liberation from the self-imposed rules and expectations that once dictated my days. When I was pregnant, I gave myself permission to skip a day of exercise, take a midday nap, down a second plate of pasta without hating myself when my pants cinched at the waist or my feet disappeared beneath my breasts and abdomen. When I was pregnant, I gave myself permission to disconnect the telephone, turn down unwanted invitations, roll over when my husband came close without feeling guilty when the calls went unanswered, the mail unopened, or my husband unfulfilled. Only when I was pregnant did I routinely grant myself indulgences, make allowances, let go and let down without berating myself for vegging out or pigging out or copping out. Because when I was pregnant, everything I did was for the baby. I needed to rest for the baby. I needed to read for the baby. I needed to eat for the baby. The baby, a built-in excuse to baby me. Like my mother, I have never again been able to be so kind to myself, or so forgiving.

The Invitation to this chapter encourages you to reflect back on your pregnancies or near pregnancies—a time few of us can describe *without* the use of qualifiers (sorry, Strunk and White).

INVITATION

✧ *9 Questions, 9 Quickwrites.* This Invitation asks you to complete a series of quickwrites—short, timed writings in response to a question or prompt. Quickwrites are an excellent way to jump-start your pen or to warm up for more sustained writing. For each one, copy down the question in your notebook, then give yourself five minutes to answer it. Use a kitchen timer or stopwatch. You may want to do two or three quickwrites each day, or, if you're on a roll, try doing all nine in a single sitting. The questions are designed to spark your memory, but if you draw a blank, simply write down whatever you *don't* remember. Be sure to follow the ABC's of *Writing Motherhood*. Do not ponder or plan what you will write. Do not stop to edit or rewrite. Let the writing go wherever it wants. As you follow along, you should try to let go, too—of expectations, inhibitions, and judgments.

1. What do you remember about being pregnant, trying to get pregnant, or waiting to adopt?
2. What books did you read or classes did you take during that time?
3. What foods did you crave or smells did you abhor?
4. What clothes did you wear? Which ones have you kept?
5. What physical symptoms did you suffer? Did you sweat or smell? Were you nauseated?
6. Did you make any changes in lifestyle or acquire any new habits?
7. What rituals did you follow or superstitions did you develop?

8. How did other people treat you: your lover, mother, colleagues, strangers?
9. What did you fear most?

INSPIRATIONS

I've learned from [my mother] that it doesn't always take faith to become pregnant, but it does take faith to have a child. I'm not talking about religious faith, but instead something purely, instinctively human. (CLAUDIA O'KEEFE)

My experience as a pregnant woman has shown me that the process of holding life within you changes you. For the pregnant woman the physical changes are numerous and humbling. The changes in the heart are greater.
(JULIE DONOVAN MASSEY)

Throughout the experience, in spite of her growing discomfort, she'd been astonished by her body's ability to make life, exactly as her mother and grandmother and all her great-grandmothers had done.
(NARRATOR OF *THE NAMESAKE* BY JHUMPA LAHIRI)

5

Birth Stories and Other Beginnings

I came to my first class of *Writing Motherhood* with the naïveté of a teenager arriving in Times Square from Des Moines, Iowa, via Greyhound bus. Convinced that birth was the logical place to begin, I asked students to tell their birth stories. I had not anticipated such stark accounts of late-term stillbirths, emergency C-sections, and postnatal intensive care, nor had I considered that some women might have alternative birth stories to tell. A full year later, one Writing Mother, Fran, returned for a workshop in memoir. As she began talking about her adopted son, Jordan, I experienced the jolt a teacher feels when, minutes after the class is dismissed, she discovers her blouse is unbuttoned. "What did you say when I invited students to tell their birth stories the first day of *Writing Motherhood*?" I asked her. Fran beamed her beatific smile. "I told the story of my airplane ride from Newark to Denver, how I cried the whole way until they placed my son in my arms, and I became a mother."

Whether we deliver our babies by natural childbirth or cesarean, use an egg donor or adopt a two-year-old from China, each of us has a birth story to tell—a story that begins months, sometimes years, before our baby is born and continues well beyond the moment he or she is placed in our arms. As author

Susan Cheever writes in her memoir of motherhood, *As Good as I Could Be,* "Childbirth is just one point on the continuum." Notwithstanding the 6.5 billion birth stories in the world today, yours is as magical and mystifying and earth-shattering as any other. But how do you reduce an event as monumental as birth to a page in your Mother's Notebook? You begin by telling birth stories.

I got the idea from Nancy Hokenson, a relative through marriage and a mother of mythical proportions. From sunup until way past sundown, she tirelessly moves from the stove to the dining table to the laundry room to the toolshed to the vegetable garden to the station wagon to her office, where she heals ailing patients with herbs and acupuncture. To mark the birthdays of each of her five children, Nancy retells the story of their birth— how Michael was almost born in the backseat of their Volvo when the hood of the car flew up en route to the hospital; how Leah was delivered, as planned, on their living room couch by her father, who used a yellow Tupperware bowl to catch the placenta; and how Joanna was also delivered at home by her father, this time because the doctor got lost and arrived too late. The details Nancy leaves out her children fill in. Telling their birth stories has become a birthday ritual as meaningful to the Hokensons as lighting candles and opening presents.

The birth stories I invite students to tell in class, however, are not necessarily the ones we would tell our children. As models and for inspiration, we read published stories that reveal the naked truth of childbirth—in fiction and in memoir, in detail and with humor. Bonnie, the twenty-year-old protagonist of the short story "Before" by Mary Grimm, gets pregnant on her honeymoon because she is too embarrassed to cruise the feminine-hygiene aisle of the local drugstore. In a tough-edged, witty voice, she recounts the events leading up to the birth of her baby nine months later: the unwelcome advice of nosy relatives, the frightening inevitability of pain, the widening gulf between her body and her husband's, the alienation from friends who chat across her swelling stomach about shopping and boyfriends and work. Only once she is wheeled into the delivery room does Bonnie stop begrudging the past and start welcoming the future as it rushes toward her: "[her] life changing, the old familiar parts of it crumbling away and a new shape emerging." Students are often amazed to discover that the author wrote "Before" twenty years *after* the birth of her first child—what Grimm later described as "the cataclysmic event that changed [her] from a girl into a woman and a mother." Sometimes it takes that long for birth stories to simmer.

Rahna Reiko Rizzuto, on the other hand, wrote her birth story, "What My Mother Never Told Me," while her children were still small. In her frank and funny essay, she vows to tell the truth about childbirth, even if the details "tend to be smelly and wet." So shockingly graphic are the details she recounts—of amniotic fluid and mucous plugs and vomit—that I always worry some of my students will hand in their notebooks and ask for a refund. No one has yet quit.

Rizzuto explains that she has bought every book and taken every class on childbirth only to discover that, come her due date, she is not privy to the insider's information she so desperately needs: "how to keep my sense of humor when I was two weeks overdue in an un-air-conditioned house in July; that Pitocin-induced contractions feel like, oh, having your teeth smashed in with a hammer; whether I should bring my own airbag to protect myself as my hospital cot ricocheted toward the operating room, where my emergency cesarean section would be performed." Humor, it turns out, is what carries Rizzuto through the mishaps and miseries of her first delivery and her second, and the telling of both. Humor lets her write about unhappiness and ugliness without becoming squeamish or sentimental. So don't be afraid to use humor in telling your birth stories. As writing teacher William Zinsser says, "Humor is the writer's armor against the hard emotions."

More important than humor, however, is the willingness to slow down when you tell your birth story. Rizzuto, for example, takes a full page to describe the mad dash from the top floor of her residence to the backseat of the car her father will drive to the hospital: "Feel my contraction subsiding, run to the hall; have another contraction; stumble down the first flight of stairs (we live in a brownstone, and, of course, I was on the top floor); lean over our unstable banister to have another contraction . . ." And so on. Striving to be literal instead of literary, daring to write about a mystical event in mundane language, the author slows time down to a near standstill, so that we can see the second hand on the stopwatch we imagine her husband holding as he counts her contractions. These details are not boring. They are the heartbeat of the story.

To help students remember the details of their birth stories, I encourage them to bring a prop to class: sonogram films, birth certificates, adoption records, airplane tickets, hospital gowns, baby blankets, birth announcements, baby diaries, photographs—anything that brings back a memory. One student, Maisie, passed around a tiny red leather sandal purchased in Zhuzhou, in China's Hunan province, the birthplace of her adopted daughter, Ava. Maisie told us that when her daughter-to-be was less than a week old, she was left on the steps of a bustling, multistory marketplace that sold nothing but shoes. Early the next morning, a shopkeeper discovered the crying bundle and summoned the police, who delivered the abandoned baby to a nearby orphanage. Before Maisie returned home to the United States with her child, she insisted on traveling to Zhuzhou to buy a pair of shoes as a way of weaving Ava's birth story into her own version. You see, every birth story has multiple strands, each worth remembering and telling.

More than anything, the birth stories we hear and the ones we tell remind us that when a baby is born, another birth takes place: the birth of you as a mother. You may see the outward metamorphosis of your body as it swells with new life, but inner transformations are also taking place: changes in your perspective, your priorities, your interests, your dreams, your nightmares, your friendships, your marriage. For birth is a beginning. Not unlike the day you started your period or got your driver's license, you sit at the edge of time the first moment you cradle your baby in your arms—a mother being born.

INVITATIONS

- *Birthday Rituals.* Children delight in hearing stories about themselves. They listen with eyes wide, recognizing and not recognizing themselves in the story. Make a ritual of telling your children their birth story on their birthdays. If your parents are living, ask them to tell you *your* birth story. Let birth stories become a part of your family's birthday rituals.

- *Birth Stories.* Like my students, you may find it easier to tell your birth story before trying to write it down. Get together with other mothers and share birth stories. Remind one another that stories about infertility, artificial insemination, and adoption count—as does any story that marks the arrival of your child. Use a prop to help you recall the details. Don't be afraid to use humor. Remember to slow down. Notice which stories hold the most interest. Go home and write your story down the same way you told it.

- *What Your Mother Never Told You.* Use the titles of published birth stories as starting points for your own writing. For ideas, scan the contents of parenting magazines or collections of essays and short stories about motherhood. You may begin with these two titles I use as writing starts in my classes: "What my mother never told me" (from *Mothers Who Think: Tales of*

Real-Life Parenthood) and "Before" (from *Mothers: Twenty Stories of Contemporary Motherhood*). What did your mother never tell you? About birth and parenting and marriage after children? What was your life like *before* you became a mother? What did you do? Where did you live? How did you spend your days? Keep a list of titles in your notebook and use them as writing starts.

Inspirations

There is nothing on earth like the moment of seeing one's first baby. Men scale other heights, but there is no height like this simple one, occurring continuously throughout the ages in musty bedrooms, in palaces, in caves and desert places.
(Katharine Trevelyan)

Giving birth is little more than a set of muscular contractions granting passage of a child. Then the mother is born.
(Erma Bombeck)

The birth of my daughter divided my life into a one-dimensional "before" and a rich, deep, and human "after."
(Susan Cheever)

WRITING MOTHER'S HELPER

Sometimes You Can't Say It Without Sounding Sappy

In Tim O'Brien's award-winning novel *The Things They Carried,* the narrator tells the story of the man he considers to be the hero of his life. "How do I say this without sounding sappy?" the narrator asks. He can't, so he goes ahead and says it anyway: "The man saved me." In writing about pregnancy and birth and babies, you, too, may sometimes sound sappy, crossing the line from sentiment (sincere emotion) into sentimentality (mawkish affectation). It's hard to talk about motherhood without cooing. Even published writers, many of them well-schooled and well-respected, sometimes sound sappy when writing about motherhood. If, however, you want to find a way to be truthful without being tearful, to be candid without being corny, then consider these age-old writing tips:

Avoid clichés—we've heard them so often they make us cringe.
Children, like puppies, give love until it breaks your heart.
(from *What Do You Do All Day?* by Amy Scheibe)

Use metaphor sparingly—comparisons must emerge organically, not be pasted on artificially, such as this one.
Her smile was like a rainbow after a sudden storm. (Colette)

Avoid grandiose generalizations—they lack authenticity.
I can't get over the miracle of giving birth. (Jane Fonda)

Be as specific as you can—details are believable.
Rocking, breathing, groaning, mouthing circles of distress, laughing, whistling, pounding, wavering, digging, pulling, pushing—labor is the most involuntary work we do.
(Louise Erdrich)

Don't just *tell* us how you feel.
I loved the smell and feel of him. (Rosalynn Carter)

Show us how you feel.
I would lean over that crib and bury my face in her neck and inhale her smell until my back gave out or I began to hyperventilate. (Dena Shottenkirk)

When all else fails . . . try for humor.
I was doing the family grocery shopping accompanied by two children, an event I hope to see included in the Olympics in the near future. (Anna Quindlen)

SAMPLE MOTHER PAGE

Waiting for Spring
by Fran Greenbaum

Spring is
    supposed to be a time of rebirth and renewal
    of the trees and the flowers and the earth
Instead here I am feeling upset and saddened
    by all the pregnant women around me
Seeing all the new babies emerging in their
    strollers and snugglies
Even the farm animals are madly reproducing
    and birthing
Why not me?

I'm tired of all the tests
the invasions
the questions
not only from the doctors
but now uninvited from friends and
    colleagues

"When are you going to start a family?"
"What are you waiting for?"

Next, endless discussions and more discussions
Conferences, networking and meetings
Agencies say we're nice people but unfortunately
    the wrong age, wrong religion, wrong
    something
Lawyers tell us the ups and downs of advertising
in state, out of state, country to country, open vs.
    traditional
Learning more than we ever wanted to know
about the 3 r's of adoption
regulations, reciprocity and relinquishment

Finally we join the arena of future parents-in-
    waiting
With our requisite ongoing stress and anxiety
keeping us company
Gathering our reference letters
"Mr and Mrs G would make ideal parents"
they all say

And so another year and a half go by
Turns out our names have finally hit the top of the
    Ohio lawyers list
Our classified ad will run the following Sunday
"Dear Birth Mother
We are a loving and secure
couple who can give your baby a good life
Please call us anytime"

The very next day
we get an unrelated call
from a Colorado lawyer we had engaged
over two years before

"Good news," he says
"I think I've got the perfect birth mother
for you
Take the next plane out and come meet her"

There we are
limboing over the clouds into the Colorado Rockies
We meet her and instantly feel a bond
She's everything he said
It feels so right to us

Oh please pick us
We are so ready to be parents
We promise to keep in touch
to send pictures and letters
Oh please let this be our time

To every time there is a season
and springtime seems to be ours
as I begin my letter
"Dear Susan
He's had another great year
and has gotten so tall
Can you believe that he's almost sixteen?"

6

Baby Names

The first gift we give our children is a name. Whether they love it or hate it or change it, they will carry this name from the crib to the schoolyard, where it will be shouted out or kicked around or ignored. They will carry this name from the podium at graduation to the altar on their wedding day, where it may merge with another name. They will carry this name, finally, to the graveyard, where it will be etched in marble or in granite so that their children will have a way to remember them. For just as a person carries a name throughout his or her life, that name carries a story that survives even death.

To mark the second anniversary of September 11, New York City held a memorial ceremony that included the naming of every man, woman, and child who had lost his or her life in the 2001 bombing of the World Trade Center. One by one, relatives of the victims stood at the podium and recited half a dozen names, ending always with the mother, father, or uncle he or she had lost. The naming proceeded alphabetically, beginning with the *A*'s, then the *B*'s, and so on, and I thought, *Ugh, this will take all day.* And it did. But instead of being bored, I was transfixed. As I listened to the names—all 2,645 of them—projected across the sound system and broadcast across the country, I understood how names help us remember.

When I teach *Writing Motherhood,* I sometimes invite partic-
ipants to tell a story about their name. I begin by saying that my
name was more a curse than a gift when I was a child. In the
schoolroom, I was dubbed Lisa 1 or Lisa 2 (Lisa 3 when things got
out of hand) as teachers struggled to keep straight the duplicate
names in a class of thirty or more. My students, many of them
baby boomers like me, have similar stories to tell. In a recent
course, Diane expressed a vehement dislike for her name, a name
she considered too common, until, at age thirteen, she changed
the spelling to *Dyan.* Rebecca, who still cringes at her childhood
nickname Becky, confessed to feeling shortchanged for never
having had a middle name. Another student admitted that she
had always hated her middle name, Joan, so she changed it in college to June. Patricia, hearing this, announced that she had chosen the name Joan for herself on her confirmation day, to honor
Joan of Arc, the saint she most admired. Judi told us that her parents were undecided until the moment of her birth, when they
named her after a nurse in the delivery room. She could never get
over the arbitrary circumstances of her naming, and so as an
adult she changed the *y* to *i* to stamp her own personality on the
borrowed namesake. Again and again, we are reminded of the
character in Lucy Maud Montgomery's *Anne of Green Gables,*
who insisted she was Anne with an *e* all the while she dreamed of
being the elegant Cordelia.

As students tell their stories, I encourage them to learn one
another's names. I know this is not easy. Before I graduated from
Teachers College, a professor asked my class what we feared most
as we set out to become educators. I wasn't daunted by the
thought of standing in front of a classroom, pacifying irate parents, or doing cafeteria duty. All that seemed surmountable. The
really scary part for me was having to remember the names of
twenty or thirty students in a classroom when, at a cocktail party,
I am prone to forget a person's name three seconds after we are

introduced. Over the years, I have developed all sorts of sneaky ways to remember names—seating charts, name tags, alliterations (*Little Leslie*), rhymes (*Happy Kappy*), associations (*reminds me of Aunt Estelle*), identifying features (*funky glasses, cracks gum*). I try hard to remember names because I know that names are important. I have listened to the stories people tell about their names, and I have watched the moment of recognition on their face when I call them by their name. A name embodies who we are—where we came from, and whom we want to be. When you call a person by her name, you honor her.

In writing, too, it is important to use names—not just the names of people, but also the names of places and things. Natalie Goldberg says, "Give things the dignity of their names." Don't write *fruit*, she advises; write *apple*. Better yet, write *Macoun*. More than the word *apple*, the name *Macoun* carries a story, the story of me at eleven, keeping watch for cars along South Mountain Road where it winds past the Orchards of Concklin, while my best friend, Pamela, who, at ten, is more brazen and adventurous than I will ever be, hops the fence, shimmies up the nearest tree, and tosses down a dozen Macouns, which we eat until our stomachs cramp.

In the same way that names carry stories, they also cast shadows. I can never meet a Peter without thinking of the big-eared boy I befriended in kindergarten whose father called him a sissy for playing with us girls and whose mother would appear at recess stark naked inside a trench coat. I can never meet a Julie without thinking of the green-eyed girl I knew in high school who, as a child, had hoarded her Halloween candy all the way until Easter, but as a teenager, guzzled concoctions of club soda, red-wine vinegar, Dijon mustard, Heinz ketchup, sweet pickle relish, and whatever else might induce her to throw up the food she had just wolfed down. I can never meet a Dylan without thinking of the man I dated in college who was found early one morning curled up in the backseat of his car asphyxiated from carbon monoxide poisoning. Do you notice how a person becomes a name, and that name lives forever?

I like to imagine, sometimes, the stories my children will tell about their names. I wonder if my daughter, Colette, will resent having been given such an unusual name, an obvious reaction to my common one, when all she ever wanted as a child was to fit in. I wonder if she will complain about seeing her name misspelled, with two *l*s instead of one, year after year in programs for ballet recitals and school concerts. I wonder if she will remember the humiliation she endured during an interview at a private high school in Manhattan when the interviewer, a native of France and a French teacher, could not get over her shock that a girl with the authentically French name Colette Garrigues could not speak a word of the Romance language. But these will be our children's stories. We can only tell the stories of how we came to choose their names.

When I ask Writing Mothers to write down these stories, their pens fly across the page with none of the indecision and deliberation that typically go into the naming of a baby. One mother named her son Nicholas because she and her husband spent their first date at a Knicks basketball game at Madison Square Garden. Another mother wanted a name to reflect her gratitude for having adopted her daughter, and so chose Theodora, Greek for "gift of God." One mother picked Colin after the protagonist in her favorite childhood book, *The Secret Garden*. Another mother, desperate because her husband rejected every "normal" name she suggested, settled on Salen, the name of a small town she had seen written on a road sign in Scotland. Whether we choose a name for its popularity or its uniqueness, from the Bible or a baby-name book, to honor a family tradition or observe a religious rite, in memory of an ancestor, a saint, or a Hollywood star, the stories of how we came to name our children often reveal deep truths about ourselves, our relationships, and our dreams.

INVITATIONS

☙ *Baby Names.* How did you choose a name for your child? What other names did you consider? Who was involved in the decision? In two Mother Pages, write down the story of your child's birth name.

☙ *Grown-Up Names.* Write about your own name. What was your name at birth? How did your parents come to choose that name? Did you like it? Did you change your name at any time? When you went to college? When you got married? Divorced? Write down one story about your name.

☙ *Nicknames.* On one Mother Page, make a list of all the nicknames you have been called in your lifetime—both the ones you hated and the ones you found endearing. On another page, make a list of all the nicknames your children have been called. Compare lists. What do you notice? Any similarities? Differences? Who makes up nicknames? Why are some so hurtful? Which ones expose a truth? In your notebook, write down the writing start *nicknames* and write without stopping until you fill two Mother Pages.

INSPIRATIONS

Seeing names makes us remember. A name is what we carry all our lives, and we respond to its call in a classroom, to its pronunciation at a graduation, or to our name whispered in the night. (NATALIE GOLDBERG)

Consciously or unconsciously, we all have private pictures of the people who answer to certain names. (BRUCE LANSKY)

He wonders how many times he has written his old name,
at the tops of how many tests and quizzes, how many
homework assignments, how many year-book inscriptions
to friends. How many times does a person write his name
in a lifetime—a million? Two million?

(NARRATOR OF *THE NAMESAKE* BY JHUMPA LAHIRI)

7

FIRST WORDS AND
OTHER FIRSTS

My husband and I joke that our son came into the world talking, but when Miles asks me what his first word was, I can't remember, so I tell him it was *Mama,* of course. Colette, on the other hand, has always been pensive and reserved. I well remember her first word: *more,* pronounced *maw,* an expression of universal want—more soup, more Elmo, more hugs.

When my children were small, I set aside a page toward the back of my Mother's Notebook for *childisms*: first words, invented words, and *mis*words—words they misused, mispronounced, misunderstood, or misspelled. *Anthony is so unbehaved. Terry is my garden angel. Why do Jewish boys wear Yamahas?* More than being cute, these "linguistic gems," as writing teacher Tom Romano calls them, provide nuggets for writing at the same time that they give us insight into how our children construct their world through language.

Sometimes our children's first words are branded on the hides of our memory. More often, though, they are erased by time. My friend Pamela, a psychologist and poet, recently wrote this poem lamenting the loss of her son's first words, and with them, the loss of his innocence and childhood:

WORDS TO REMIND ME
by Pamela Hill Epps

When you leave for good
will I remember what you said
yesterday or the way you see
the world like a Garfield comic?

What were your first words?

I have already forgotten and
desperately reach for this present:
your irreverent hair, the last breath
of babyness plumping your cheeks.

Later when your legs are long
and your father's stoop is yours
I will have only this poem
these paltry words to remind me.

Not only are first words significant, but so is every other first. Open any baby diary and you will find whole pages devoted to firsts: first impressions, first visitors, first outing, first smile, first sadness, first friends, first mischief, first books, first birthday. So insistent was my focus on firsts that I used to call our pediatrician every third day, frantic because my friend's baby, born two weeks after mine, was already scurrying across the floor or reciting her ABC's while my daughter was still rocking on all fours and uttering incoherent grunts. Dr. Skog, perennially patient, would tell me again that my child would learn to walk and talk in her own time. His advice, however sound it may have been, did little to allay my anxiety, nor did it render my baby's firsts any less momentous or memorable.

I later discovered that firsts do not end with babyhood. Last September, I attended a meeting of a national organization for mothers. I had seen their notices in the papers for years, once went so far as to Google the name, and finally, after much self-talk, showed up for the first fall gathering of my local chapter. The minute I walked into the meeting room, I knew I had made a mistake. I was greeted by the chapter's president, who ushered me over to the head of membership, who introduced me to various committee chairs, the fund-raising committee, the party committee, the book club. These women took their jobs seriously, that much I could tell.

The meeting was soon called to order. We heard first from the president, who then invited us to introduce ourselves one by one. That's when I should have left. "Hi, my name is Nancy," one woman said. "Today was my daughter's first day of preschool." There was a general expression of empathy, as close to a group hug as a formal gathering can come. "Hi, I'm Heather, and today was my son's first day of kindergarten," said another woman. Heather told us she had cried the whole way home. Lots of head nods from the crowd. "I'm Cathy, and tonight is the first time I'm leaving my newborn with a babysitter." Cathy roused a round of applause.

I was beginning to obsess about the wrinkles around my eyes and the strands of gray in my hair when I noticed that everyone was looking at me. "Hi, I'm Lisa," I began, but then I stopped, uncertain what to say next. All these first-time mothers with their firstborn babies. It seemed like eons since I had dropped off my son and daughter for their first day of preschool. The president nodded at me reassuringly. Suddenly I remembered that I had a first, too, so I said, perhaps a tad bit too excitedly, "Today my son started ninth grade, his first day of high school!" There was no clapping, no collective compassion, just an awkward shuffling of feet as the other mothers blinked at me from across the great expanse of parenthood. Standing on the distant shoreline, I wanted to shout to them that there will always be firsts—the first day of sleepaway camp, the first day of college, the first grandchild.

Whether we are watching our baby roll over for the first time or teaching our firstborn how to drive a stick shift, firsts wake us up. Which is why writers love to write about them. In *Becoming a Man*, Paul Monette wrote about his first day at Andover, when the shame of being a nonathlete overshadowed the stigma of being a scholarship student. In *Death in the Afternoon*, Ernest Hemingway wrote about his first bullfight. In *What Work Is*, Philip Levine wrote about the first time he drank gin. In the collection of short shorts titled *Three Minutes or Less*, Reginald McKnight described his first love, at the age of four, and Gloria Naylor recalled the first time her mother took her to a low brick building in the Bronx and told her that once she could write her name, all of the books that lined the dark walnut shelves would be hers. A new writer, Minter Krotzer, is at work on her first book, an anthology of firsts—"First Crush," "First Electrical Shock," "First Metaphysical Moment."

In my notebook, I wrote this page about the first time I saw my husband, the summer he was working as a hotshot firefighter for the U.S. Forest Service. The entry is dated June 10, 1998—twenty years to the day after we met:

The first time I saw him he was standing in the doorway, all limbs, the moon on his teeth. He leaned lazily against the door jamb, and I believed then that his broad shoulders could hold up the house should the beams give way. The long length of his body filled the outline like a child's coloring book, sketchy, uneven, jagged, with white spaces showing under the arms, in the crook of the elbow, in the gulf of his neck where it broadened out along the shore of his shoulder. My eyes glued on even before I opened the car door and exited the life I had known up until that moonlit midnight in the Umatilla Forest.

He stood jauntily on two black boots that were half military, half lumberjack, the waffled Vibram soles visible from the distance. Stiff leather shoelaces fanned off the uppers like cat whiskers, untied yet untangled. His left foot swung casually over the right and balanced on point, while his hands pocketed a pair of faded jeans that hugged his narrow hips and belled over his work boots. He wore a green and beige plaid woolen work shirt, collared at the neck and buttoned up the front, and over that a down vest, also green. Apparently, it was cold inside the lodge still in early June. The date was June 10. I remember because it was the day I met the man who would become my lover, my husband, my children's father, standing there in the doorway with the night on his shoulders, the moon on his teeth, and me for the taking.

Why are firsts so significant? Because they represent a beginning. Because they push us beyond what is familiar and comfortable. Because they jolt us out of the numbness of everyday life and bring us back to our primitive selves when we saw the world through a child's eyes.

INVITATIONS

➳ *A List of Childisms.* Set aside a page at the back of your Mother's Notebook and label it "Childisms." Keep a running list of your children's first words, invented words, and *miswords*—words and sayings they misuse, mispronounce, misunderstand, or misspell. If your children are full grown, search your memory or ask members of your family what they remember. Use the list as inspiration for writing, or preserve it as an artifact in your Mother's Notebook.

↝ *First Words and Other Firsts.* What were your child's first words? What do you remember about his learning to read or write? What were her favorite books or songs? Begin with the writing start *first words* and write down whatever you recall about your child's acquisition of language. Tomorrow you may start writing about other firsts. Use the writing start *the first time* and write down the first thing that comes to mind: the first time your baby belly laughed, the first time you left your child with a babysitter, the first time your toddler threw a tantrum, his first day of kindergarten or middle school, her first kiss. Get in the habit of writing about firsts as you witness them. And don't be surprised if you find yourself writing about your own firsts: the first time you got a speeding ticket, got drunk, made love.

INSPIRATIONS

There is no doubt that these first things are magical, that you hunch over the changing table waiting for another smile, that you shriek, "You rolled over!" as though the next step will be the Nobel or the presidency, that a first step is like watching the history of human civilization from small fishy things to Neanderthals unravel in one instant before your eyes.
(ANNA QUINDLEN)

I love being a mom for all the same reasons other moms do. For all the firsts that we've already had—his first bath, the first time he laughed out loud, his first tears, his first

*Halloween, the first time he rolled over—and for all the firsts
to come: his first day of school, his first T-ball game.*
(THERESE J. BORCHARD)

**Writers, when they write, need to approach things for the
first time each time.** (NATALIE GOLDBERG)

WRITING MOTHER'S HELPER

Unforgettable First Lines

Writers spend a great deal of time crafting the first lines of their
stories. Why are first lines so important? What makes a first line
compelling or memorable? Go to your bookshelf or bookstore and
randomly open a dozen or more volumes. Notice how writers start
their stories. Through dialogue, scene, or setting, they try to grab,
lure, shake, lull, seduce, shock, or otherwise hook the reader. Copy
down your favorite first lines and use them as writing starts. You
may "talk back" to the line, supporting or refuting its argument, or
you may use it as a springboard for your own writing. Here are a
few first lines—some of them famous, all of them unforgettable—
to get you started:

"In my younger and more vulnerable years my father gave me
some advice that I've been turning over in my mind ever since."
(*The Great Gatsby* by F. Scott Fitzgerald)

"I had the story bit by bit, from various people, and, as generally
happens in such cases, each time it was a different story."
(*Ethan Frome* by Edith Wharton)

"It was her fortieth birthday." (*Pavilion of Women* by Pearl S. Buck)

"These are the things I must not forget." ("Immortal Heart" by Amy Tan)

"A few months ago, I stopped opening my mother's letters." ("Thinking of You" by Rose Stoll)

"I'm mostly a mother." (as told by Marney Price in *Strong Stuff: Mothers' Stories,* by Emily Moore)

"Everyone said I was lucky they were boys." ("Stepmother" by Alex Witchel)

"I have to tell you: I hate rap." ("Prayin' Hard for Better Dayz" by Camille Peri)

"I don't have anything against dolls, but part of me has always found them a little creepy. . . ." ("Material Girls" by Margaret Talbot)

"I still remember the grief and gratitude I felt when I first opened *What to Expect When You're Expecting.*" ("Expecting the Worst" by Jennifer Reese)

"We take our mothers where we can get them—and they are not always the women who gave us life." ("My Other Mother" by Lori Leibovich)

"Once upon a time . . ."

8

FAMILY ALBUM:
FROM BABY PICTURES TO
PHOTO STORIES

Stephen King begins his memoir, *On Writing,* with a disclaimer: Because of his sketchy memory and helter-skelter childhood, he can recall only snapshots of his early years—most of them out of focus and out of sequence. His memory is better than mine. My earliest childhood memories, I have discovered, are not memories at all; they are black-and-white photographs taken by my aunt Estelle's first husband, Alan, a professional photographer whom she married at the then spinsterly age of thirty-five and divorced by forty when she figured out that he was more interested in men than in marriage. All is forgiven. Had it not been for Uncle Alan, my early years would be a whiteout.

I carry the memory of one photograph in particular, taken of me at age three or four. In the photo, I am seated before an easel, paintbrush in hand, a plastic smock tied twice around my waist. I am looking not at the camera but sideways, presumably at my mother, who is, I imagine, standing next to me at her own easel. With one finger, I am pointing to my painting, apparently asking my mother to admire my artwork, but from the look in my eyes you can tell that I am admiring my mother. She was a painter in those days, and my happiest memories (or are they photographs?)

are of painting alongside her. A few years ago, at the suggestion of her neurologist, I enrolled my mother in an art class for Alzheimer's patients. She had not picked up a paintbrush in twenty-five years. The new canvases frightened me. They were abstract, like the old ones, but had none of the earth tones and organic textures typical of her early work. Instead, the shapes were grotesque and the colors garish, like the reds, grapes, and lime-greens of frozen-fruit bars. I look back at the photograph of me looking at my mother and try to remember the way I saw her then. I can't. For photographs not only tell the story of things that were; they also tell the story of things to come.

I invite my students to bring to class a photograph from their family album—either of their children or from their childhood. We begin by swapping photos. I instruct students to look closely at the unfamiliar faces pictured in someone else's photo and to describe in detail what they see: *untied shoelaces, checkered bandanna, scraggly hair, squinting eyes, sun low on the horizon.* Next I encourage students to focus more sharply and speculate about what they don't see. *Who are these people? What are they doing? Where are they going? Why are they dressed this way? What took place just before or after this frozen moment? What lies just beyond the frame of the photo?* We read aloud our invented stories, then listen to the owner of each photograph tell the "real" story. (You can try this exercise with pictures from newspapers, magazines, or art books. Just avoid looking at the captions or headlines until after you have written your version.) Sometimes students come surprisingly close to the truth; other times they could not fall farther from the mark. Regardless, students go home ready to write their own photo story.

The best example I know of a photo story—a story that emerges from a photograph the way an image takes shape on Polaroid film—is "Mom" by Anne Lamott. "Mom" is the first story in what amounts to a family album of short narratives published in her book *Traveling Mercies,* each devoted to one member of the author's family: her mother, her father, her sister, her baby. "Mom" begins with a description of a recent photograph of Lamott and her mother taken at Stinson Beach on the Fourth of July. They are holding hands, the mother unsteady in her midseventies, the daughter with an expression of "enormous gentleness" on her face. In the photo, the mother appears eager to please and the daughter ready to help, but behind the mutual adoration, Lamott tells us, is annoyance, resentment, and disappointment that her mother has suddenly become so needy. Again and again, the author looks at the photograph, is softened by the love and forgiveness evident in the faces, then returns to another time when her mother seemed less vulnerable behind her mask of makeup. Through the author's eyes we see her mother the way she is in the photograph, a gray-haired woman toddling across the sand, and we see her the way she was years before the picture was taken, as a young wife, a law student, a new grandmother. "Mom" is fundamentally about accepting our mothers, surrendering them, mothering them—not an easy evolution for any of us. But what I love most about the story is the smart and seamless way the author uses a photograph as both a lens for remembering and a frame for storytelling.

Before I send students home to write their own photo stories, we read a fictional short story by Molly Giles, called "Baby Pictures," about a young woman who struggles to reconcile the demands of mothering with her dream of being a professional photographer. "Do you know what's in my portfolio?" the narrator complains to her best friend, Leslie. "Baby pictures," she says bitterly. Her son—an hour old, a day old, a month old, in a basket, a backpack, a walker. With a toddler on the go and a baby on the way, she has no time to take real pictures, much less to build the darkroom she so desperately wants. When Leslie rises to leave, the narrator turns to see her little boy watching her from the doorway, a shaft of midmorning sun ablaze in his hair. Without shifting her focus, she reaches for the camera on top of the refrigerator, uncaps the lens, and catches the boy the moment he turns on his heels to run. In the end, the narrator understands that these are the photographs she must take now, quickly, before the light changes, and her son is half-gone. This is the same reason you are a Writing Mother: to capture on paper the fleeting moments a photographer strives to capture on film.

INVITATION

⤙ *Photo Stories.* Flip through family albums, scrapbooks, and baby diaries in search of photographs of your children or from your childhood. Choose one that intrigues you (it doesn't have to be a baby picture). Begin by transcribing the photo into words. Describe in detail exactly what you see so that someone else can see it, too. Use bullet points if that helps. Focus on the faces. Examine the clothing. Look closely at the hands and feet. Don't overlook the setting. What is the weather? Now zoom in and write a photo story. What do you know that is not visible in the picture? Whose eyes did she inherit? What news did she just receive? Who is she about to meet? What would you tell her if you could? Who took the picture? Photo stories begin with what was, but they move on to what will be or could have been. Write two Mother Pages. Tomorrow you can write a different photo story.

INSPIRATIONS

Cameras spit out images that help us remember where we were, who we were with, moments of our lives. And while I love photographs and spent years as a photographer, writing can be an even more effective way to secure certain kinds of memories. (BARBARA DeMARCO-BARRETT)

When I look at photographs of my childhood, I am gathering shards of the past, trying to make meaning out of its fragments. Sometimes they bring back a forgotten moment: the time at the Sandwich Fair when I ate caramel apples; me in my new strawberry dress and hat; my best friend's dog, Laddie. Photographs make me laugh or remember with a stab of regret. Photographs demand that stories be told around them. (GEORGIA HEARD)

In the photograph by my bed my mother is perpetually smiling on me. I guess I have forgiven us both, although sometimes in the night my dreams will take me back to the sadness and I have to wake up and forgive us again. (SUE MONK KIDD)

SAMPLE MOTHER PAGE

Photo Story
by Phyllis Rosenthal

It's a warm day for September as Sarah and her best friend Charlie pose for a picture on the first day of sixth grade. They are both wearing short-sleeved tee shirts. Sarah, age eleven, is unhappy with her thighs so she wears khaki pants. Charlie wears shorts. Their new backpacks are stiff and light because there is nothing in them but brown bag lunches.

Cherubic and so young, they stand fidgeting and shoving one another from side to side. This year the sixth grade has been divided into houses and Sarah and Charlie will be in one together. This is the last September they will ever spend as friends.

By the end of seventh grade Charlie shows signs of bipolar disorder, and Sarah of depression and attention deficit. The houses turn out to be horrible for them. There is too much work and teachers with too little patience. Charlie struggles with paranoia and becomes an outsider developing few friendships. Sarah's year is full of pop quizzes because she is not focused enough in class to hear when tests are announced. Her few friends make fun of her low grades and fogginess. Her self-image plummets.

They become wary of one another. Loath to be associated, they don't hang out after school anymore, or go to the movies together on weekends. There are no emails late at night. By eighth grade Charlie is speaking very little to anyone, and almost never to Sarah. She rarely goes to school, and spends most of her time alone listening to sad music. Sarah goes on to a small private high school and Charlie to the public school in their town. They no longer speak at all. Wounds are too deep, scars too thick.

If I had known that the photo taken that morning was to be the last of Sarah and Charlie as children what would I have done? What could I have done? Even mothers can't change outcomes.

9

THE ESSENTIAL QUESTION: *Why?*

Every parent knows the torment of a four-year-old's interrogation. *Why is the sky blue? How do birds fly? Where did I come from?* Even though we know that curiosity is a good thing, we often deflect our children's questions—either because we are too busy or too tired or because, frankly, we do not know. In time, children stop asking questions, teenagers think they know all the answers, and adults take for granted the wonders of the world. How unfortunate! Questions are the backflips of the mind. They are, as the early-twentieth-century explorer Frank Kingdon-Ward once said, "the creative acts of intelligence." Even when our patience is stretched and our energy depleted, we as parents need to encourage our children to ask questions, for curiosity leads to creativity, and a creative mind is never bored.

The moment a child asks a question, he or she sets out on a *quest*—in search of knowledge, adventure, or enlightenment. One New York City father went along for the ride. By his own admission, he was increasingly frustrated by his six-year-old's questions: "What would hurt more: getting run over by a car or stung by a jellyfish?" "Why do ships have round windows?" "Why are there sidewalks on both sides of the street?" "What happens when lava goes on dirt?" "Is hummus like dinosaur poop?" So the father went straight to the experts who knew the answers: a doctor of pain medicine at New York–Presbyterian Hospital, a professor of engineering at a maritime college, the commissioner of the New York City Department of Transportation, a professor of earth science at Columbia University, a curator of dinosaur paleontology at the American Museum of Natural History. Not only did his research satisfy the boy's curiosity, but it also spawned an article in the *New York Times* and an online discussion aptly titled "When *Because* Just Won't Do." I am told the father is now at work on a book, so much did his subject resonate with parents.

Sometimes, though, we learn less from the answers than we do from the questions themselves. I recently invited a group of Writing Mothers to jot down the questions their children ask in a day. Jordan, at fifteen, was relentless: "Why can't you ever buy anything good to eat?" "Why do I need new shoes?" "Why can't I get a tattoo?" "Why do I have to go to college?" James, at four, was philosophical: "Who made me?" "Who made you?" "Does everyone die in this whole world?" "Where do they go?" Behind our children's questions lurk a host of emotions: curiosity and concern, shame and pride, flashes of boastfulness followed by flickers of doubt, both the desire to please and the impulse to defy. When we pay attention to the questions our children ask, we come to know what they care about, what they worry about, what they want and need and dream.

I encourage my students—all of them grown women—to ask questions, too. We begin by asking ourselves, "Why do people write?" For answers, we think of all the places one finds writing: in books, newspapers, and instruction manuals; on billboards, road signs, and postcards; on take-out menus, in song lyrics, in the Bible. It becomes clear that people write for lots of different reasons: for validation, communication, and entertainment; to immortalize ourselves or to edify others; to teach, to learn, to heal, to remember, to understand. I next ask students to ponder their own reasons for wanting to write—a question I have encountered in nearly every book on writing I have ever read. It seems we human beings not only share a deep need to represent our experience in writing, but we also want to understand *why* we write:

- Because I have so much to say.
- Because no one will listen.
- Because I have a poor memory.
- Because I want to hold on.
- Because I need to let go.
- Because my life is my legacy.
- Because I don't want my children to grow up and myself to grow old without paying attention.

Go ahead and ask yourself, *Why do I want to write?* Some of you may secretly dream of seeing your name on the best-seller list. Others may want to pass on what you have lived and learned and known—in Lynn Lauber's words, to use writing as a kind of bequeathment, a way of "reaching out a hand in kinship across time." Most of you, however, probably want to write for yourself alone—for comfort, for clarity, for sanity. Here's what I wrote in my notebook on March 23, 2000, in answer to the question *Why do I write?*

I write because I like to be alone with my thoughts, in a place where telephones don't ring and cash registers don't clang and cars don't honk. I write because I like to bushwhack through the overgrown trails of my mind. Writing is an excuse to follow those paths, to take detours, to journey far and wide. I write because it brings great satisfaction, especially when I am surprised by what I have just written down, excited by the promise of an idea forming. I write because I need discipline, a task to do every day. And because I crave companionship; my stories stay with me like friends along for the ride. They join me at the gym. They come along to the supermarket. They sit next to me on long drives. They lie on my pillow at night. I write because I need a purpose. I need to believe that life is more than doing laundry and making beds. I write because it feels empowering to tell people that I write, even though I cannot yet say the words, "I am a writer." I write because I am private. How else will anyone know what I am thinking? I write because I am shy. How else will anyone know what I have to say? I write because I cannot accept that only children have dreams. I have a dream. It is to write. There. I said it. Better yet, I wrote it down.

Don't be surprised if your reasons for writing change over time. Mine have. And don't be embarrassed if they sound silly. Maybe you want to practice your penmanship, or perhaps you have a weakness for stationery supplies. Whatever the reason, if we know *why* we want to do something, we are far more likely to do it.

Asking ourselves why we want to write is not unlike asking why we want to mother. Some women know from a young age that they want to raise a family. They even know how many children they plan to have. Other women remain undecided well into their childbearing years. I had never thought about being a mother until the age of twenty-seven, when in the span of one month I found my first gray hair and discovered I needed prescription glasses. For the next three years, I thought of nothing else. Was my biological clock ticking? Or were there other reasons why I suddenly, desperately, wanted to become a mother? Almost twenty years later, I ask myself the same question: *Why did I want to become a mother?*

- Because I wanted to repay my parents.
- Because I wanted to do better than they did.
- Because I was afraid I would otherwise evaporate.
- Because 1 + 1 = 3.
- Because I wanted to know what unconditional love is.
- Because I have a fetish for small fingers and tiny toes.
- Because I have things to give and stories to tell.
- Because it was my turn.

Our motivation to mother, like our impetus to write, remains elusive. We do it because we want to. We do it because we have no choice. We do it because it is in our blood.

INVITATIONS

❧ *Copy Down Your Children's Questions.* Begin to pay attention to your children's questions. What do their questions reveal about their personality, their preoccupations, their dreams? Make a regular practice of jotting down the questions they ask you in a single day. Then choose one question, and answer it in writing. You might also want to write down a question you would like to ask your child but can't, or a question you do *not* want your child to ask you. If you do this Invitation periodically, you will notice how the nature of your children's questions changes over time.

❧ *Why Write?* Make a list of ten reasons you want to write, however grandiose or picayune they may seem. If you are writing for your own edification, that is fine. If you dream of recognition and fame, that is okay, too. But try to remember that writing, like mothering, is not about being discovered. It is about discovering—who you are, where you came from, and where you are going. In your notebook, explain your reasons for wanting to write. Begin with the phrase *I want to write because . . .* and finish the sentence. Keep writing until you fill two Mother Pages.

↦ *Why Mother?* Make a list of ten reasons you wanted to become a mother. Was this a decision you took for granted, never giving it much thought? Or did you agonize over it through years of blind dates and failed romances? One friend, who adopted a child after years of unsuccessful infertility treatments, described her wish to become a mother as an ache, not unlike the ache she still feels to write a novel. You, too, may discover that your motivations to write are similar to your motivations to mother. Compare the two lists. What's similar? What's different? Jot down the writing start *I wanted to become a mother because . . .* and write two Mother Pages.

INSPIRATIONS

> *To be, or not to be: that is the question.*
> (WILLIAM SHAKESPEARE)

> *What makes a story worthwhile is the question or questions it poses.* (AMY TAN)

> *If we can teach our children that speech is the means of formulating their endless questions, and if we can learn from our children to sincerely ask questions, then something really good has taken place. Our children will talk sooner and learn more; we will talk less and learn sooner (and more).*
> (POLLY BERRIEN BERENDS)

> *The important thing is not to stop questioning.*
> (ROBERT FROST)

WRITING MOTHER'S HELPER

Why Writers Write

Writers claim to write for lots of different reasons: to teach, learn, heal, understand, remember, forget, immortalize themselves, or edify others. To help you articulate your own motives, consider what other writers have to say about why they write.

"Writers write to learn, to explore, to discover, to hear themselves saying what they do not expect to say." (Donald Murray)

"We write because we want to understand our lives. This is why my closets are filled with boxes and boxes of musty old journals. It is why I found pages of poetry under my stepdaughter Kira's mattress when she went off to camp. It is why my father tells me he will soon begin his memoirs." (Lucy Calkins)

"I have written for love, for money, for escape, for grounding, to tune out, to tune in, and to do almost anything that writing could be made to do." (Julia Cameron)

"When I began to write, I found this was the best way to make sense of my life." (John Cheever)

"We are a species that needs and wants to understand who we are. Sheep lice do not seem to share this longing, which is one reason they write so very little. But we do. We have so much we want to say and figure out." (Anne Lamott)

"Writing is an opportunity to take the emotions we have felt many times and give them light, color, and a story." (Natalie Goldberg)

"In many ways writing is the act of saying *I*, of imposing oneself upon other people, of saying listen to me, see it my way, change your mind." (Joan Didion)

"Writing is a form of therapy; sometimes I wonder how all those who do not write, compose or paint can manage to escape the madness, the melancholia, the panic fear which is inherent in the human situation." (Graham Greene)

"I did not look on my work as therapy, and still don't. Yet . . . the act of writing had led me through a swirl of memories that might otherwise have ended in paralysis or worse. By telling stories, you objectify your own experience. You separate it from yourself. You pin down certain truths. You make up others." (Tim O'Brien)

"To insist that writing always has to become something is like barging into someone's shower while she's singing and asking: 'What are you planning to do with that song?' There is no reason why you shouldn't continue writing in this way for your own self-discovery and pleasure." (Lynn Lauber)

"Writing is not life, but I think that sometimes it can be a way back to life." (Stephen King)

"I have to write as if my life depends on it, and of course, it does." (Hortense Calisher)

"The role of a writer is not to say what we all can say, but what we are unable to say." (Anaïs Nin)

"I write to discover what I don't know." (Flannery O'Connor)

"I write because I have questions about life, not answers. . . . I write because often I can't express myself any other way, and I think I'll implode if I don't find the words. . . . I write for very much the same reasons that I read: to startle my mind, to churn my heart, to tingle my spine, to knock the blinders off my eyes and allow me to see beyond the pale.
(Amy Tan)

"I must write, I must write at all costs. For writing is more than living, it is being conscious of living." (Anne Morrow Lindbergh)

"To write is to write is to write is to write is to write is to write is to write." (Gertrude Stein)

SAMPLE MOTHER PAGES

Questions Children Ask

Jordan, age 15
(Fran Greenbaum)

Mom, do you have to work tomorrow?
Mom, what time will you be home?
Mom, what is for dinner?
Can Dave and Tom and Josh come over today?
Can Dave, Josh, Mitch, Tom, and maybe
*   someone else sleep over?*
Will you be home all afternoon?
Can you take us to town?
Can you pick up Olivia at the train station?
Why do I have to go with you to Roberta's?
Why can't you ever buy anything good to eat?
Why do I have to have an uneven amount of kids
*   over when you're gone?*
When can Olivia come over?
Why do I have to have a guitar lesson today?
Why can't I go to that concert?
Why do I need new shoes?

Why do I have to get your car?

Does it drive well?

Can I drive it into the garage?

Why do we have to go to Paramus Park to
    practice driving?

Why can't I get a tattoo?

Why can't I get a piercing? Everyone else is.

Why do I have to go to college? Recording school is
    much cooler.

Anna Christine, age 6
(Amy Carr Wojnarowski)

Momma?

Momma?

Where are you?

Is this real?

What's the matter, Mommy? Are you sad?

Why won't Salami [our male cat] have babies?

What is the best house you ever lived in?

Why does it rain? Where does rain come from?

Mommy?

Momma?

Where are you?

Can we get a Pocahontas costume?

Can we go to Disney World when Ben turns four?

When do I have school next?

Mommy?

What princess would you like to be?

Even if you or Daddy are mad at us, you still love
    us, right?

I'm scared. Will the ghosts hurt me?

Do you believe in ghosts?
I'm shy, Mommy. Is that ok?
Momma?
Where are you?
Can I lay down with you?
Don't leave me, Mommy, ok?

Crissy, age 30
(Barbara Hymans)

Did you have a good trip?
Would you like a glass of something? Water? Diet
    Pepsi?
Do you want your own popcorn bowl?
How long do you cook scallops?
I'm going to make dinner, do you want to come in
    the kitchen and keep me company?
Did you sleep?
Did Jake wake up happy?
Did Jake eat everything?
What did you write about today?
Oh, Mom, you haven't been able to write, have
    you?

James, age 4
(Winnie Atterbury O'Keefe)

Is five minutes longer than ten minutes?
Why did the police go through the red light?
What kind of rig is that?

Are we going on the highway?
What are those warning lights for?
Who made me?
Who made you?
Who made Daddy?
Who made Grandma?
Who made Grandpa?
Does everyone die in this whole world?
Where do they go?
Will Spider-Man go to heaven?
Will Batman go to heaven?
Will Superman go to heaven?
Who goes to hell?
Does the bad guy go to hell?
Is Batman a friend of Spider-Man?
Is Spider-Man a friend of Superman?
Is Superman a friend of Batman?
Do they fight the police?
Mom, will you look at my police truck?
Mom, what is our errand?
Is it long?

In the Middle—
Finding Your Balance

Society perpetuates as many myths about motherhood as we do about writing—myths that often stand in stark contrast to reality. Legends about such literary giants as William Shakespeare, Virginia Woolf, and Ernest Hemingway fool us into thinking that all writers are born geniuses, suicidal depressives, or alcoholic adventurers, generalizations that only distance us from our dream to write. And we seem to have invented equally misleading myths about mothers. The new mother whose infant won't latch on wonders what has become of maternal instinct. The go-to-work mother who, for the second time in a week, drops her third grader at school eight minutes after the bell and is herself late for a meeting feels like anything but the supermom she has read so much about. The stay-at-home mother who screams at her son for leaving a wet towel on the wood floor—*again*—forgets momentarily the meaning of unconditional love. At no time is it more difficult for mothers to maintain our equilibrium than when we find ourselves in the middle—in middle age with growing children and aging parents. But mothers at every stage of parenting can feel unsettled and off-balance. No wonder so many of us wake up many days with what I call irritable morning syndrome! In this section of

Writing Motherhood, I will help you separate fact from fiction as you try to find your balance somewhere in the middle.

INSPIRATIONS

> *On the one hand, everyone wants their mom to be a regular mom, whatever that thing is. They want their moms to make pancakes and be there for them. Even nowadays, when there are almost no "regular moms" left in America, I think people still have a yearning for this fantasy, Hallmark-card mom.*
> (NORA EPHRON)

> *What made my predicament worse was that I had come to believe one of the great American myths—the myth of the natural mother. I grew up thinking that parenting in general and mothering in particular was something a woman could just do without preparation. . . . We all thought that a "good mother" didn't need lessons.* (SUSAN CHEEVER)

> *We've finally stopped falling for the great palace lie that such a person [as a normal mother] exists. Somewhere along the way, we figured out that normal is a setting on the dryer.*
> (ANNE LAMOTT)

10

ONE DAY IN THE LIFE
OF A MOTHER

I have always wanted to write a weekly column for my local newspaper that would cover one day in the life of a typical town employee: a kindergarten teacher, a sanitation worker, a volunteer fireman, the meter maid. I imagined shadowing the person from sunup until sundown, recording the minute details of his or her day, then spinning those strands into the stuff of story. I am sure I could have sold the idea to the editor of the *Ridgewood News*, but I wonder if she would have approved a profile of the worker who interests me the most: the mother.

I am a fan of the magazine *Working Mother*, but its title offends me. I know women with MBAs and law degrees from Columbia and Yale who, after holding high-powered jobs at high-octane firms, have opted to stay home with their children. I know other women who juggle part- or full-time jobs with parenting. All mothers work, whether we get paid for it or not.

When my son was in the fourth grade, he turned to me one morning before school and asked, in a voice more condescending than curious, "What do you *do* all day?" My first reaction was to chuckle at his egocentric view of the world. At ten years of age, Miles was not able to imagine that I had a life separate from his. But when I tried to give him an honest answer, my amusement turned by degrees to uncertainty and then to defensiveness. What *do* I do all day?

Whether in answer to my son's question or in validation of my life as a mother, I began to examine my days through a magnifying glass and to record the fine print in my Mother's Notebook. Here's one page, dated October 11, 2000:

6:30 AM

The alarm cuts into my dream and jolts me into wakefulness. Mark stands stretching, naked, at the edge of the bed. Not fully awake, I feel a pang of guilt over another night without intimacy. I throw back the covers, pull on my tattered terry robe and shift into first gear. Mental checklist: Colette must get to school early for retest; Miles must wear layers for field trip; they'll need a protein breakfast for brain power; leave time to pack brown bag lunches; recyclables must go out; when should I go to the gym; I want to write first thing; then there are telephone calls to make and bills to pay. Now I'm in high speed. Unloading the dishwasher. Slicing French bread. Beating eggs. Slathering Hellmann's mayonnaise onto squares of whole wheat bread. Coaxing the kids out of bed. Miles, at 10, smells like a boy-man, Dove soap mixed in with sweat and the sour stench of retainer mouth. Colette, now 12, emits a she-smell, strong and decisive; she will make an impression on the world. The kids are eating breakfast: sliced bananas with cinnamon, French toast with Vermont maple syrup, Tropicana orange juice, No Pulp. I know I am doing something right because they say thank you even with their eyes at half-mast and their bodies buoyant with sleep. Miles especially resists waking up, just as he regrets growing up, not wanting the time to pass so quickly. I glance at the clock and tell them it is time for school.

The tedium of daily life lulls us into boredom, tricks us into thinking that what we do every day as mothers is not important. Then we witness a mini-milestone or a fleeting show of humanity—a kiss, a kindness—and we know that motherhood is at once mythical and mundane. Granted, there is nothing enchanting about neon Band-Aids, carrot sticks, or No. 2 pencils, small everyday things sold on supermarket shelves, but there is something miraculous about ten tiny fingers and toes. There is nothing heroic about fixing peanut butter and jelly sandwiches, broken shoelaces, or scraped knees, but there is something transformative about healing hurt feelings. There is nothing enlightening about showing your child how to ride a two-wheeler or do long division, but there is something magical about a first word or a first step. When you burrow in the small details of your days, you begin to illuminate the bigness of your life. You begin to see the magnitude in the minutiae.

Many years ago, at a cocktail party, someone asked my husband, "What do you do?" I will always adore him for his answer. "I'm a dad," he said. Mothers may not receive paychecks or benefits, raises or promotions, but as my husband suggested, we do the most important job of all: raising a child—one day at a time.

INVITATIONS

- ☙ *One Day in Your Life as a Mother.* Pretend you are a reporter researching a story about the life of a mother. In your

Mother's Notebook, record your daily doings for an entire week. Narrow your focus each day to one block of time: breakfast, nap time, bedtime. Be as specific as you can and use as much detail as possible. If you are writing about doing the breakfast dishes, tell me whether you were using Palmolive or Ajax. Were you wearing rubber gloves? What color were they? How many times were you interrupted—by the telephone or the doorbell or the cat? By the end of the week, you will have written an accurate chronicle of one day in your life as a mother.

❧ *Help Wanted: Mother.* Make a T-chart on a blank page in your Mother's Notebook. In the left column, list ten to fifteen activities you do as a mother. Again, be as specific as you can: *change diapers, tie shoelaces, braid pigtails, schedule playdates, referee fights, bake cupcakes, recite the "Itsy Bitsy Spider" fifteen times a day, grocery shop, help with homework, drive to baseball and ballet and back again, carve Halloween pumpkins, finger paint, gift wrap birthday presents, scrub grass stains from the knees of jeans, pay the babysitter and the dentist and the math tutor.* On the right column of your T-chart, list ten to fifteen personality traits of a mother—the ones you possess and the ones you wish you did: *selfless, generous, loving, trusting, playful, wise, patient, creative, artsy, nurturing, calm, energetic, youthful, forgiving.* Look over both lists and highlight the words and phrases that startle, inform, or amuse you. Use those phrases to draft a help-wanted ad for a replacement mother. Read the ads in your local newspaper for ideas. Consider how to advertise the salary, the benefits, the hours. Is the work full- or part-time? You may want to write the ad in the form of a poem, with each item printed on its own line. Title the poem "Help Wanted: Mother," and post it on your refrigerator or paste it into your Mother's Notebook. Be honest. Be bold. Have fun.

INSPIRATIONS

It's easy to lose sight of the larger perspective when we're caught up in daily life—signing permission slips, making lunches, teaching our children to be kind to one another. It doesn't always feel as if we're doing anything truly profound. And yet with each kiss, with each lesson, we are doing the work of the ages. (DENISE ROY)

Motherhood is a job. With most jobs, the more you do it, the better you get at it. There's a certain learning curve and then you're fine. Motherhood is a job where the learning curve never ends. You're constantly trying to figure out the parameters of what's expected of you. (KATE MOSES)

If this were a job, you'd quit! (KATHE RUTLER)

SAMPLE MOTHER PAGE

Wanted: Replacement Mother
by Kathe Rutler

Large family
In need of
Replacement mother.

Erratic hours
On call 24/7
Compensation variable
Days off subject to last minute cancellation

Must be able to
Function coherently on very little sleep
Communicate effectively with all age groups
Negotiate sibling skirmishes and teenage strife
Be extremely diplomatic about friends
Listen without overreacting
Patch up wounds without flinching
Make large quantities of white sticky rice
Without burning the pot
As good with the brown paper bag as you are at
    picking out a prom dress.
And don't worry about a little sand in the car.

A sense of humor is a must
Tasteful wackiness is acceptable
But please don't get carried away
You will, above all, be required to set a good example
Creativity is encouraged
You should be subtly intelligent and discreet
It is not necessary to play a musical instrument
But you must be willing to
Sing at the top of your lungs when the situation
    calls for it.

Have a poker face ready at all times
Wear flipflops in the winter just for fun
Be clever at planning the future
While remaining present at all times.

Must sign up for the long haul
Meaning birthdays, graduations, weddings
Anniversaries, grandchildren and family reunions
Never lose sight of the important things
The big picture
The little details
And most of all love.

WRITING MOTHER'S HELPER

Every Day Is Mother's Day: A History of the Holiday

Hallmark did not invent Mother's Day. Nor did President Woodrow Wilson, who proclaimed the day a national holiday in 1914. Mother's Day can be traced to ancient times, when the Greeks held spring festivals to commemorate Rhea, mother of the Olympian gods. Centuries later, in the 1600s, England set aside the fourth Sunday in Lent, called Mothering Sunday, first in honor of Mary, mother of Christ, and later expanded to honor mothers everywhere. Today, countries around the world celebrate Mother's Day in different ways and at different times throughout the year.

In the United States, Mother's Day started as a day devoted to peace. Beginning in 1872 and for several years thereafter, Julia Ward Howe, a poet, pacifist, and suffragist, held an annual Mother's Day rally for peace because she believed that mothers bore the greatest toll of wartime casualties. Years later, in 1907, Anna Jarvis of Grafton, West Virginia, launched a campaign to commemorate the life and work of her mother, an Appalachian homemaker and advocate for the poor. Legend has it that Jarvis's mother said, in a Sunday school lesson, "I hope and pray that someone, sometime, will found a memorial mother's day. There are many days for men, but none for mothers." Little did she know that her own daughter would be the one to commemorate this day.

Jarvis and her supporters lobbied prominent businessmen and politicians in their quest for a national observance of mothers. Jarvis chose the second Sunday in May and established the custom of wearing a carnation, her mother's favorite flower. To this day, many people wear a colored carnation if their mother is living, a white one if she is dead. In 1914, President Woodrow Wilson signed a joint resolution of Congress recommending that the legislative and executive branches of government observe Mother's Day. He was authorized the next year to proclaim Mother's Day a national holiday.

Jarvis eventually became enraged by the increasing commercialism of Mother's Day, fearing that the day's sentiment was being sacrificed for profit. Nonetheless, the second Sunday of May has become the most popular day of the year to dine out, send flowers, and place long-distance telephone calls, as sons and daughters at home and abroad seek ways to venerate their mothers.

11

BEDTIME STORIES

For as long as there has been someone to listen, human beings have felt compelled to tell their stories. In prehistoric times, cave dwellers etched crude pictographs of hunts and herds on stone walls. Thousands of years later, the bards of ancient Greece sang songs of the heroes, gods, and monsters. Since before the time of Christ, priests and prophets have told of the miracles and miseries of men—stories that came to be written down in the Old and New Testaments. Whether to educate or edify, to explain or entertain, to soothe or frighten, stories have been passed down from one generation to the next like heirlooms. The timeless themes of struggle and triumph, of good and evil, appear again and again in myths and legends, in fairy tales and folklore. They have become a part of our collective unconscious.

Even so, I grew up in a house without story. My parents were atheists, so I never heard the stories of the Torah or Bible. Their parents were immigrants, interested more in learning the ways of the new country than in teaching the ways of the old. My grandparents handed down no rites, no rituals, hardly even any recipes, other than one for kugel and another for piroshki, both of which my mother has long forgotten how to make. Like many of their generations, my parents and grandparents traded in tradition and story for innovation and change.

When my children were little, I began telling them stories not so much out of reverence for a lost art as out of desperation—to distract them when they were hungry, to pacify them when they were afraid, to quiet them when they grew fidgety. I felt self-conscious at first, like when I try to speak French with a native (*Je parle français un peu*). Then my father-in-law came to visit, and I became hopelessly tongue-tied.

Bebop, as my children call him, has the mystique and comportment of a real live storyteller. Originally six feet six inches tall (rumor has it that he grew one foot the summer between his sophomore and junior year of high school), he now stoops on a bony frame, ties his hair in a wispy ponytail, and flaunts a bushy, white beard and eyebrows to match. Every night at bedtime, Bebop would ask each of my children to name an animal, and then, spontaneously and without forethought, he would weave together the convoluted fate of a boa constrictor and a bat, a muskrat and a cougar, an elephant and a rainbow trout. Listening to Bebop's stories made me think of the movie *Out of Africa*, in which the main character enchants her fellow expatriates with stories spun from someone else's first line. Listening to his stories also made me want to give up storytelling altogether.

I knew that I could never learn to tell stories like Bebop, especially fantastical tales of wild animals and exotic places. I also knew that I didn't want my children to grow up, as I had, without story. Convinced that I lacked the confidence and the imagination to make up stories on the spot, I signed up for a class in storytelling. There I picked up a few tricks of the trade—the importance of varying tempo and pacing, when to use hand gestures and facial expressions, how to elicit audience participation. But ultimately I learned how to tell stories the same way I learned how to write: by telling them.

Every one of us has a storyteller somewhere inside. All we have to do is find her and wake her up. More important, each of us has a limitless storehouse of stories waiting to be told. As author Katrina Kenison writes in her book *Mitten Strings for God: Reflections for Mothers in a Hurry,* "Someplace deep within me, I carry every story I have ever heard, every story I have ever lived, every story I will ever need." So do you. Some stories you have inherited; others you will invent. But the majority of your stories will come from having lived them—from school and books, memories and dreams, nature and the cosmos, leaving home and coming home, growing up and growing old.

Because I believe that the best way to get to know someone is through story, I begin each session of *Writing Motherhood* by inviting students to introduce themselves with a personal anecdote: the etymology of their name, something about themselves that could not be true for anyone else in the room, an event in their life that reads like a fairy tale or a ghost story. Without fail, storytelling is an instant icebreaker for students new to *Writing Motherhood* but in the weeks that follow it proves to be a great warm-up for writing as well. Whether we are recounting birth stories, photo stories, or toy stories, students share their histories with one another in class, then go home primed to write them down. Natalie Goldberg says that talk is the exercise ground for writing. When we tell stories, we notice what draws listeners in, what makes them laugh, what lulls them to sleep. We limber up for the strenuous work ahead.

Whether or not you find it easier to put on paper a story you have told out loud, I'm sure you will agree that writing and storytelling come from the same primal place—the oldest human longing for self-revelation. Stories may not immortalize you and me, the way the Greek myths immortalized Achilles and Odysseus, but they allow us to pass on who we are and where we came from. They connect one generation to the next—parent to child to grandchild. That's what stories are for. As Tim O'Brien writes in his autobiographical novel *The Things They Carried,* "Stories are for joining the past to the future. Stories are for those late hours in the night when you can't remember how you got from where you were to where you are. Stories are for eternity, when memory is erased, when there is nothing to remember except the story."

Long after you and I are gone, our children and our grand-children will remember our stories.

INVITATIONS

꘎ *Story Starts.* On a blank page in your Mother's Notebook, make a list of the stories you were brought up on—the ones you were told by your parents and grandparents, aunts and uncles. Make a second list of the stories you have told again and again—to your children, your lovers, your friends. Now make a third list of the stories you have never dared to tell— because they are too shameful or embarrassing or disap-pointing. Circle one story each day and write it down. Write it the way you would tell it to a friend, with lapses and dis-connects and interjections. Since you are not writing for publication, feel free to exaggerate, invent, or add color if fic-tion brings you closer to the truth than fact. As Tim O'Brien tells us, "Story truth is truer sometimes than happening truth." Begin anywhere, and stop when you fill two Mother Pages. Consider these writings "story starts." You can return to them later to fill in the gaps, flush out the excess, and test for authenticity.

꘎ *Bedtime Stories.* What are your children's favorite bedtime stories? Which books do you read aloud night after night? What stories do you tell over and over? What were *your* favorite bedtime stories as a child? Regardless of your chil-dren's ages, write down the writing start *bedtime stories* and tell me how storytelling is (or was) a part of your nighttime ritual.

INSPIRATIONS

Every one of you is a storyteller. Your ancestors sat around a campfire or a sweat lodge or a table and recorded their histories by telling their stories. Now you tell them. (NANCY SLONIM ARONIE)

The fact is that stories matter deeply to us; we yearn both to hear and to tell them. We are tuned, as if exquisite instruments, for beginnings, middles, and endings. (LYNN LAUBER)

Every person is born into life as a blank page—and every person leaves life as a full book. Our lives are our story, and our story is our life. (CHRISTINA BALDWIN)

WRITING MOTHER'S HELPER

Learn to Listen

According to author Katrina Kenison, our first task as storytellers is to learn to listen. And to learn to listen, she says, we must first practice being quiet—not an easy task for mothers, who are used to barking orders, giving instructions, and doling out advice. Much of the time, I am so busy being noisy—talking on the telephone, vacuuming the carpet, answering the doorbell—that I don't hear what my children are saying. Again and again, they have to ask me, for a second and a third time, to sign a permission slip or pick up a bottle of Wite-Out. "I must have early Alzheimer's," I tell them sheepishly. "No," they insist. "You just don't listen." Which makes me feel, of course, like a Bad Mother. Worse, it makes me wonder what else I didn't hear all those times I wasn't listening. Natalie Goldberg says that writing is 90 percent listening. You take in the world around you—not just with your eyes and ears but with your whole body as well—and you churn it out on paper. Mothering, too, is 90 percent listening. Sometimes all we do is talk when all we need to do is listen.

INSPIRATIONS

Writers have to cultivate the habit early in life of listening to people other than themselves. (RUSSELL BAKER)

Writing is a way of listening to ourselves, putting an ear to the wall of our interiors, discerning the rustle of our souls. (LYNN LAUBER)

12

BODY LANGUAGE

I could tell you a story about my teeth, how my brother tormented me with the nickname Buck Tooth all the years my parents drove me an hour and twenty minutes every six weeks to a progressive orthodontist who gently coaxed my mammoth front teeth into place. I could tell you a story about my breasts, how they stopped me finally from dancing onstage because, after puberty, they fell one beat behind the rest of my body. I could tell you a story about the scar on my right breast, but the scar is still purple, so it is too soon to tell that story. I could tell you a story about my hands, how they are identical to my mother's hands, so that when we interlace fingers I cannot tell where mine end and hers begin, which is a story that has haunted me my whole life, the fear that I will become my mother. These are the stories our bodies carry, if we let our bodies talk.

Knowing that our bodies are topographical maps of the physical and emotional journeys we have traveled so far, I developed a class for *Writing Motherhood* called "Body Language." Its focus is not so much on how our bodies manifest experience through shrugs and postures and mannerisms, what we typically associate with body language, but instead on how experience etches itself on our bodies in the form of moles and scars, stretch marks and age spots, broken bones and fallen arches—life marks as compared with birth marks. I think of the Wallace Stegner character in *Crossing to Safety* who, as an old man looking back on his life, says, "I set out to make my mark on the world, but the world instead left its marks on me." No one among us escapes unscathed.

Writing is a natural way to communicate body language, for writing is not just a mental exertion. Like crunches and squats, it is physical, too. The day I conceptualized the class on body language coincided with my weekly grocery shopping. As I stood in line to check out, absentmindedly placing the lettuce, the toilet paper, the salami, on the conveyor belt, my eye landed on the cover of *Self* magazine, which touted, among other promises, "The Perfect 10-Minute Workout." With only ten minutes of exercise a day, I could have the perfect abs, the perfect thighs, the perfect butt. Isn't this the same promise I extend to Writing Mothers? In just fifteen minutes of daily writing—two Mother Pages—you can whip your writing muscles into shape.

When I write, I get in and out of my chair. I circle around the butcher block in my kitchen. I stand before the living room window and stare out. I stretch, I squirm, I slouch, I grow still. This is not procrastinating; this is preparing. Sometimes when I write, I laugh or cry. Always I speak the words out loud so that I can hear the music and rhythm of the writing. Sometimes when I write, my heart quickens and I notice damp circles under my arms. Or my mouth waters, my nose itches, a muscle twinges as a memory awakens—what I call *muscle memory* in writing. Indeed, writing is as physical as it is cerebral. Which is why you may feel exhausted, then invigorated, after you write.

The first day I taught a class on body language, I remember pulling up in front of the building, pausing a moment before turning off the ignition, knowing that with the engine my cell phone, too, would power down, deciding to leave the phone in the car mount since I would turn it off inside the classroom anyway, even though my daughter was home sick. She was nearly sixteen and could manage for two hours on her own. An hour later, while my students were writing about an accident or an illness, about a scar or a mole, about sagging skin or cracked nipples, Colette accidentally stabbed herself with a pair of sewing scissors. The scissors stuck in her knee, and when she dislodged them, she had to cup the blood with both hands to avoid staining the beige carpet. She telephoned me but my cell phone was off, so she telephoned her father, who could, fortunately, take her to Urgent Care. Ten stitches, sloppily threaded—they have left a nasty scar, a *scary* one. When Colette grows up, she can write down the story of how her mother wasn't there when she needed her, which is, of course, any child's greatest fear, but especially hers—that I won't be there to pick out her dress for the senior prom, to pack her trunk for college, to answer the telephone when she calls to tell me she has finally met someone she loves.

Later that night, I took Colette with me to see my therapist. Dr. Lynne suggested, ever so subtly, that perhaps the stabbing was not entirely accidental, at which point Colette, who had been dozing off, snapped to attention. She knows about self-mutilation, knows a flamboyant boy named Josh who once carved her initials into his right thigh and vowed to do it again if she did not remain his friend. When I told Colette that maybe I had not been paying enough attention to her—first because of my brother's illness and then following my own diagnosis—but that she had better believe she had my attention now, Colette objected. She said that she felt negligent toward me, preoccupied with her teenage dramas when I was playing out the drama of life and death. Ten black stitches. Dried blood. Regret. A scar that will forever remind us of the year they cremated my brother's body and cut open my breast. Now Colette can say she is nearly an adult, old enough to carry in her body the wounds of childhood and the scars of adolescence. She is forever marked.

All women are. I recently heard that two editors wanted to compile a collection of personal stories by women about their bodies. Their idea was to assign each writer one anatomical part or feature: her feet, nose, breasts, hair, stature, weight—whatever roused the most pain or shame. I don't know what came of the project, but I do know that it speaks to the ways in which we women wrestle with body image in a nip-and-tuck culture that idolizes youth and beauty. Over the years, my students have written so many stories about their bodies that we could easily compile our own anthology.

At the end of one class on body language, one of my longtime students, who had been struggling with her writing for weeks, approached me and said, "Finally, this is a subject I can write about. I have reams to write about my body." I'm sure you do, too.

INVITATIONS

↬ *Our Bodies, Our Stories.* Set aside ten minutes when you are home alone. Stand naked in front of a mirror and inspect your body the way a dermatologist would. Take note of scars and moles, lines and wrinkles, freckles and age spots. Which parts of your body do you like? Which ones have you always regretted? What has changed over the years? Each day this week, write about one body part or one marking on your body. Alternatively, you can use any of these writing starts: *I have always hated my . . . , I still have pretty . . . ; write about breasts, my stomach, footprints, holding hands, fingernails; tell me a story about your teeth, a bad haircut; write about your oldest or newest scar, broken bones, an accident, an illness, sore muscles.* Or simply write down the writing start *body language* and start writing.

↬ *Their Bodies, Their Stories.* Jot down ten events in the life of your child's body. Think of accidents, illnesses, hospitalizations, growth spurts, trips to the emergency room, a fall, a broken bone, a bad sunburn, a bout with poison ivy, a piercing or tattoo. To help you remember, do a mental scan of their body, starting with the scalp and moving down to the soles of their feet. Even young children have scars and moles and freckles that carry stories. And don't forget the psychic scars, the ones that may not be visible to the eye. Now circle those events that cause a physiological reaction when you think of them, perhaps because you felt responsible or because you felt powerless. Write one body story each day. Begin with the facts (the fall from the swing set when you turned your back, the screams in the ER when the doctor set the bones, the tiny plaster cast that still sits in his closet) and move on to the feelings (the terror turned to anger then relief).

Inspirations

I say all writers, no matter how fat, thin, or flabby, have good figures. They are always working out. Remember this. They are in tune, toned up, in rhythm with the hills, the highway, and can go for long stretches and many miles of paper. They move with grace in and out of many worlds.
(Natalie Goldberg)

As a young woman, I thought about my body all the time: how to disguise it, to shape it, to present it, to comfort it; what everyone else thought of it. Motherhood taught me to live in it. (Kate Moses)

I can't argue with those who told me my life would completely change with eight pounds of love. My stretch marks are proof of that. And if you think the ones on my stomach are bad, you should see my heart.
(Therese J. Borchard)

WRITING MOTHER'S HELPER

Let Your Body Talk

The English language is filled with idiomatic expressions that derive from the human body: *I put my foot in my mouth. She is head over heels in love. He has broad shoulders.* In your Mother's Notebook, use body parts as verbs and adjectives to make your writing more visceral. *I toed my way down in the dark. She is sure-footed. He thumbed a ride. I couldn't stomach the news. He elbowed his way through the crowd.* As you begin writing about your body, let your body talk.

SAMPLE MOTHER PAGE

A Reflection on the Not-So-Bodacious Bodies of Middle-Aged Matrons
by Mary Jo Freebody

I regret the mocha coffee drink
And the sweet corn with butter
As I slide into my cotton nightie.
My guilt rides rampant at the end of a day
Without my three-mile walk.
I am depressed by my drooping eyelids
And dismayed by my dimpled and pillowy padded
*   parts.*

But wait!

Here is a creative idea.
Maybe, just maybe, this is all
Part of God's grand design.

Our laps are soft
And our breasts are full
So grandchildren can be comforted by our warm
    closeness.
Our firmly planted feet
And well-worn faces
Give encouragement
To our uncertain adult children.
Our square, stable, solid bodies
Give support to our frail, leaning parents.

I am comforted to think that those I love the
    most
Might benefit from the parts of me I like the least.
Was that part of God's plan?

13

Copycats

As parents, we want our sons and daughters to stand out from the crowd. As children, they just want to fit in. As parents, we want them to be leaders. As children, they sometimes prefer to follow. So your daughter throws away her ballet slippers the day after her friend quits dance class. Your son shoulders a lacrosse stick to school now that the popular boys do. No matter what we say or do, our children become carbon copies of their friends. They dress alike, walk alike, and talk alike. Pretty soon, you can hardly tell them apart.

As developing writers, we would do well to follow our children's example. Just as they will define their own identity by mirroring their friends, so you will discover your own style by imitating other writers. Attach yourself to a writer you love. Read everything he has written. Notice the moves she makes: how she exaggerates character, employs street talk, uses detail. Don't worry if you never took college English. You don't need to know the literary terms to appreciate their effect, any more than a writer consciously decides now is a good time to plug in hyperbole (extravagant exaggeration) or alliteration (recurrent consonant sounds). As you read, just begin to pay attention to *how* an author writes, not only *what* he writes. Does she use punctuation or capitalization in an unusual way? Does he juxtapose long sentences with short ones? Does she embed lists or recipes or dialogue in the narrative? Paying such close attention to craft will not impede your reading; it will enrich it. With practice, you will find yourself reading like a writer—reading with a writer's eyes.

For every book you read, ask yourself, *What did I learn about writing from this author?* (And keep in mind that you can learn as much—sometimes more—from the books you do not like as from those you do like.) Write the lessons down in your Mother's Notebook. Then, the next time you write your Mother Pages, try on one aspect of the writer's style. Steal a word or phrase and use it as a writing start. Borrow a metaphor and apply it to your own life. Imitate an element of craft: try writing in dialect, use swear words, throw in a one-line paragraph. One of my favorite professors at Teachers College described this exercise as writing *after* an author. She didn't invent it, though. For as long as books have been written, writers have taken on other writers as models and mentors.

I witness this phenomenon in my classes every day. One student's phrase suddenly turns up in another student's writing, usually without her intending it. I think this happens because writers have big ears. We are always listening for language, and when we take in good language, that is what comes out. One time, a student was offended. She sought me out after class and cried, "Did you hear that? She copied me! That was like the piece I wrote last week."

"She's just trying you on for size," I told her. "Take it as a compliment."

No matter how hard we strive to be original, every sentence we write is in some way shaped by something we have read or heard. This is not plagiarism; we are not publishing someone else's words in our own name. This is apprenticeship; we are studying someone else's style as we develop our own. This is how artists learn their craft, how writers learn how to write. As Natalie Goldberg says, "We are carried on the backs of all the writers who came before us."

In fact, I borrowed the idea for this chapter from a line in *Writing Down the Bones,* Goldberg's first book. I don't think she would mind. Several years ago, I attended one of her weeklong writing workshops in Taos, New Mexico. On the last day of the workshop, she told us, "You are part of a long lineage of writers. Read them and steal from them." One participant raised his hand and asked, "Would you mind if I titled my next book *Far Silent Freeway?*"—an obvious reference to *Long Quiet Highway,* the memoir Goldberg had just published. The room went silent; then we erupted in laughter. "Go ahead," Goldberg said, smiling. Anyone can copy an author's words, but no one can tell someone else's story because no one can live another person's life.

Echoing the voices of other writers is an essential practice in finding your own voice. Like speaking in a foreign accent or wearing a costume to a party, imitating another writer's style takes daring. But it can also be liberating. By assuming someone else's persona—in writing or in life—you may discover a part of yourself you didn't know was there. So go ahead and follow your children's example. Be a copycat.

INVITATIONS

- ◆ *Read Like a Writer.* For every book you read, identify five things you learned about writing from the author—not just the techniques you may want to emulate, but also those you will want to avoid. Write the lessons down in your Mother's Notebook. Then, if you feel so inspired, try them out in your Mother Pages. Even if you don't make a conscious effort to write "after" an author, you will naturally take what works and make it your own.

- ◆ *Copycats.* Think of a time your child followed the crowd or succumbed to peer pressure. Perhaps it was innocent, such as straightening her hair, wearing Bermuda shorts, or playing poker. Perhaps it was not so innocent, such as urinating on the radiator in the school bathroom or playing chicken with trains. Now think of a time your child did not follow the crowd, a time she stood up for her beliefs rather than standing by her friends. Choose one incident and write two Mother Pages. Or jot down the writing start *copycats* and see where it takes you.

INSPIRATIONS

It is the ego's demand that our work be totally original—as if such a thing were possible. All work is influenced by other work. All people are influenced by other people.
(JULIA CAMERON)

Don't ever hesitate to imitate another writer—every artist learning his craft needs some models. Eventually you'll find your own voice and shed the skin of the writer you imitated.
(WILLIAM ZINSSER)

Every book you pick up has its own lesson or lessons, and quite often the bad books have more to teach than the good ones. (STEPHEN KING)

14

LEFT OUT

When Miles was in the seventh grade, he called after school one day to say he was staying late for a game of basketball. Twenty minutes later he called again, this time asking to be picked up. "Something happened," he said. But he wouldn't say more until he was safely in the car. He and three friends were playing two-on-two in the schoolyard when a large and rowdy group of boys approached their court and suggested they play a tournament game. Four captains were selected. The remaining seventeen boys lined up against the wall. One by one, each boy bounded off the wall when his name was called until all four teams had an even five players. Only Miles was left to hold up the wall. "You can take Miles," TG said to Pat. "Naw, you take 'im," Pat answered. Whereby Miles gathered up his backpack and his basketball and muttered, "I gotta go anyway." Ernie ran after him, begging Miles to leave his ball behind. The boys needed two balls to play the game, Ernie urged. Ernie himself would return the ball to Miles first thing tomorrow. He promised.

From the kitchen window, I watched Miles shoot hoops alone on our dead-end street. While he attempted to heal his wounds through physical exertion, I plotted ways to retaliate. I could cut off every mother whose child was party to my son's ostracizing. I could publish an editorial in the *Ridgewood News* exposing the pimply barbarians. I could transfer Miles to another school where he would unanimously be voted captain of the basketball team, if not class president. I could telephone the principal of the middle school or the mayor of Ridgewood or the president of the United States and protest. Surely someone—or something—could make things right for my son.

Instead, I went to my bookshelf, took down a copy of Anne Lamott's *Operating Instructions,* and reread for the forty-second time that year the passage in which the author states that her greatest fear in bringing a child into this world—a fear more worrisome than infant inoculations, automobile accidents, and drunken teenagers, a fear more troubling than school violence, terrorist attacks, and global warming—is the knowledge that "he or she is eventually going to have to go through the seventh and eighth grades." For Lamott, who remembers this age as a kind of living hell, a pit into which she descended from the light and laughter of the elementary years, middle school was about feeling, in her words, "completely other." For my son, then in the winter of his seventh-grade year—the stark middle of middle school—it was about feeling left out.

I can tell you that the only thing as bad as being a child who feels left out is being the parent of a child who feels left out. Which may explain why I cried throughout back-to-school night each September my two children entered middle school—both in memory of my own experience and in anticipation of theirs. Since then, I have seen mothers of middle schoolers pick up the telephone when their sons did not receive an invitation to a birthday party or a bar mitzvah. I have watched fathers reprimand coaches when their daughters spent more time on the bench than on the playing field. I have overheard parents challenge teachers when their child did not get a part in the school play. Such actions rarely help; more often, they hurt. I know because I have stooped to them all—and not just during the middle school years. I can remember placing those pushy telephone calls as far back as the first grade, when Miles was elbowed out of the sandbox by a boy twice his bulk.

In my experience, other than talking gently with my child, the only act that helps to heal and clarify is to open my notebook and write the details down. Try it. The next time you are seething or hyperventilating because you or your child has been left out, sit down and write two Mother Pages. Or simply write the writing start *left out,* and see where it takes you. From listening to the stories Writing Mothers have read aloud, I know that there is no getting around the feeling. But there is getting through it. After seventh grade there will be eighth grade and high school and eventually college. And in a world where slavery and the Holocaust and 9/11 can happen, knowing how it feels to be left out or singled out may not be such a bad thing.

INVITATIONS

↦ *Left Out.* Write down the writing start *left out* and start writing. One mother in my classes wrote about the season her son was the only one of his friends who did not make the travel basketball team. Another wrote about the September her daughter ate lunch in a stall in the girls' bathroom because nobody would offer her a seat in the cafeteria. My writing partner, Deborah, wrote about feeling like an outsider among her closest friends, all of whom were pregnant at the time she was undergoing infertility treatments. Over the years, Writing Mothers have written about being left out and left back and left behind, and they have written about leftovers. As you will discover, there are many ways to feel left out.

↦ *Cafeteria Confidential.* First documented in Rosalind Wiseman's book *Queen Bees and Wannabes* and later popularized in the movie *Mean Girls,* the school cafeteria can be as socially segregated as any major metropolitan area, with separate tables for the Asians and the African-Americans, the nerds and the jocks, the creative types and the popular kids. The lunch-room is where children come to know who is in and who is out. If you could spend a lunch period in the cafeteria of your children's school, what might you see? What would look famil-iar? What has changed since your day? Write down the writ-ing start *cafeteria confidential* and recount a lunchroom story, anecdote, or memory about your child or from your child-hood. Remember to mention the brown bag lunches, the wet plastic trays, the soggy french fries, the sticky linoleum floor. Don't leave anything out.

INSPIRATIONS

*Many girls can describe a universal American phenomenon—
the scapegoating of girls by one another. . . . Scapegoats are
shunned, teased, bullied and harassed in a hundred different
ways. Girls who are smart, assertive, confident, too pretty
or not pretty enough are likely to be scapegoated.*
(MARY PIPHER)

*Margaret wasn't Margaret; she was Maggie Rogers, one of
the most impossible girls in my grade. She hung out with the
ultracool crowd, the kids who never, ever, talk to anyone but
themselves. I shoved my hands into my pockets and turned
green.* (NARRATOR OF *JACK* BY A. M. HOMES)

SAMPLE MOTHER PAGE

Left Out
by Deborah Chiel

I often feel left out by Michelle. She is everything that I am not, and in spite of all my years in therapy, still yearn to be: polished, confident, tastefully dressed, happy, confident. She has the perfect baby and a handsome husband who doesn't buy his clothes at Antique Boutique or look like a derelict on weekends, even when he hasn't shaved.

When I spend time with both Michelle and Jackie, I envy not that they gave birth to their children, but their shared experience of raising their babies from infancy. They ask each other questions and give advice. I keep silent. What do I know about breast-feeding or teething? My daughter was thirteen months old and already had all her baby teeth when I first held her in my arms.

I remember feeling left out when the two of them were pregnant at the same time. I wanted to be a part of their pregnancy club. I wanted to have morning sickness and a fat belly and swollen ankles. My friends gave birth to boys two weeks apart. They bought themselves special watches to keep track of when they had to nurse their babies. I made fun of those watches behind their backs, but I desperately wanted one, too.

Owning that watch symbolized being part of the "in" crowd, a status that eluded me all through high school, when I could never figure out the secret language that all the popular girls spoke. I wanted to live near them, up on Richardson Road. I wanted my curly hair to hang straight and end in a flip at my shoulders as theirs did, instead of exploding into a huge ball of frizz whenever the weather turned damp. I wanted to wear Fair Isle sweaters. I wanted a boyfriend who would make out with me at the parties to which I was never invited.

I had none of these. My hair would not be tamed. My mother refused to buy me any of the sweaters I coveted. I never visited any of those Richardson Road homes, and I went dateless every weekend. Instead, I hung out with girls who were friends with me because they, too, felt left out.

15

DUMP TRUCK

One Sunday night when Colette was in the ninth grade, rather than stay up with the family to watch a movie, I decided to go to bed early so that I could wake up at six o'clock the next morning to write. Otherwise, with the children home from school for winter break, I would have no time to myself. No sooner did I close my eyes than I heard the door creak open and felt a weight settle at the edge of my bed. It was my daughter backing up her dump truck. "I'm sorry," Colette said. She had ostensibly come in to apologize (for rolling her eyes, slamming her door, and behaving generally like a teenager), but she really wanted to unload, which she did for over an hour.

She confessed that she had been playing her guitar instead of cleaning up her room. She had been watching reruns of *Friends* instead of studying for midterms. She had been text-messaging her own friends instead of writing her term paper. She was frightened, she admitted, by her lack of motivation, her apathy. I became frightened when she cupped her hands in front of her face, as if drinking from a stream, and said that she was trying to hold the pieces of her life together but feared that it would at any moment shatter. Without so much as blinking, I said a silent prayer to the Goddess of Mothers. *Make me strong and wise,* I prayed, *so that I will say the right thing.* Mostly I did. Colette went to bed relieved and reassured. I, of course, went to bed concerned, my sleep flea-bitten with worry.

I awoke every two hours from dreams littered with the debris of our conversation. Recycling every parenting decision I had ever made, I went as far back as the choice of preschool. I remembered soliciting recommendations, touring facilities, and interviewing administrators at practically every preschool in Bergen County until at last I narrowed the choice to two. I made a T-chart, listed the pros and cons of each, called my therapist, asked my father for his opinion, slept on it, asked my father for his opinion again, finally flipped a coin. Years later, my daughter told me that she had hated her preschool. So you can imagine the agony I endured when it came time to choose a high school. That Sunday night in December, I lay in bed cringing at the thought of the college process.

At dawn, I hauled myself out of bed, opened my Mother's Notebook, and unloaded on paper the same way Colette had unloaded on me. I complained. I kvetched. I carried on. One of my students calls these entries "whining pages," and she is not alone. Many professional writers confess to such literary unloading. Julia Cameron scribbles three pages of stream-of-consciousness writing every morning, what she calls "brain drain"—the premise behind her method for clear-cutting a path to creativity. Natalie Goldberg, in her daily practice, feels free to write "the worst junk in America." And Anne Lamott admits to writing "shitty first drafts," claims all authors do, thus dispelling the myth that writers take dictation from a divine source. So while my family slept on, I sat at the kitchen counter and wrote down every fear, every regret, every worry—page after page of garbage. Trust me, nothing junkier had ever been written. Afterward, I felt relieved. I actually felt lighter. And I knew, not for the first time, that if I do not allow myself some days to unload in my Mother's Notebook, then I will walk around all day with a heavy heart. Worse, I will dump on everyone else.

INVITATION

ↄ *Dump Truck.* Your Mother Pages do not have to be poetry. They don't even have to be good prose. Some days you may be capable of spewing nothing but garbage. Just back up your truck and dump. Complain. Kvetch. Rant and rave. If it helps, call these entries "whining pages." Only once you dump your load will you clear a space to get on with your writing.

INSPIRATIONS

All that angry, whiny, petty stuff that you write down in the morning stands between you and your creativity. Worrying about the job, the laundry, the funny knock in the car, the weird look in your lover's eye—this stuff eddies through our subconscious and muddies our days. Get it on the page.
(JULIA CAMERON)

For me and most writers I know, writing is not rapturous. In fact, the only way I get anything written at all is to write really, really shitty first drafts. (ANNE LAMOTT)

16

Fathers
(or Marriage after Motherhood)

The summer I met Mark, the man I would marry, he was living in a backwoods lodge forty miles from the nearest telephone and two hundred miles from a major town. As I watched him drive a pickup, wield an ax, and clear-cut a fire trail, I wondered if he would know how to order prime rib in a restaurant on Madison Avenue, if he could sit through an all-Beethoven performance of the Beaux Arts Trio at Lincoln Center, if he had read *Paradise Lost*. Of all the things I wondered, it never so much as occurred to me to consider the kind of father he would be.

Not that I could have known anyway.

I was nineteen; he was twenty-three. I was a junior in a music conservatory in New York; he had just graduated from U.C. Berkeley. I played the cello; he played poker. Both of us were vegetarians. I didn't wear a bra underneath my peasant blouses; he didn't wear boxers underneath his Hash jeans. We both wore bell-bottoms. I grew up in a cooperative community within driving distance of Manhattan; he was born in the Haight-Ashbury section of San Francisco. Our mothers both painted. My parents were still married; his were divorced. I didn't shave my legs or underarms; he sported a mustache. We both smoked pot. For extra cash, he sold inlaid boxes and stone scarabs he had imported from Egypt; I had $211 in the bank. It was 1978. The last thing on either of our minds was marriage—or family.

My first vision of Mark as a father was ten years later in the delivery room at New York Hospital. Never mind that throughout my pregnancy he had given up wine and chocolate, rarely missed a Lamaze class, and gallantly stood between my expanding belly and oncoming buses on Broadway. The first moment he became a father in my eyes was when the nurse handed him our baby, swathed and swaddled, and he whispered father love in her doll-sized ear while Dr. Thornton sewed up my episiotomy. Mark had a look of fierce gentleness on his face, and I knew then that this man would do everything in his power to protect our children.

And he has.

Still, I have at times felt the need to protect our children from their father. Especially at the dinner table. I mean, what was God thinking when, two years after our daughter was born, he gave my husband a son who doesn't eat? Mark, at six feet four inches and 205 pounds, loves to boast about his appetite: the summer he traded freshwater trout for platefuls of pancakes and eggs on the John Muir Trail, the Thanksgiving he ate four helpings of turkey and stuffing to win my mother's heart. Mark idolizes his paternal grandfather, Marcel, who downed twenty-five hot dogs in under three hours to win first place in an eating contest—reportedly after finishing a full-course French dinner! Miles, on the other hand, at fifteen years of age, will not so much as look at a hot dog, nor will he eat a hamburger or barbecued chicken or grilled fish or roast beef or veal Parmesan or vegetarian lasagna or spaghetti and meatballs or scrambled eggs and bacon or tuna-fish sandwiches or almost any other meal I place on the table other than plain pasta, grilled cheese, or peanut butter and jelly.

All the books tell you, don't make a fuss over food. My husband cannot stop himself. His big joke at the dinner table is that Miles eats less than Baby Ross, the two-year-old next door. But it's no joke. Over the years, our dinner table has been witness to snide remarks, cruel insults, yelling matches, silent treatments, angry insistence, willful resistance, threats, tears, slammed doors, notes saying *Never come into my bedroom ever again,* apologies, and forgiveness—the cycle repeated over and over, prompting me to confide in friends, talk to teachers, consult the pediatrician, hire a therapist, and still I cannot help but defy my husband in front of the children even though everyone tells us that no matter what we must present a united force. There have been times I could just hate Mark.

Except that I love him.

I love him for the way he used to toss Colette, when she was a baby, four feet into the air in spite of my protests. I love him for the time he strode out to the pitcher's mound after Miles, then eight, had thrown the losing pitch in the semifinals of a national baseball tournament and slung him, like a hero or a wounded soldier, over his shoulder. I love him for making sure that our kids chew their food with their mouths closed. I love him for leading our family, from the time the kids first walked, over some of the highest mountain passes in the world, in the Sierras, the Rockies, and the Alps. I love him for the day in Rome when he muscled over a taxi driver who had, without provocation, shoved our friend Larry onto the pavement while we mothers and children watched helplessly from the sidewalk. I love him for all the times he says yes, and for the times he says no. I love him for having been my brother's friend before he got sick and after, when he took Jason in his wheelchair to Disneyland. I love him for the easy way he has with old people, refereeing races across the living room between my mother and my aunt, both pushing walkers and laughing like little girls. And I love him for the year I traveled through breast cancer and back again and he stood by my side every step of the way.

Even so, to be honest, I must admit that I don't love Mark the same way I loved him the summer we met, when we couldn't keep our eyes or our hands off each other. This may explain why I quit reading "Modern Love"—the first column in the *New York*

Times I turn to every Sunday morning—for two months after the week it featured a piece by Ayelet Waldman on sex after motherhood. Waldman writes about a phenomenon she has witnessed among married couples with children—what she calls "bed death," a total lack of sex because we mothers are too sore or too tired or too wrapped up in our kids. Adding insult to injury, Waldman goes on to claim to be the only mother in America who is "getting any" (or at least in Berkeley, California, where she lives with her husband, the Pulitzer Prize–winning author Michael Chabon). If you detect a shred of animosity or envy on my part, know that I am not alone. The essay incited so much antipathy from mothers across the country that the author ended up on *Oprah,* which according to Mary Gordon is the writer's equivalent of winning the lottery (as if we didn't already have reason enough to be envious of Ayelet). In contrast to Waldman's experience, in the years since my husband and I started a family, it has been hard for me to switch from mother to lover and back again.

Neither teenagers nor time has helped.

During a book signing several years ago, Susan Cheever, in answer to a question, said, "There's no such thing as marriage after motherhood." I disagree. True, much of my marriage is now conducted over telephone wires. True, my husband and I rarely make love anymore in dark alleyways and other forbidden places. Still, there is something darkly sexual about a man who is a father and all the unspoken acts fatherhood implies. Sometimes when I catch sight of Mark, my breath comes short. But then I breathe deeply with the knowledge that when my children leave home, their father will stay behind.

INVITATIONS

↬ *Fathers.* If you want to know what kind of husband a man will make, age-old wisdom tells you to look at the way he treats his mother. To my knowledge, no such barometer exists to predict the kind of father a man will be. Describe the father of your children. (In the case of a separation or divorce, you may want to write about the person who plays the role of stepfather, or, if no father figure is present, consider writing about the father you wish your children could have.) What are his most endearing qualities as a father? Most aggravating? What about him do you most appreciate? What would you change if you could? To help you begin writing about the man who is father to your children, try this writing start: *I never expected* _____ *to be so* _____ *as a father.* Just fill in the blanks and start writing. Each day this week, pick up where you left off the day before and write two more Mother Pages. Alternatively, use the writing start *fathers,* and you may find yourself writing about your own father as well.

↬ *Marriage after Motherhood.* How has your marriage or relationship changed since you had children? What activities did you once enjoy that you no longer do together? What do you talk about now that you never talked about then? What else has changed: how you spend your vacations, your Friday nights, your Sunday mornings? What about your sex life? In what way is your relationship better or worse? Write down the writing start *marriage after motherhood* and see where it takes you.

INSPIRATIONS

In their study of marriage and the transition to parenthood, psychologists wonder why some couples deal with the arrival of a baby so smoothly and others suffer so acutely. They often find that a key factor in a couple's harmonious transition is whether the father joins the mother in undergoing a transformation, whether he consents to share the world of parenting and she allows him in. (DAPHNE DE MARNEFFE)

When my first daughter was born my husband held her in his hands, her face peering from underneath a pink acrylic hospital hat, her mouth a round O of surprise at having been tugged from the wound of my incised abdomen. His face softened and got all bleary, the way it does when we make love. . . . He turned to me and said, "My God, she's so beautiful." (AYELET WALDMAN)

17

IMPROVISING MOTHERHOOD

As a girl, I usually brought my cello with me whenever I went to Pamela's house for a sleepover. Everyone there played a musical instrument: her older sister, two brothers, two stepsisters, even her stepfather. Only her mother didn't play music; Zelda, or Selma as we knew her then, was tone-deaf.

I remember playing my cello one evening inside the narrow rectangle of Pamela's bedroom. The space was so small that the frog of my bow jabbed the twin bed on a down-bow, the tip stabbed the desk on an up-bow. Danny Toan was stretched out on the bed, his mile-long legs dangling off the end, a Gibson couched in the hollow of his lap. He was picking out a harmony on his guitar to the melody I was playing on my cello, one of the Bach Suites, probably the D Minor, tentatively at first, then his fingers flying ahead of mine, strumming chords, improvising arpeggios, intuitively playing the music as it was meant to be performed. Here was Danny, in 1974, his hair below his shoulders, a Camel cigarette dangling from his lips, playing an acoustic guitar the way a baroque musician might have played a lyre or viola da gamba—improvising on the spot.

As musicians, Danny and I were polar opposites. He played rock 'n' roll; I was classically trained. He was brilliant at improvising; I needed to practice and polish. He used his ear to learn music; I needed a script, well-rehearsed, in hand. No longer. Now

I like to think of my writing, especially the impromptu writing I do every day in my Mother's Notebook, as a kind of improvising. I may know where I will start, but, like Danny on his guitar, I rarely know where I will end up. Nor do I know how I will get there. Over the years, I have learned to trust the spontaneous direction of my words, however illogical or haphazard. My writing sometimes throws me off-balance and off-course, but in the end it always leaves me feeling more grounded. I cannot tell you why, but for some reason the rectangular pages of my notebook feel more spacious and less confining to me than the rectangular bedrooms in which I practiced my cello as a teenager.

I have since discovered that mothering, too, requires improvisation, as suggested by the title of Kathryn Black's book *Mothering Without a Map*. No matter how grand your plans, every day is like a blank page in your Mother's Notebook. In the same way that you may be surprised by what you write on a given day, you never know what to expect as a mother when you wake up each morning. Your two-year-old registers a fever of 104 degrees. Your thirteen-year-old refuses to go to school because you forced him to cut his hair and now he looks dorky. Later he comes home needing help with algebra and you can't for the life of you remember the order of operations. One evening you find a lump in your breast. What do you do? There is no formula, no prescription, no one to ask. So you do what all mothers do every day: you improvise.

Mary Catherine Bateson, daughter of Margaret Mead and an accomplished anthropologist in her own right, was so intrigued by the notion of a woman's life as an improvisational art form that she traced the histories of five women in a book aptly titled *Composing a Life*. She concluded that women do not live their lives according to some preconceived master plan but instead zigzag from stage to stage, improvising along the way. Pamela's mother, Zelda, is a perfect example. A modern dancer in her youth and a social worker in her middle years, she raised four children through two marriages and three name changes before settling down with her high school sweetheart around the time Pamela left for college. Now Zelda travels, meditates, and meets with her many women's groups. At eighty-five, she is still stopped on the street by strangers who marvel at her beauty. Zelda may be tone-deaf, but she picks the strings of life with the same trust and abandon that inspired Danny Toan to jam to the Bach Suite I played on my cello all those years ago.

If, as Mary Catherine Bateson suggests, you think of your life as a composition and yourself as the artist, then anything you do—whether you are writing in your notebook or putting your baby to bed—is a creative act. And creativity demands improvisation.

INVITATIONS

- ↬ *Improvising along the Way.* Think of a time you had to improvise. Friends stopped by unexpectedly at the dinner hour. You were asked to make a toast at a birthday party or to give an impromptu speech at a PTA meeting. Your babysitter didn't show up and you were already late to work. Your child awoke with the chicken pox on Christmas morning. What did you do? How did you feel? In what ways did you improvise? Use the writing start *improvising along the way* and write down whatever comes to mind.

- ↬ *Composing a Life.* Think of a mother you know who, like Zelda, has composed a life, making bold, sometimes surprising brushstrokes rather than connecting the dots of a predictable line drawing. What have you learned from this woman about the importance of living our lives creatively? What has she taught you about the value of improvising along the way? Use this person's name as a writing start, and in two Mother Pages tell me how her life is a composition and she herself the artist.

INSPIRATIONS

> *In my recent work on the ways women combine commitments to career and family, I have been struck by how commonly women zigzag from stage to stage without a long-term plan, improvising along the way, building the future from "something old and something new."*
> (MARY CATHERINE BATESON)

> *Improvisers walk onstage and dare to make visible everything that they've ever learned—and then to learn even more right there in front of an audience. This takes courage, a willingness to test oneself in the most extreme circumstances. Nothing gets erased in a live performance. . . . To improvise is to court error, and to trust that your own artistry will prevail.*
> (KEN GORDON)

> *Raising children is a creative endeavor, an art rather than a science.* (BRUNO BETTELHEIM)

WRITING MOTHER'S HELPER

The Rhythm of Writing

In poetry, we refer to the recurrent and regular pattern of beats as *meter.* But all language—both spoken and written—has a recognizable, if variable, sequencing of sound, what we call *rhythm.* This is why so many writers are also musicians. Writers not only have an ear for language, choosing words as much for their music as for their meaning. We also have a feel for rhythm, the underlying beat or pulse in poetry and prose. While there are lots of ways to create rhythm in writing, as you will see below, rhythm is not something you think about. It is something you feel. So don't become self-conscious about generating rhythm in your writing. Just as your heart beats without your willing it, so your pen will find its own rhythm as you write. Here are some ways to make music with words:

Vary your sentences—both in length and in type. Try alternating a long complex sentence with a short simple one.

Use repetition—again and again. Begin or end consecutive sentences with the same phrase, or repeat a phrase or line throughout the writing (known as a *refrain* in poetry).

Use parallel construction —words, phrases, or clauses that have the same grammatical form. Many maxims and clichés have parallel patterns that make them easy to follow and remember (*A bird in the hand is worth two in the bush*).

Write in twos—the equivalent in music of 2/4 time. Lots of grammatical constructions generate pairs of words or phrases: *either . . . or, neither . . . nor, not only . . . but also, both x and y.* But you can also create rhythm simply by connecting pairs of words with the coordinating conjunction *and* (*He packed underwear and socks, shirts and pants, hiking boots and running shoes*).

Write in threes—the equivalent in music of 3/4 time. The number three is significant both in religion and in art. Listing items in groups of threes creates balance and harmony in writing (*She washed her face, brushed her teeth, and went to bed*).

18

MOTHERING OUR MOTHERS

I wait until the dessert is served to take my mother to the ladies' room. I don't want to have to take her twice. Earlier in the afternoon I had asked if there was a facility on the main floor of the restaurant. No way could she walk down the stairs to the public restrooms below. "Opposite the bar," the hostess told me. "But it's for handicapped only." Her eyes were on my legs.

It takes two of us, my sister and I, to hoist my mother out of her chair in the dining room. The rest of the family, gathered for my nephew's bar mitzvah, pretend not to notice. We hold her securely under both arms as she transfers her hands in one clunky motion from the table to the walker. Two squares of foam have been duct-taped to the handlebars, and two Wilson tennis balls rigged to the bottom of the legs. Little by little, the walker is being customized.

At eighty, my mother no longer walks; she shuffles. But it's not so much the age that slows her down; it's the Alzheimer's. First the walker lunges three or four inches ahead, then the left foot lurches forward, then the right drags behind, her movements clumsy and disconnected like her mind. I cannot believe that this is the same woman who was up at six o'clock every morning to walk a mile before work, who planted flats of pink impatiens each spring, then weeded the garden beds all summer long, who sewed name labels on my clothes before sleepaway camp and sneaked me care packages of Lindt chocolate, Bazooka bubble gum, and troll dolls.

She stops now and looks back over her shoulder, squinting. At first I think she has forgotten where we are going, but then she asks, "Where's Dad?" her voice timid like a little girl's. "In the dining room," I answer. We continue to inch down the long, dim hallway. She stops again, looks back over her shoulder, and asks, "Where's Dad?" her voice frightened now. "Where do you think?" I answer, testing her. By the third time, I begin to feel like Bill Murray in the movie *Groundhog Day*, only I have not yet reached the part where he grows compassionate. I am enraged.

"Where's Dad?" she asks again. Refusing to answer, I plant my feet in front of my mother, facing her, and begin to pull the walker, not speedily but steadily, daring her to keep up. She can't. Or won't. What difference does it make? Her face grows panicky, the same face she wore when I skated onto the Skyview Pond or bicycled across Route 45, and she would yell from the shoreline or doorway, "Be careful!" I stop and place both my hands on hers. They feel like piles of chicken bones. I want to cry. I want to hug her, but the walker is in the way.

"Where's Dad?" she asks again. She seems so small, standing there looking up at me. "Where's my mom?" I want to say. From the time of her diagnosis, I have dreaded the day my mother would no longer know who I am. I never imagined that one day I would no longer know who she is.

Aware that the hostess is watching us, I open the wide door to the restroom with the righteousness of an old man pulling into a handicapped parking space. Inside, I turn my back to the toilet but can see in the vanity mirror that my mother is wearing Depends now, something I suggested months ago when I opened her closet door and nearly passed out from the stench of urine. I moisten a towel and dab at her mouth, trying to erase the faded fuchsia that is smeared beyond the outline of her lips. When she stands up, I worry that she will slip on the marble floor or lose her balance as she turns to toss the hand towel into the rattan basket, which is tucked inconspicuously behind the toilet.

"Be careful!" I tell her. The last time I felt so skittish was when my children were toddlers and everywhere I saw stairs and electrical outlets. This bathroom may meet handicapped codes, but whoever designed it is not yet mothering a mother.

Psychologist Mary Pipher claims that the only thing worse than having aging parents is not having aging parents. I wonder. In one trip to the restroom, I journeyed through rage and remorse, annoyance and acceptance, greed and guilt, loss and love. In one trip to the restroom, I endured the pain of losing a mother inch by inch.

When we finally return to the dining room, my son nearly knocks my mother over, so ferocious is his hug. "Hello, Grandma!" he exclaims, not seeming to notice the souped-up walker, the smudged lipstick, the bulge of the diapers under her pants. I will never get my mother back, but maybe I can learn to love her like that again.

INVITATIONS

- *Mothering Your Mother.* Most of us expect to mother our mothers once they enter old age, but many younger women mother their mothers through illness, divorce, depression, or alcoholism. Whether your mother is living or dead, vibrant or elderly, you probably have stories to tell about mothering your mother. Most likely, the stories include run-ins with siblings or spouses. Write down the writing start *mothering my mother* and start writing. Or try to recount in two Mother Pages one interaction that illustrates the changing roles—a trip to the restroom, a telephone call, a doctor's visit. (You can follow these same prompts to write about mothering your father, as one of my students did in the sample Mother Page that follows.)

❧ *Remembering Your Mother.* When we begin to mother our mothers, or to mourn them if they are gone, we sometimes forget who they once were. Writing helps us remember. Give yourself a full week to write about your mother. Begin by making a list of five defining features, then write about one each day: *my mother's hands, my mother's eyes, my mother's hair.* Write about the perfume she wore, a meal she cooked, an expression she used. Or try this writing start: *When I think of my mother, I think of her* _____. Fill in the blank with the first word that comes to mind and write two Mother Pages.

❧ *Other Mothers.* When we become mothers, most of us hear the voice of our own mother telling us what—and what not— to do. But lots of other mothers influence how we raise our children. In your notebook, list the names of a few mothers you know under each of these categories:

- **Blood mothers**—in addition to grandmothers, include in this category godmothers, stepmothers, and mothers-in-law.
- **Co-mothers**—the mothers with whom you coordinate, collaborate, and carpool.
- **Ghost mothers**—the mothers who haunt you from childhood (your boyfriend's mother, the mother next door).
- **Surrogate mothers**—any mother you have adopted as a mentor or caregiver.
- **Celebrity mothers**—movie stars, public figures, religious icons (Mother Teresa).
- **Fictional mothers**—sitcom moms, storybook moms.

Now choose one mother from any category above and insert her name in the following writing start: *If it weren't for* _____, *I would probably never have* . . . Finish the sentence and write two Mother Pages. Tomorrow you can write about another mother.

INSPIRATIONS

They say you begin to understand your mother only when you become a mother yourself. (CHITRA DIVAKARUNI)

For the first few years of Sam's life, my mother and I finally found a consistent closeness; we were mothers together on this earth—plus, I'd given her a fantastic grandchild. She was in heaven. Then she had to go and get old. Now she wants to tie her cord to me. But I'm somebody's mom now. And I still want a mommy—I do not want to be my mommy's mommy. (ANNE LAMOTT)

You have to find a mother inside yourself. We all do. Even if we already have a mother, we still have to find this part of ourselves inside. (NARRATOR OF *THE SECRET LIFE OF BEES* BY SUE MONK KIDD)

SAMPLE MOTHER PAGE

Trip to the Teapot
By Mary Jo Freebody

The smell of cigarette smoke assaults me as I push Dad's wheelchair over the threshold of the Teapot. I have been helping Dad, and Mom, too, in and out of this unlikely place for five years. A wheelchair has replaced the walker this year, and the oxygen tank and long tubing are also new. I make quick checks to be sure the wheels of the chair are not running over the tubing that runs from Dad's nose to the tank as we make our slow way in. Mom, stooped from arthritis and angst, holds open the door and then brings up the rear, helping Dad up and then down into our booth.

The Teapot is a coffee shop in the middle of the central Michigan farm fields. A high shelf on the side wall holds nine teapots of varied colors and sizes, but the ambience is anything but tea party. It is smoky, shabby and not quite clean. Mom and Dad love the thirty-mile drive through woods and fields. They know when to watch for the pens of sheep and cows, and they watch the crops growing through the changing seasons. For years Mom drove to the Teapot with Dad strapped into the passenger seat of their rusty 1987 Oldsmobile Cutlass. This spring is different. The Olds died last month, and Mom, at 88, decided she could not see well enough to continue driving.

Dawn, Mom and Dad's favorite waitress, greets us with a boisterous "Hello! Where ya been? Want ya usuals?" She sees me and says, "Oh, your daughter from New Jersey's here again. What'll ya have, doll?" She brings coffee. This is a big day for Dad, who has not been out of their apartment for *months, except for doctors' appointments. He needs to rest, sipping his coffee, before the effort of eating his meal. His heart failure is progressing faster now. Mom and their health aide, Julie, have been caring for him all winter. Now it is April and I have come for my quarterly visit. We have driven here in my rented Ford Focus, Dad smiling and pointing out the daffodils and forsythia to Mom in the backseat. I fight the lump in my throat and wonder how many more times we will have like this.*

As it turned out, that was our last trip to the Teapot. Dad died of heart failure three months later.

WRITING MOTHER'S HELPER

How Writers Write about Their Mothers

Many of us best remember our mothers in the kitchen—chopping onions, salting potatoes, washing dishes. But there are lots of other ways to remember your mother. Take a look at the different ways writers have written about their mothers, then try one for yourself.

A WALK

In her memoir *Fierce Attachments,* Vivian Gornick recounts a walk with her elderly mother along the streets of New York. She alternately records their heated conversations about the past and describes odd interchanges with bag ladies and street people they encounter on their way.

↬ *Write about a walk you took with your mother.*

A HOBBY

James McBride, in his memoir *The Color of Water: A Black Man's Tribute to His White Mother,* writes about the old, clunky bicycle his mother hauled home one day and took to riding in slow motion all over Queens, in part because she couldn't drive a car, in part because she was grieving the sudden death of her second husband, the author's stepfather.

✧ *Write about a hobby your mother took up when you were a child.*

A CLOSET

In *French Lessons,* Alice Kaplan writes about stepping into her mother's closet as a little girl and burying her face in the bright colors, delicate patterns, and faint smell of talcum powder that made up the fabric of her mother's married life. The author then writes about stepping into the same closet three years later, after her father died, only to find it empty except for a zipped plastic bag that smelled of mothballs.

✧ *Write about your mother's closet.*

THE KITCHEN

In *A Walker in the City,* Alfred Kazin returns to the Brownsville tenement of his childhood and remembers his mother sitting in the kitchen all day at her sewing machine, hunched over the wheel, pounding away at the treadle, apparently stitching dresses for paying neighbors but really keeping her family stitched together.

✧ *Write down a memory of your mother in the kitchen.*

A RECIPE

When Elizabeth Ehrlich became a mother, she longed to resurrect the traditions of her immigrant grandmothers, by then long gone. In the kosher kitchen of her mother-in-law, a native of Poland and a survivor of the Holocaust, the author learns not only the recipes but also the rituals and stories of the Old World, as faithfully recounted in her memoir *Miriam's Kitchen.*

✎ *Write about a recipe from your mother or grandmother.*

A TELEPHONE CALL

Russell Baker begins his memoir, *Growing Up,* with a telephone call from his eighty-year-old mother, whose mind had begun to wander after her last bad fall. "Are you coming to my funeral today?" she asks briskly. The author assures himself that his mother is all right, but he knows, of course, that she isn't.

✎ *Write about a telephone call with your mother.*

Beyond Motherhood—
Holding On and Letting Go

One Christmas vacation in the Yucatán, when my daughter was seven and my son five, we hired four horses and a guide for a day trip up the coast. None of us knew how to ride horses, except the Mayan guide, who spoke no English. For most of the ride, the horses were as intractable as mules, moronically picking out yesterday's hoofprints in the sand. Only toward the end of the return trip did the horses finally respond to our ceaseless jabbing and clucking. Then there was no holding them back. When Colette's horse took off at a gallop, her feet flew out of the stirrups and she rode the final five hundred yards parallel to the horizon, her stomach one foot above the horse's back, her face buried in its mane, her small hands clinging to the short reins. As I watched helplessly from behind, I prayed that she would hold on, but I knew that there was nothing for me to do but let go. I remember thinking that this is how I would feel when she first learned to drive a car or left home for college.

Since then, I make sure my students read Sandi Kahn Shelton's essay "One Week Until College," not because I think everyone is the parent of a high school senior, but because the essay speaks to the universal theme of holding on and letting go. Although the author still remembers the day she stomped out of

her mother's house for good at the age of eighteen, she nonetheless grieves that her own daughter is distant and difficult and
condescending in the weeks before she leaves for college. The
mother desperately wants to spend time with her daughter—
shopping, reminiscing, bestowing final words of wisdom. The
daughter just wants to spend time with her friends. Finally, after
rebuffing her mother's advances for days, the daughter finds her
in the bathroom late one night, brushing her teeth, and buries
her head in her shoulder. The mother dares not utter a word, for
fear her daughter will bolt. Silently, their bodies swaying, they
hold each other for a long time. The mother knows that tomorrow they will most likely fight again. But for now, she writes, "I
am grateful to be standing in the bathroom at midnight, both of
us tired and sad, toothpaste smeared on my chin, holding tight—
while at the same time letting go of—this daughter who is trying
to say goodbye."

During a class discussion earlier this year, one of my students,
whose eldest child was four at the time, said, "This story doesn't
apply to me; my daughter is never going to college." The rest of
us laughed, but of course we understood that from the day we
become mothers we are torn between wanting to hold on and
needing to let go. My good friend Kathleen, who just turned fifty,
recently lost her mother to cancer. On the telephone the next day,
she said to me, "The umbilical cord has finally been cut." It takes
that long, from the birth of a child to the death of the parent,
before we ultimately let go. Sometimes longer.

In this section of the book, we will explore some of the issues
mothers face as our families grow up and we grow older.

INSPIRATIONS

*Motherhood has taught me more about letting go, being in
the moment, unconditional love, grace, wisdom, joy,*

*patience, and sacrifice than yoga, Buddhist meditation, Sufi
dancing, Christian prayer, and psychotherapy combined.*
(ELIZABETH LESSER)

Part of letting go, I suppose, is deciding what you hold on to.
(ANN HOOD)

*A child's departure demands perhaps a mother's greatest
performance. We must learn to let go. And yet, much as we
think we have rehearsed this act in the thousand small breaks
we've experienced over the years, the leave-taking can feel
like a death.* (KATRINA KENISON AND KATHLEEN HIRSCH)

TO A DAUGHTER LEAVING HOME
by Linda Pastan

*When I taught you
at eight to ride
a bicycle, loping along
beside you
as you wobbled away
on two round wheels,
my own mouth rounding
in surprise when you pulled
ahead down the curved
path of the park,
I kept waiting
for the thud
of your crash as I
sprinted to catch up,
while you grew
smaller, more breakable*

with distance,
pumping, pumping
for your life, screaming
with laughter,
the hair flapping
behind you like a
handkerchief waving
goodbye.

19

PORTRAIT OF MYSELF AS A
WRITING MOTHER

Writers are by nature self-reflective. Not only do we feel compelled to write, but we also feel inclined to write about our writing. A number of authors—Annie Dillard, Anne Lamott, and Stephen King among them—have published memoirs of their writing lives. In these personal pages, they celebrate influential teachers, recall favorite writing studios, and muse about the source of their writing, whether it comes more from inspiration or from industry. Before journeying further into *Writing Motherhood*, I encourage you, too, to take stock of who you are and who you want to become, both as a writer and as a mother.

In my classes, I invite students to think of a metaphor that communicates something about the process they go through when they sit down to write. Susan is a balloon that fills quickly, then deflates suddenly as she loses direction or interest or faith. Janet is a car on a winter's day, slow to start but smooth once she gets going. Michelle is Silly Putty, shaped and reshaped by books she reads and classes she takes. Elaine is a straitjacket, paralyzed by fear the moment she puts pen to paper. Debra is a leaf on a stream, writing with the changing currents of her life. Maria is a battery that loses its charge from time to time. For me, writing has always been an obsession that borders on addiction. I once wrote this metaphor in my notebook to describe myself as a writer:

> *I was born with a pen in my hand. It dangles like a cigarette between my fingers, rolling over my writer's callus, leaving a writer's smudge. After all these years, I need it the way smokers need nicotine. I need it to think. I need it to remember. I need it to know.*

Author Judy Reeves, in her book *Writing Alone, Writing Together,* typecasts a dozen or more personalities she has come across in writing groups. Her descriptions may help you clarify your characteristics and inclinations as a writer, making it easier for you to think of an apt metaphor. According to Reeves, these are the most common writer types:

- **The committed writer** manages to write no matter what arises in her life.
- **The tentative writer** is uncertain about whether—and what—she wants to write.
- **The inspired writer** seems to take dictation directly from the muse.
- **The perfectionist** is so bent on getting it right that some days she can't write at all.
- **The wounded writer** still suffers from a humiliation or insult inflicted long ago.
- **The self-deprecating writer** belittles her talents and minimizes her efforts.
- **The censored writer** chooses her words carefully, preferring to play it safe rather than tell the truth.
- **The dropout,** or on-again, off-again writer, joins a class or a group only to quit before it really gets going.

Most likely, you will recognize a part of yourself in every one of these types since all of us waffle between feeling inspired and discouraged, confident and unsure, determined and doubting. Just choose a metaphor that reflects how you feel about your writing today. Tomorrow you can think of a different one. Like a painter's self-portraits, your metaphor will change over time as you overcome some hurdles and encounter others.

Most women in my classes have no trouble thinking of a metaphor that describes themselves as writers, but for some, visualizing an image that sums up who they are as mothers proves more challenging. I begin by asking students to write down on an index card a definition of *mother*. There are as many definitions as there are women in the room:

- A mother is someone who provides nurturing care and unconditional love to another.
- A mother is someone you can come home to no matter what.
- A mother holds things together even when she is falling apart.
- A mother has the only job in the world that you can't quit.
- A mother is the one person who worries more about someone else than she does about herself.

Next, I hand one student my torn edition of *Webster's Collegiate Dictionary* and ask her to read aloud the definition of *mother*:

1. **a:** a female parent **b:** (1) a woman in authority (2) an old or elderly woman
2. source, origin
3. maternal tenderness or affection
4. [short for *motherfucker*]: one that is particularly impressive or contemptible—sometimes considered vulgar

Afterward, she looks up and exclaims, "Whoever wrote that definition is definitely *not* a mother!"

Why don't you come up with your own definition of *mother*? Write it down on a page in your Mother's Notebook. If it helps, think of common mothering styles. You already know about the supermom, the mother who does it all seemingly without effort. But maybe you haven't yet heard about the alpha mom, a new breed of so-called "go-to" mothers, professional women who bring to motherhood the skill set of a CEO. Many mothering styles, though, go well beyond the simplistic division between mothers who stay at home and those who go to work. Here are just a few, but I'm sure you and your friends will have fun coming up with more:

- **The stage mom** will do anything to promote her child's stardom.
- **The soccer mom** lives in her car and on the sidelines of games and tournaments.
- **The hands-on mom** insists on scheduling every minute of her child's day.
- **The laissez-faire mom** still believes in plenty of downtime.
- **The Martha Stewart mother** sews her child's costumes for Halloween and bakes cupcakes for birthdays.
- **The Earth mother** does not allow refined white sugar in the house, nor does she believe in fast food.
- **The Jewish mother,** a perennial worrier, sacrifices her own needs and wants in a self-denying determination to provide for her children.

Again, you will probably recognize yourself or someone you know in every one of these mothering styles. That's the point. *Webster's* aside, it is not so easy to reduce motherhood to a neat package or a clear-cut definition.

The poet Georgia Heard once was asked to name an image

that represents her life. Without hesitation, she said, "Layers," as in archaeology or geology. Rather than ask students to think of a metaphor that represents motherhood, I bring to class a variety of objects that reveal some truth about what it means to be a mother today. The objects are commonplace—everyday things gathered from my kitchen, bathroom, garage, and backyard: a painter's palette, a kitchen timer, car keys, a rock, Elmer's glue, a box of Band-Aids, a thermometer, a flashlight, a Halloween mask, a woolen hat, a pair of eyeglasses.

I encourage students to think metaphorically, not just literally, as they write an answer to this question: *In what way does this object represent me as a mother?* Car keys, for example, may inspire someone to write about all the hours she spends driving her kids back and forth, but it may also suggest that as a mother she is "in the driver's seat." Elmer's glue may remind someone of crafts projects and schoolwork, but it may also prompt her to write about the different ways in which a mother is the glue that holds her family together. After fifteen minutes, we swap objects and write again. Without fail, every one of my students sees herself mirrored in every object I bring to class.

When we sketch portraits of ourselves as writers and mothers, I invite students to think in metaphor because the comparison between two seemingly unrelated things lets us see truths we might not otherwise notice. For example, when we compare a writer and a car, we understand that a writer needs fuel to keep going. When we compare a mother and a rock, we know that motherhood is hard, but it is also grounding. That is not to say that you should weigh down your writing with metaphors. In fact, writers disagree wildly on this point. At one end of the spectrum is Ernest Hemingway, who claimed that metaphors should be used only when they are absolutely essential, which according to him is almost never. At the other end of the spectrum is Anne Lamott, who has been known to use up to three unrelated metaphors in a single sentence. I fall somewhere in between. In my Mother Pages, I am liberal in my use of metaphor, freely experimenting with unlikely and at times cacophonous comparisons. When I come out of the notebook, into second and third drafts, I use metaphor sparingly, choosing only those images that shed light in otherwise dark corners.

The key, according to Mary Catherine Bateson, is that through metaphor we learn something about ourselves and our world. As she wrote in her book *Peripheral Visions,* "A metaphorical approach to the world is endlessly fertile and involves constant learning. A good metaphor continues to instruct." As long as metaphor can teach you something about who you are as a writer or a mother, feel free to use it.

INVITATIONS

◈ *Myself as a Writer.* How would you characterize yourself as a writer? How would you describe the process you go through when you sit down to write? Do you have trouble getting started? Are you easily distracted? Do you lose momentum after a while? Think of a metaphor that reveals something important about how you write. Over the years, my students have compared themselves to a windup toy, a freight train, a thunderstorm, an ice cube, a ruler, a battery, a kite, a roller coaster, a turtle hidden inside its shell. Write two Mother Pages explaining how your metaphor illustrates who you are as a writer. It's a good idea to try this exercise periodically. Your responses will expose the shifting shoreline of your writing life.

◈ *Myself as a Mother.* Walk around your house or yard and find an object that reveals some truth about who you are as a mother. Feel free to choose one of the objects I use in my classes, but there are countless others: a picture frame, a checkbook, a ruler, a camera, a sponge, a flashlight, a pair of running shoes. You might even consider the telephone, the television, or the refrigerator. On two Mother Pages, tell me all the different ways you see yourself reflected in this object, both literally and metaphorically. What can this object teach you about your experience of motherhood?

INSPIRATIONS

Metaphor: a figure of speech in which a word or phrase literally denoting one kind of object or idea is used in place of another to suggest a likeness or analogy between them. (MERRIAM WEBSTER'S NEW COLLEGIATE DICTIONARY, NINTH EDITION)

Metaphors and similes remind us of the power of language to take an ordinary experience and preserve it forever. After reading a good one, you may never look at something the same way again. (LYNN LAUBER)

Metaphor must come from a very different place than that of the logical, intelligent mind. It comes from a place that is very courageous, willing to step out of our preconceived ways of seeing things and open so large that it can see the oneness in an ant and in an elephant. (NATALIE GOLDBERG)

WRITING MOTHER'S HELPER

Me, Myself, and I

You have been writing your Mother Pages now for six or twelve or twenty weeks. Maybe longer. Take a few minutes to flip back through the pages and notice how you begin each entry. How often do you start with the first-person pronoun *I*? How frequently do you use some form of the first-person pronoun, *me, myself,* or *I*? Count the occurrences on random pages. If you are like me, you will be amazed, perhaps mortified, by the number. This can signal a danger point for a Writing Mother. We begin to feel trapped inside our head. We grow tired of our petty, self-pitying voice. So we stop writing. Please don't!

Personal writing is necessarily preoccupied with the self, so don't decide you are a hopeless egomaniac. Just push yourself some days to take off the blinders and look at the world through someone else's eyes. You already do this every day as a mother. Instinctively, you know what your child is feeling, you imagine what he is thinking, you anticipate what she will say. You can train yourself to do the same as a writer.

Here are some ways to step out of your mind and onto the page:

Me as she. Try writing in the third person, referring to yourself as *she* instead of *I*. Writing in the third person lends objectivity and insight to the otherwise narrow perspective of personal narrative.

Myself as journalist. Describe an event—a dinner party, a birthday party, a playdate—with the detachment of a newspaper reporter. Who was invited? Who arrived late? What were they wearing? What did they say? Describe the room, the food, the weather. Write as though you are an observer or outsider, not a participant.

Double vision. Describe a person, place, or event first from the perspective of an adult (not necessarily you), then from the perspective of a child (not necessarily yours). Write one page from each perspective. Describe the entryway to a grand house, a meeting with the school principal, a "Mommy and Me" class.

Three versions of the same story. Write about breakfast or bedtime, a car ride or a carnival, from the point of view of three different people—yourself, your husband, your nanny, your mother, your child, your boss, whoever was present. Choose a short event and limit each version to one page. You may write in the first or the third person, but each time you must replay the story from someone else's perspective.

Character portrait. Write about someone you recently met. Sketch this "character" with a painter's attention to detail: describe her physical features, facial expressions, mannerisms, quirks. What do you imagine she is thinking? What are her dreams? Alternatively, write about a person you knew in childhood but have not seen since. According to Virginia Woolf, memories of people we knew in childhood remain fixed; we see them now exactly as we saw them then.

Still life. Choose an object or collection of objects and arrange them on your writing table. Paint a still life with words. Describe how the object feels in your hand, its color and texture, the shadow and light. Tell a story (real or imagined) about the object.

20

THE THINGS WE CARRY

In 1979, less than a year after my husband and I met, we traveled around the world for eight months, flying red-eyes and hopping trains and buses from San Francisco to New York to London to Athens to New Delhi to Srinagar to Kathmandu to Bangkok to Honolulu and home again. What I wasn't wearing on my body I carried on my back: one pair of jeans, one pair of shorts, three underpants, one bra, two T-shirts, one long-sleeved cotton shirt, one woolen button-down shirt, a Sierra Designs down vest, a Speedo one-piece bathing suit, new Nike running shoes, flip-flops, a journal and pen, two paperback novels, a modest cosmetic kit (with Dr. Bronner's doing triple duty as shampoo, body soap, and laundry detergent), a comprehensive but compact first-aid kit (including moleskin, malaria pills, and Imodium), a Swiss Army knife (complete with corkscrew, scissors, and toothpick), a money belt (crammed with passport, traveler's checks, and fourth-class tickets), a deck of playing cards, lightweight binoculars, and a Frisbee. My backpack measured no bigger than the ones my children now carry to school, and it weighed considerably less.

Last year, when my family of four traveled to the Dominican Republic for winter break, I had to hire an extra-large car from Airbrook Limousine Service to drive us to Newark Airport. In addition to the daypack each of us carried on the plane, we checked six pieces of luggage: a twenty-nine-inch hard-side suit-case, which weighed forty-nine pounds packed to the max; a twenty-seven-inch soft nylon upright, which weighed thirty-six pounds; a second upright, twenty-four inches and twenty-three pounds with room to spare; a thirty-inch expedition duffel, forty-two pounds stuffed; a twenty-four-inch weekend duffel, twenty-six pounds and bulging; and a carry-along cosmetic tote, measuring twelve by fourteen inches and weighing just under twelve pounds. I remember the weight of each piece of luggage because Continental Airlines imposed restrictions: fifty pounds per bag and two bags per person. Clearly, the days of traveling light are long gone.

I have concluded that mothers are like tribal packhorses. We carry our children first in our womb and then on our hips. In our purses, we carry pacifiers and baby pictures; in our pockets, car keys and crayons. From our ancestors, we carry heirlooms that have been handed down from one generation to the next, along with the genes that determine whether we will have brown eyes or blue, whether we will be bipolar or diabetic. From our parents, we carry ambition or altruism, gratitude or guilt. For our chil-dren, we carry hope. Just look at the variety of carriers for moth-ers on the market today—from strollers to diaper bags to backpacks—and you will begin to appreciate the weight of the things we carry, not least of which is the unweighed love and fear.

Inspired by Tim O'Brien's novel *The Things They Carried*, I invite students in my classes to empty their bags and catalog the things they carry—not just the literal things but also the metaphorical ones, the things we carry *inside*: memories, super-stitions, shame, worry, disappointment, dreams. Cathy carries a compact mirror and a stick of Clinique black honey gloss, though she rarely wears lipstick these days. Karen carries a nail file to keep herself from picking at ragged edges, a bad habit she carries from childhood. Jennifer carries tissues for runny noses and Cheerios for empty tummies. Betsy carries worry lines on her brow, as well as the memory of the year her daughter started to cut herself. Dana carries a green leather case with slots for twelve cards that hint at where she spends her days—CVS, Pet Goods, Costco, the Gap, Barnes & Noble, Toys "R" Us, the A&P, the public library. Madeleine carries stories to enchant and stories to distract. I carry a prescription bottle of tamoxifen and the daily reminder that I will not live forever. We all carry cell phones, set on vibrate, because on top of all the things we mothers carry is the understanding that no matter what, we must carry on.

When we write about the things we carry, we typically find ourselves writing lists. That is good. Writers incorporate lists in their narrative all the time (no one more skillfully than Tim O'Brien) because lists ground the writing in real things. I once took a workshop in which all we did was write lists. The teacher would call out a category—say, trees—and for five minutes we would generate in our notebook a list of examples: redwood, poplar, black oak, white ash, ponderosa pine, Norway spruce, saguaro—on and on until our minds emptied and our hands cramped. As a mother, you already know about lists: grocery lists, back-to-school lists, camp lists, packing lists, to-do lists. I still have the checklist I wrote in the fall of 1988 of all the things I would need in the months after I came home from the hospital with my baby: bassinet, crib, musical mobile, changing table, diaper pail, rocking chair, nursery monitor, high chair, bibs, infant car seat, stroller, baby bathtub, nursing bras, breast pump, rectal thermometer, infant Tylenol, miniature nail clippers—four pages typed and single-spaced. I wish I could tell you that as my children have gotten taller my lists have gotten shorter. They haven't. On my computer, in a folder for travel, I have a file of packing lists for every trip we have taken since the children were born, each as long as the one we used to pack for the Dominican Republic last year.

Sometimes I feel weighed down by all the things I carry, but then I remember that each of these things carries a story that wants to be told. The poet Georgia Heard said that writing hides in the most ordinary and familiar places. Pablo Neruda, in his *Odes to Common Things,* shows us where: in a pair of socks, a bar of soap, an onion, french fries, a dog, a cat, a dictionary, a pair of scissors, a cluster of violets. Whenever I feel uninspired, I walk around my house and choose an everyday object to write about. I begin by describing its physical dimensions, but I invariably end up uncovering the story hidden inside—how we came to own it, what happened when it nearly broke, whose feelings got hurt. Over the years, I have written about a baseball glove, a Barbie doll, a cello bow, a stuffed animal, a picture book, cookie cutters. the kitchen table, my coffee mug, pointe shoes, buttons, my mother's wedding ring. In one notebook, I wrote again and again about our laundry hamper:

April 17, 2000

The hamper makes a mockery of my life. No sooner do I empty it than it is full again. Baseball uniforms with green dreams ground into the knees. Socks balled up and caked with infield dirt. Leotards stiff with sweat and reeking of dead shoes. Pockets that jingle with old pennies and plastic LEGOs from a day spent foraging in gutters and schoolyards. T-shirts stained red from Bing cherries. Underpants crusty with discharge or old blood. Silk camisoles that speak of whispered nights between damp sheets. Tossed inside the hamper along with the dirty laundry are the stories of what we do, where we shop, how we eat, when we make love. My family soiled and stripped naked, waiting to be washed and folded.

I could just as well have cataloged the contents of the kitchen sink or the dishwasher or the refrigerator, any object that demands my constant attention in caring for my family.

Because our lives are so cluttered with things, you will probably need extra time to complete the Invitations to this chapter. Most of us have pages and pages to write about pockets and closets, toy chests and trunks, attics and basements, the things we have lost and the things we have found. And while you write about the things you carry, I will show you, in the Writing Mother's Helper that follows, how to pay attention to the weight of words.

INVITATIONS

↪ *What Are the Things You Carry?* Empty your purse and make a list of the things you carry. Be specific. Name the color of the lipstick, the brand of the wallet, the make of the pen. If you have a kitchen scale on hand, record the weight of each thing. Now write two Mother Pages explaining where you bought each item, why you need it, when you use it. As a second activity, use the writing start *These are the things I carry* and write for fifteen minutes. You may notice how the assortment of things you carry changes depending on where you are going, what you are doing, and whom you are with. And don't forget to mention the metaphorical things, the emotional baggage we all carry with us wherever we go.

↪ *Find the Stories Hidden in Things.* Look around your house at all the things your family owns. What have you saved or lost? What have you inherited? What have you preserved? What has broken? Each day this week, choose one object in your house and write down the story hidden inside. Poke around your attic and write about the Depression-era Christmas ornaments you inherited from your grandmother. Rummage through your basement and write about the binder of baseball cards your son collected in elementary school. Catalog the contents of your medicine cabinet, then write about the year your daughter had strep throat nine times. Look in your cupboard or pantry and find the story in a can of Campbell's soup or a box of Kraft macaroni and cheese. Open a drawer—ideally one that's crammed shut—and write about the dinosaur ice tray you bought at the American Museum of Natural History eleven years ago. Scan your bookshelves and write about the time your child sobbed on your shoulder after reading *Bridge to Terabithia.* On two Mother Pages write about a treasure or a piece of junk, an heirloom or a hand-me-down, something you kept or something you threw away—any *thing* that carries a story.

↬ *Toy Stories.* Long before the Disney movie appeared on-screen, mothers have written toy stories—stories inspired by toys that are lost, then found; discarded, then rediscovered; toys that grow old as our children grow up. Look through toy chests and closets, bedrooms and playrooms, in search of favorite or forgotten toys. Pay particular attention to the things your children have collected over the years—Beanie Babies, Pokémon cards, rocks, seashells, coins—because collections are often filled with *re*collections. Now choose one toy and write a toy story on two Mother Pages. Keep in mind that toy stories often have less to do with the toy itself than with the child who adores or abandons it.

INSPIRATIONS

No ideas but in things. (WILLIAM CARLOS WILLIAMS)

I have a crazy, crazy love of things. (PABLO NERUDA)

How could I have become so dependent on a dusty little thing [a stuffed tiger], I wondered. But deep down, I knew: The thing wasn't just a thing. (JOYCE MILLMAN)

SAMPLE MOTHER PAGE

The Things I Carry
by Jill Jenks McKeon

Today I carry the weight of the knowledge that my little sister is miscarrying. I carry my cell phone in case she calls. I carry my tampons because I too am hemorrhaging. I carry my running watch and my minivan car keys. I carry my notebook because I need to write all this stuff down. My notebook carries my words, my worries, my neuroses, my kids' drawings, my goals, my running achievements, cards my kids have made and their words, and the uplifting air of possibility. It is a dense notebook and I carry it because I need to.

I carry lavender hand cream, a gift from a new coworker whom I find passive aggressive and annoying. The hand cream, however, is rich and soothing. I carry lollipops from the pediatrician's office where Miranda received a negative throat culture. I carry a general mistrust of all doctors and their mantra of words about kids and coughs, antibiotics and rashes.

I carry my home equity checkbook because you never know when the last of our forty-thousand-dollar construction bills will come in. I carry the weight of the two thousand things I must do for the house like order master closet shelving, pick out mail slot, pick up doorbell, find rug for master bath, design mudroom cubbies for all the things that they will carry. And then I carry the knowledge—or rather the shame—that these materialistic obsessions occupy the forefront of my mind while things like miscarriages are going on. A friend of mine just finished her surgery for breast cancer. Another friend just checked into an AA rehab after blacking out behind the wheel, and her husband may be going to jail for his third DUI. A seven-year-old girl was beaten to death by her father over the course of a few days, a story my newspaper carried, and I carry a vision of her final hours around with me still. Did she know she was going to die? What was heavier for her, the emotional pain or the physical pain? What does her father carry now? His bag must be heavier than mine.

WRITING MOTHER'S HELPER

The Weight of Words

I used to be so skinny that my classmates taunted me with nicknames like "rubber band" and "string bean." Then I hit puberty and became, well, voluptuous. Ever since, I have sampled every weight-loss fad from the grapefruit diet to the rotation diet to South Beach. I remember exactly what I weighed on my wedding day, and I can tell you how many pounds I gained, then lost, for each of my pregnancies. To say that I am weight-conscious is an understatement; like most women living in the United States today, I am weight-obsessed.

Words, too, carry weight. I do not just mean metaphorical weight, the so-called "loaded" words that carry the weight of shame and hatred and history—words like *nigger* and *faggot* and *cunt*. I also mean literal weight—heavy words that clunk around in the back of your mouth like an extra pair of molars.

On a blank page in your Mother's Notebook, make a T-chart titled "The Weight of Words." Label the left column *Heavy Words* and the right column *Light Words.* List ten or more words for each column.

HEAVY WORDS	LIGHT WORDS
rock	feather
dagger	slippery
gun	drizzle
boulder	tease
thunder	fly
terror	pirouette
gangster	please
anger	pebble
break	fracture
hard	soft

Say the words out loud. Notice how they feel in your mouth. Typically, heavy words are made up of hard consonants formed at the back of the mouth (*r*, *g*, and *k*), whereas light words are made up of soft consonants formed with the lips or front teeth (*p*, *s*, and *f*). Heavy words bear down on your lower jaw, as compared to light words that slip off the tip of your tongue and tickle your lips.

As you write, choose words that carry the weight of your subject. When you write about weighty topics, such as pregnancy or mothering your mother or the things you carry, choose heavy words. When you write about moments of revelation or inspiration, such as the first glimmer of a smile on your newborn's face or a fleeting kiss from your thirteen-year-old son, use light words. But don't become self-conscious about the weight of words the way most of us are self-conscious about the weight of our bodies. In fact, you never need to think about the weight of words again. From now on, you will naturally notice which words are burdens and which words are blessings.

21

Push Me, Pull You

I vividly remember, at sixteen, hugging my mother one minute for having given me the keys to her Karmann Ghia, no questions asked, and barking at her the next for saying, "Drive safely, honey." "No," I said with as much venom and sarcasm as I could muster. "I'm going to drive dangerously." And by way of demonstration, I screeched out of the driveway without looking in my rearview mirror. I never imagined that one day my own daughter would be as contrary as I was. Nor do I believe that my son, now in the throes of adolescence, will spare me.

A couple of years ago, Colette and I were invited to a Passover seder at my sister's house in Riverdale. Miles and Mark were at a tennis tournament and wouldn't be home until late. Colette, racing to flatiron her hair, mask her blemishes, and lose five pounds before sundown, asked me to help her choose a top to wear with her black slacks.

"How about this?" I suggested, holding up a black lace blouse.

"Mah-um," she said derisively, dragging the one-syllable word into two. "Aunt Rena's seders are conservative," as if I didn't know.

"Well, what about this sweater?" I tried again.

"Not dressy enough."

"And this?" I asked, handing her an oxford, button-down shirt.

"Too preppy."

And so we proceeded through her closet until the bulk of her wardrobe was heaped in a reject pile on her bed.

Eventually, we got to the shoes. She screamed at me first for suggesting a pair of boots (too wintry for April), and then for suggesting sandals (too summery). That's when I quit. "Just tell me when you're ready to go," I said, walking out of the room. Five minutes later, Colette found me in my own closet, throwing on whatever clothes were in easy reach. Pleading, her voice sugary, she said, "I'm sorry, Mom." Then she added, "Would you *please* help me choose a purse?"

In the half-hour car ride to Riverdale, Colette sat grinning at the cell phone in her lap, thumbing text messages to her friends. As we were crossing the George Washington Bridge, she turned to me and, without preface, asked what I thought about smoking pot. I noticed that she called it *pot*, not *marijuana*, the word teachers use in health class. At fifteen, she said, she was the only one among her friends who had not tried it. I thought, *How lucky I am to have a teenager who still talks to me.* Then I tried to cop a casual tone so that she would keep on talking. But later that evening, because I would not let her sleep over at a friend's house just blocks from my sister's, since it was a school night, she wouldn't say a word the whole way home. Once inside the house, she slammed her door in my face and went to bed without saying good-night.

Carl Jung tells us that the heart is "the place of the coincidence of opposites." No one better understands the wisdom of these words than a mother. We are used to doing the do-si-do with our children, welcoming their advances, then dodging their blows, stepping forward and back, then forward and back again. As partners in this dance, we are pushed and pulled by our own opposing emotions as well. On any given day, we may feel cultish adoration and fiendish hatred, we may experience anger and forgiveness, doubt and trust, fear and hope. At no time in a mother's life is this dance more lively than when our children are in adolescence, but from the beginning we are torn between the instinct to pull our children close and the impulse to push them away.

An Amazon search assures me that I am not the only mother bungee jumping through her daughter's teenage years. As many as 21,294 hits resulted from a search of these three words: *mothers, daughters, adolescence*. Among them I found such encouraging titles as *Hold Me Close, Let Me Go: A Mother, a Daughter and an Adolescence Survived; When We're in Public, Pretend You Don't Know Me: Surviving Your Daughter's Adolescence So You Don't Look Like an Idiot and She Still Talks to You;* and *Get out of My Life, but First Could You Drive Me and Cheryl to the Mall.*

As much comfort as these books may provide, however, I still gain the most solace from remembering my favorite Dr. Dolittle character, the Pushmi-Pullyu. A llama with two heads at opposite ends, this fictional character speaks more to the truth about mothering adolescents than any pop psychology book does. Why I was fascinated by this beast as a child I cannot say, but now that I am a mother, he makes me smile when I might otherwise scream from being pushed and pulled at the same time.

Invitation

↬ *Pushmi-Pullyu.* A child does not need to be in adolescence to behave like Dr. Dolittle's fickle two-headed beast. Write down the writing start *Pushmi-Pullyu*. On one page, write about a time your child pulled you close: climbed onto your lap, asked for your advice, revealed a secret. On the next page, write about a time he or she pushed you away: let go of your hand, rejected your counsel, slammed the door in your face. The two incidents may be years apart or they may be minutes apart. By writing about them in one sitting, you will begin to appreciate the humor that inspired Hugh Lofting to invent his fictional jungle character.

INSPIRATIONS

Being a mother is a lifelong lesson in embracing contradiction. (CAMILLE PERI AND KATE MOSES)

As anyone who has raised children can attest, motherhood is the world's most intensive course in love. We may experience it, by turns, as a state of grace or oblivion, entrapment or exaltation, profound joy or numbing fatigue. Sometimes we pass through all these emotions in the course of a single day. And yet, the next morning, we are ready to resume.
(KATRINA KENISON AND KATHLEEN HIRSCH)

WRITING MOTHER'S HELPER

Writing from Opposite Ends of the Story

Go to any children's bookstore and you will find lots of picture books about opposites: *Alone Together; Up, Down, All Around; Wet Foot, Dry Foot, Low Foot, High Foot.* Books about opposites help us teach toddlers about the complexities and contradictions of the human heart. They also can give us guidance for writing. If you find yourself struggling with a writing start, sometimes it helps to approach the subject from the opposite end. If you are writing today about something you found, then try writing tomorrow about something you lost. If you are writing today about your child's first words, then try writing tomorrow about your father's last words. If you are writing today about having a son, then write tomorrow about having (or not having) a daughter. In writing, as in life, if you find that the front door is locked, try knocking on the back door.

You can write from opposite ends of almost any writing start. Begin with these, then make your own list of opposites:

- *I remember . . . I don't remember*
- *my mother told me . . . my mother never told me*
- *a food my child hates . . . a food he loves*
- *the color pink . . . the color blue*
- *before I became a mother . . . after I became a mother*
- *the first day of school . . . the last day of school*
- *leaving home for camp or college . . . coming home from camp or college*

22

LOVE LETTERS

One Valentine's Day, when my children were still young enough to be put to bed by seven-thirty, I prepared a candlelit dinner for two. I took the recipes from a Williams-Sonoma glossy cookbook called *Festive Occasions*:

Roast Lobster with Meyer Lemon Butter
Broiled Squabs in Honey Marinade
Wild Rice
Pear, Fennel, and Frisée Salad
Chocolate Pots de Crème with Candied Rose Petals

The hardest part was finding the ingredients: Meyer lemons, star anise, cardamom pods, ripe Comice pears. The rest was just a matter of following the instructions. I set the table with my grandmother's china, my husband's grandmother's silver, and odd pieces of beautiful gold-rimmed crystal from my mother-in-law, Claire, an antiques dealer. In the middle of the table, tied with a red ribbon, I placed a bundle of love letters my husband had written to me the autumn after we met, when we were living on opposite coasts.

Mark has a gift for letter writing, one he developed the year he traveled alone from Egypt through the Middle East to India and Nepal. It was well before the age of the Internet, when international telephone calling was costly and unreliable, so his family depended on those letters as their only source of news, even if the news was old by the time the letters made their way to San Francisco from Cairo or Damascus or Kathmandu. To my knowledge, those faded blue aerograms postmarked 1976 are the only written artifacts that have survived from the years before I met my husband. Which is one reason why I have safeguarded the bundle of love letters he addressed to me the fall of 1978. Now Mark writes to me three times a year: on my birthday, on our anniversary, and on Valentine's Day. I save those letters, too.

I worry about children growing up nowadays because they have no incentive to write letters—other than e-mails, instant messages, and text messages, all of which get sucked up into cyberspace. So much of what we know today about people from another time—writers and artists, pioneers and politicians, our own ancestors—comes from the personal letters they left behind. When the Pulitzer Prize–winning author Russell Baker was writing a memoir of growing up in the Depression, he stumbled upon an old trunk kept by his mother, not an unusual possession for a Southern woman. Inside the trunk, however, he discovered something unusual: a stack of love letters sent to his mother between 1932 and 1933 by an immigrant Dane named Oluf. Had it not been for those letters, Baker would never have known of the clandestine correspondence, nor would he have known of his mother's unconsummated love for this man. Baker felt that he could not write honestly about his mother without mentioning those letters, that to leave out the love affair would leave a great hollow at the heart of his book.

Conversation—whether it is conducted in person, on the telephone, or online—may be the most direct form of communication, but letter writing is the most intimate. When we write a letter, we hold a piece of paper in our hands, caressing it. When we write a letter, we let our guard down; we say what we mean and we mean what we say. Typically when we write a letter, we don't worry about grammar or spelling; our style is conversational and informal, the tone confessional and familiar. Many writers claim that writing a letter jump-starts their pens when they are stuck—more so than writing in a journal. Perhaps this is because when you write a letter, you are speaking directly to someone, and that someone is listening. Whether you send the letter is unimportant; what matters is that you are writing with the knowledge of being heard.

When my daughter was in the eighth grade, she applied for admission to several independent high schools in New York City. Most of the schools required the standard application essay—a short paragraph explaining the candidate's strengths and weaknesses or describing an event that had changed his or her life. One school, known for its progressive educational philosophy, required instead two personal letters, one written by the child addressed to a parent, the other written by the parent addressed to the child. For the better part of a Sunday, Colette and I sat side by side on my bed, each drafting a letter to the other.

In my letter, I told Colette that when I was her age, my best friend, Pamela, and I had promised each other that we would raise our families side by side in a cooperative community like the one in which we were growing up. I apologized to Colette for having broken that promise and expressed the hope that one day she would find a community like Skyview Acres. Colette wrote about her memories of September 11, 2001—the day she almost lost her father in the attack on the World Trade Center. Instead of becoming afraid, she wrote, she became bold. She realized that her hometown is not insulated from the world, and that her world will not forever be defined by her hometown. We had never before verbalized these sentiments to each other. I suppose some feelings are more easily expressed on paper than in person.

Unfortunately, the only time most of us exchange letters with our children is when they are away from home. My friend Kathleen once told me that Camp Dudley was worth every penny just to read her thirteen-year-old son's words: "I love you . . . I miss you." But you don't need to send your children to sleepaway camp to initiate letter writing. Authors Carol Sperandeo and Bill Zimmerman published a book called *Lunch Box Letters* in which they urge parents to write short notes of love and encouragement to their children every day. You can stash the letters not only in a lunch box, as the authors suggest, but also in a backpack or book, in a violin case or tennis bag, under a pillow or taped to a computer screen. Equally meaningful and perhaps more lasting, one mother I know, Kimberly Colvin, keeps a separate notebook for each of her children in which she writes a letter once a year on their birthday. When Kasey, her eldest, left for college, Kim gave her the notebook, nineteen letters she had written since the day her daughter was born.

You may also want to get in the habit of saving the notes your children write to you. For years, I have saved birthday cards, Mother's Day cards, thank-you notes, letters to Santa, and messages to the tooth fairy. And I don't only save the happy letters, just as I don't only save the photographs that show my kids smiling. Wedged in one notebook is a letter written by my daughter the first week of sleepaway camp, the word E-M-E-R-G-E-N-C-Y written at the top in bold capital letters and accentuated with five exclamation points. Pasted in another notebook is a collection of Post-its scribbled by my son in fits of anger and stuck on his bedroom door—eighteen variations on the theme "Keep out!" These spontaneous writings document a moment in time—words uttered in a ten-year-old's voice or penned in an eight-year-old's hand.

My favorite professor at Teachers College claims to have kept every letter she has ever received from a student or parent in all her years of teaching. *Love letters,* she calls them. For most mothers, notes from our children (and, if we are lucky, from our spouses as well) are the only love letters we can hope to receive!

Why not save them—in a shoebox, in a scrapbook, or between the pages of your Mother's Notebook.

Invitations

↬ *The Art of Letter Writing.* Resurrect the long-lost art of letter writing in your household. If your children are young, try writing Lunch Box letters. If they are older, consider communicating by e-mail. Just be sure to print out the e-mails from time to time. You can store them in a folder or paste them into your Mother's Notebook.

↬ *Unsent Letters.* Each day this week, write your Mother Pages in the form of a letter you don't intend to send. Use the suggestions in the Writing Mother's Helper that follows, or invent your own. Alternatively, you can try these writing starts: *love letters, write about a letter of acceptance, tell me what you know about rejection letters, junk mail, postcards, letters of recommendation.* Just jot down a writing start and start writing.

Inspirations

The letter is a form that encourages a sense of immediacy and the feeling that you are speaking directly to someone. Being aware that the letter will never be sent allows you to be candid and free. (Lynn Lauber)

When you don't know what else to do, when you're really stuck and filled with despair and self-loathing and boredom, but you can't just leave your work alone for a while and wait, you might try telling part of your history—part of a character's history—in the form of a letter. The letter's informality just might free you from the tyranny of perfectionism. (ANNE LAMOTT)

Letters to friends are more relaxed, less rule-bound, and more conversational than most other forms of writing. We feel known and understood as we write to a friend, and this in itself can be verbally liberating.
(TODD WALTON AND MINDY TOOMAY)

WRITING MOTHER'S HELPER

Unsent Letters

Writing a letter you don't intend to send has all of the promise but none of the pressure of being heard. You get to say what you want and need to say without worrying about who might get hurt. Here are some creative ways to write letters you don't intend to send. Copy the letters directly into the pages of your Mother's Notebook.

Write a letter to your mother or father. Share a memory about something he did or said. Tell her something you have never told her before. Franz Kafka wrote (and later published) a forty-five-page letter to his father in hopes of renewing a relationship that had become estranged. Sadly, the letter was returned unopened, but I would like to believe the act of writing it was healing for the son.

Write a letter to an ancestor you have never met. Ask a question you have always wanted answered—about your crazy aunt Bessie or the disappearance of the family fortune.

Write a letter to your child. Tell her something about your past that she doesn't know (and hopefully won't find out). Tell him your fears and prayers for what lies ahead.

Write five postcards—to your child's best friend, fiercest rival, least favorite teacher, coach, and school principal or guidance counselor. Tell her something she does not know about your child. Ask him for a favor.

Write a letter to someone you have lost—either through the years or through death. Write about the last time you saw the person. Tell him something you wish you had told him then. Tell her one thing about your life today that would surprise her.

Write a letter to yourself at a different age. Knowing what you know now, what advice might you give yourself at ten or twenty or thirty? What do you hope you will still remember about the present moment at sixty or seventy or eighty?

23

CLOSED DOORS

Writing Motherhood met for years every Thursday afternoon in the South Lounge of the YWCA on Oak Street in Ridgewood, before construction reconfigured the building and relocated my classroom. Tall, curtained windows rose from the scuffed linoleum floor to flank the sunny south wall of the rectangular room. In the far corner stood an old-fashioned, wood-framed blackboard on wheels that needed oiling. No matter how many swipes I made with the eraser, chalk marks from long-ago classes would surface on the board like lilies on a pond.

Earlier in the week, the room hosted a variety of enrichment seminars, including *Discover the Powerful You!, Why Are My Kids Licking the Table? and Other Enigmas of Parenthood,* and *The Triple Decker Sandwich Generation.* With a mix of curiosity and self-consciousness, I looked forward to reading the blackboard after these other classes had met—the same way a mother might snoop through the trash, sniff crumpled plastic cups, and smooth the craters on the couch while tidying up the morning after her teenager's party. *What did they talk about? What did they do? Did they kiss?*

On one Thursday, the blackboard was pitted with chalk marks that hinted at an especially animated discussion. The topic was "How to Communicate with Your Child," and the suggestions were, for the most part, common sense: *Kneel down to your child's level. Listen with your full attention. Don't ask too many questions. Don't provide all the answers.* One suggestion I had to read twice: *Don't tell your child everything about your personal life; tell only what is age-appropriate.* Earlier that month, Colette and I had gone to a Broadway show with another mother and daughter, then new friends to us both. We dined at a trendy restaurant on Broadway and Forty-second Street called the Blue Fin. Customers shimmered like tropical fish feeding at white-cloaked tables behind a wall of windows that opened onto Broadway. Everything was transparent—the windows, the interior glass walls, the glass escalator, the fish tanks, the translucent curtains, even our conversation.

I had intended to order a glass of chardonnay, but when the other mother ordered Perrier with lime, I did the same. Over sodas, she told the story of how she, a Jewish woman from Brooklyn, had in her early thirties met her husband, a middle-aged jazz pianist from Barcelona. Her daughter, just turned twelve, knew the story by heart, coaxing the mother through the pauses, filling in the lines she left out. Only this was no ordinary "boy meets girl" story. This was a story of racy romance, cocaine addiction, withdrawal, rehabilitation, and eventual reconciliation that ended happily in marriage and family. I sipped my Perrier and hoped Colette was too busy sawing her filet mignon to hear the naked details.

As a child, I remember distinctly *not* wanting to know the particulars of my parents' personal lives. My friend Pamela, who shouldered the smugness of someone a full year younger but several years wiser, announced one day that adults have sex not just for babies but also for fun. *Maybe* your *parents do,* I thought. Late that night, sleepless and unsettled, I pressed my ear against the closed door to my parents' bedroom. I felt thankful not to hear the noises Pamela had told me to listen for.

Even at fourteen, Colette and her friends still claimed that there were some things they did not want to know, thank you very much. One April, in the school cafeteria, the girls asked one another what each had given up for Lent. Abigail had given up potato chips; Sophie, Ben & Jerry's ice cream; Katie, nightly reruns of *Friends*. Morgan said her mother had given up Diet Coke, which was major because she downs a twelve-pack a day. Then Emily announced that her parents had given up sex. The girls shuddered and changed the subject to soccer. Less than two years later, however, Colette turned to me one morning at breakfast and said, "You lived with Daddy *before* you got married, right?"

Ironically, as our children gradually want to know more about our lives, they begin to reveal less about theirs. They begin to spend increasingly more time behind closed doors. One of my students, let's call her Joanne, in response to the writing start *Do Not Enter*, wrote that the road sign may as well have been emblazoned on the door to her daughter's bedroom. Then she remembered that as a teenager she, too, had not allowed her mother to enter her bedroom. One day, when Joanne was at a sleepover, her mother entered her room uninvited, ostensibly to straighten up. She found buried in the dark green shag carpet a tiny, round pill with a shiny coating, white with a strip of red. All night long, Joanne's mother bemoaned the realization that her daughter was on drugs. This was the seventies. She heard the stories. She read the newspapers. When Joanne returned home the next morning, her mother, red-eyed and puffy-faced, palmed the pill under her daughter's nose and demanded, "What's this?" Joanne answered, "Dristan." Then she stomped upstairs and slammed shut the door to her bedroom.

Every mother must decide for herself how much to pry and how much to tell. Several years ago, I sat with five other mothers at Kathleen's kitchen table swapping stories of times we were abused, humiliated, or taken advantage of as teenagers. I told about the time I was driving my parents' 1968 Volkswagen bus in the slow lane of the Garden State Parkway when I felt the presence of another car shadowing mine to the left. I looked down.

The driver, a middle-aged man, was smiling up at me. It was an odd sort of smile, but, being eighteen, I smiled back. Then I noticed his right hand working up and down the bony flesh out of his open fly. My head snapped straight ahead. I accelerated. He accelerated. I decelerated. He decelerated. I will never forget the powerlessness, the humiliation, the horror. I didn't even think to copy down his license plate when finally he sped away. My friends told similar stories. We listened. We laughed. We cried. Then we fell silent at the realization that each of us had a daughter on the brink of adolescence. Can our stories save our children, or will they only embarrass—or, worse, frighten—them?

When we raise a child, pieces from our past have a way of surfacing like old chalk marks on a blackboard. We can never erase those memories, but that doesn't mean we have to share them with our children. I think there is a difference between privacy and secrecy. Privacy is protective; it is about honoring what is sacred. Secrecy is insidious; it is about burying what is true. As a child, I did not want to open the door to my parents' bedroom. That was private. Now as a parent, I must decide which doors to open to my children—and when. But for all the doors that remain closed, I can open my notebook and write the stories down. And in time, I will begin to see a ray of light peeking through the crack under the door.

INVITATION

↜ *Closed Doors.* When you grew up, what took place behind closed doors—in your home, in your best friend's house, in your school? Which doors are open and which doors are closed in your house today? Metaphorically, what parts of yourself or your past remain hidden behind closed doors? Copy down the writing start *Closed Doors* and write two Mother Pages. Or try *Do Not Enter* and see where it takes you.

INSPIRATIONS

I get the willies when I see closed doors.
(NARRATOR OF *SOMETHING HAPPENED* BY JOSEPH HELLER)

Good personal boundaries make us distinct from one another and connect us at the same time.
(JEANNE ELIUM AND DON ELIUM)

24

BACKFLIPS

I have been walking around with a sore lower back, and it occurs to me that I have been doing too many backflips for my children. I am not talking about the triple flips, such as giving birth, putting away money for college, or teaching a toddler how to snowplow down the bunny slope in fifteen below. I am talking about the single flips we mothers do every day.

Take Sunday, 9 p.m. Colette needs to write a critique of the film *A Passage to India*, which she viewed in history class the week before. I sit on a stool by her computer as she shapes her ideas into a one-page essay. I keep her company because it is late, and because she is tired. Then she asks if I would stay a bit longer while she crafts sentences for a list of vocabulary words from Book Ten of *The Odyssey*. Some of the words neither of us has heard before, such as *historicity*, but with help from *Merriam-Webster OnLine* she manages to get through all twenty. By now it is ten o'clock, and Colette suddenly remembers that she has to bring cookies to school for a bake sale. Not just any cookies, mind you. Sugar cookies. At eleven, I am punching three-inch stars out of homemade cookie dough, then sprinkling them with star dust in shades of purple, pink, and blue. By the time the cookies are baked and cooled and packaged on a serving tray, it is midnight.

Fast forward to the next day. The one-page essay, it turns out, is supposed to be three. So Colette and I sit down again at the computer and discuss how she might stretch the argument to the requisite length. Now it is Miles who wants help; he is putting together a chapbook of poems for English class. Now it is Colette; she is writing a character sketch of the loyal swineherd in *The Odyssey*. I last read Homer in college, for goodness' sake, but I hold her hand anyway. I vault from room to room, doing somersaults and cartwheels and backflips. At eleven-thirty, Colette remembers that tomorrow she is supposed to bring bagels for her advisory group, so I set my alarm a half hour early, for 5:30 a.m., because I am not confident that my usual bagel store will be open in time. I may need to drive to Dunkin' Donuts. I am in bed now, worrying because Miles went to sleep with a sore throat, when I notice the light still on in the hallway—twelve forty-five and Colette is still up. I yell, though my voice sounds feeble because I am worn-out from a night of calisthenics. At my side, my husband stirs, but the last thing I feel is sexy. Besides, my back hurts. I slip into sleep and wait for the alarm to hurdle me out of bed and into the next flip.

As mothers, we naturally bend over backward for our children, but sometimes we bend too far. Sometimes, no matter how good our intentions, help can actually be a hindrance. When my daughter was in the fifth grade, her teacher advised us parents to stop jumping in to save our children. If they forget their bag lunch, let them mooch off their friends. If they forget a homework assignment, let them take the demerit. "Better to let them fall now," Mrs. Wiss said, "when the landing is soft." Five grades later and I am still trying to cushion their falls. My children are old enough now to land on their own two feet. And I am getting too old to do backflips anymore.

INVITATION

↬ *Backflips.* As you go through a given day, make a mental note of the backflips you do for your children. *Drive her to school so she can sleep an extra ten minutes. Drop off his trombone, a homework assignment, a bag lunch—whatever he left on the kitchen counter. Brave the crowds at Party City the night before Halloween because she decided, after all, that she doesn't like the outrageously expensive witch costume I special-ordered a month ago. Race to Barnes & Noble to replace the library book he lost. Cook three different entrées for dinner because my husband wants to lose weight, my daughter is a vegetarian, and my son won't eat fish. (Is it just me, or do you do these things, too?)* Now write down the writing start *backflips* and write two Mother Pages.

INSPIRATIONS

Never miss an opportunity to allow a child to do something she can and wants to on her own. Sometimes we're in too much of a rush—and she might spill something, or do it wrong. But whenever possible she needs to learn, error by error, lesson by lesson, to do it better. And the more she is able to learn by herself the more she gets the message that she's a kid who can. (POLLY BERRIEN BERENDS)

In our house, my husband is a scientist and I am a writer, but neither of us is a teacher, and there is a constant question of how much help is too much. . . . On the one hand, I am well positioned to help with their writing. Not to do it for them, but to read what they write and send them back to revise. On the other hand, is that helping or hurting? (LISA BELKIN)

25

Making Scents of Womanhood

I am standing in the feminine-hygiene aisle at the CVS off Goffle Road in Midland Park. Before me is a dizzying assortment of sanitary napkins and tampons: o.b., Tampax, Playtex, Kotex, Carefree, Stayfree, Always—everything from ultrathin pantiliners to overnight maxipads, with or without wings; from plastic applicators to biodegradable cardboard, deodorant or unscented. On the third shelf I manage to locate the brand I'm after. Now I just need to select the appropriate level of absorbency. The tampons are not for me; they are for my daughter. I have not had my period in twelve months.

Dr. Leipzig telephoned yesterday with my hormone levels, but I didn't need to hear the numbers to know that I am perimenopausal. For months I have been waking up every night in my very own sauna. Last night my husband and I had sex without protection for the first time since we last tried to get pregnant sixteen years ago. Afterward, Mark nestled his nose in my armpit and said, not unkindly, "You smell." It was a faint smell, and vaguely familiar to me. Like refrigerator air or dried mushrooms or a memory of being homesick. Something inside of me shriveled up and crawled away.

I was two months shy of thirteen when I started to menstruate. I had been inspecting my underpants religiously since the day Erica Goldstein had gotten her period, repeatedly mistaking the red flower petals on my cotton-print panties for the first show of menses. When finally it came, there was no mistaking it. I don't remember telling my mother, but I do remember telephoning Erica, who had stood vigil with me for weeks. Exactly thirty years later, on the eve of my daughter's thirteenth birthday, she announced matter-of-factly that she had gotten her period while her father and I were out for dinner with the Hoppers. I sat Colette down on the living room couch and insisted that we commemorate the event by each drafting a letter addressed to her, to be opened on her eighteenth birthday. Colette is seventeen now, and I can't for the life of me remember where I stashed those letters.

We celebrated Colette's thirteenth birthday with a goddess party that included makeovers, manicures, and perfume-making. Her grandparents from Bolinas, California, provided the essential supplies. Bebop has been concocting his own essences for years, traveling the globe in search of fragrant oils and forbidden musks, including one he smuggled out of Egypt, made from the scent gland of a male musk deer and reputed to be an aphrodisiac. For the party, he and Grandma Mary sent a dozen one-ounce, indigo blue and emerald green glass vials, a dozen tiny eyedroppers, and a collection of essential oils from San Francisco's Chinatown. As I watched the girls count out eighty drops of odorless almond oil, then mix in twenty drops of ylang-ylang or lotus, sandalwood or jasmine, I wondered what kind of woman each girl would become. There was no way of knowing at twelve or thirteen.

Still, no amount of fragrance could mask the sharp scent of awakening womanhood. Several weeks after the party, I came home one afternoon and heard Colette and her friends giggling behind her closed bedroom door. I don't remember if I knocked, but when I opened the door I saw strewn across the carpet the contents of my lingerie drawer. One girl was wearing a pair of my thongs over her Nike breakaways; another, my lace bra over her Adidas T-shirt. As my eyes adjusted to this image of dress-up adolescent-style, my nose registered an odor that nearly made me gag. It did not resemble the smell in my car when I pick up my son and his friends after baseball practice, nor was it reminiscent of gym lockers or athletic shoes worn too many days in a row. The smell was primal—one of those smells you think you can't bear a moment longer, but then, like rubber cement or Japanese wasabi or anxiety, the intensity recedes and you can breathe again. Now, at seventeen, my daughter smells like Dove deodorant, Bumble and Bumble shampoo, and Ruehl fragrance for women.

I was seventeen when I first had sex, although I tell Colette it was sometime in college. I also tell her (and this much is true) that I lost my virginity to a long-term boyfriend under the protection of a diaphragm I had fitted at the Planned Parenthood in Nyack. In the Dominican Republic this Christmas, Colette had her first bona fide love affair, with a Parisian boy named Raphael. Night after night she stayed out long after the rest of us had gone to bed, often past her curfew, until the last night, when she crept in at 1:36 a.m. I remember the time because I was watching the clock. The next morning at breakfast I turned to Colette confidentially, the way one girlfriend might look to another, and said, "So?" All she said was that after kissing a French boy she would never again be able to kiss an American. Neither that day nor during the weeks and months to follow has she offered me a single detail. I'm not sure I want to know more. As it is, I have to keep reminding myself that my daughter is seventeen. When Dr. Leipzig called with my hormone levels, I asked if I should schedule an appointment for Colette. Dr. Leipzig was quiet a moment, then she said, "The door opens. One steps in, one steps out." Her words wrapped around me like a hug.

Like many other mothers, I am entering menopause at the same time that I am raising adolescents. But whatever the timing, as we witness our children's awakening sexuality, we tend to flip-flop between the past and the present, comparing our experiences to theirs. Whenever I write about a subject as laden as this one, I find it helpful to elicit the sense of smell. In fact, these days I can hardly write about my daughter without writing about the way she smells. The same is true for my mother and for my brother. Growing up, I remember my mother smelling of A and D ointment, turpentine, Beefeater gin, Clorox bleach, raw onions, and day-old Chanel No. 5. My brother smelled of marijuana smoke, poorly ventilated fireplaces, and, after law school, designer fragrances. I recently found a bottle of the cologne Jason used to wear, wedged inside the glove compartment of his Jaguar. The silver label is too worn to read and the bottle is nearly empty. Sometimes, when I really miss him, I uncap the bottle, but not too often for fear the liquid will evaporate and then I will have no way to remember how my brother smelled before he got sick. Afterward, he smelled like lavender and hospital rooms and a hint of the grave.

I call this technique "writing with my nose," and I invite you to try it, too. Just follow the instructions in the Invitations below. You may want to use it, as I do, to push yourself to write about a subject you have been avoiding—a person, a place, a particular time in your life that evokes mixed emotions or unfinished memories. Or you can simply choose a scent, take a whiff, and ride the sense memory wherever it takes you. One of my students chose Pine-Sol and wrote about Wednesdays, the one day of the week when she can leave the house with the beds unmade and the dishes unwashed only to return several hours later to the squeaky smells of laundry detergent and household cleaners. Another student chose rubbing alcohol and wrote about the antiseptic examination room and the icy hands of Dr. Karpinski, her childhood pediatrician. A third chose a floral body lotion and wrote about forays into Victoria's Secret and other stores she would never have set foot in had she not birthed a daughter on the heels of two sons thirty years ago. The more you practice writing with your nose, the sooner you will develop a writer's keen sense of smell. And the closer you will come to making sense of your life.

INVITATIONS

↪ *Writing with Your Nose.* Write down the names of ten significant people in your life: your children, spouse, parents, grandparents, an old lover, a mentor, a best friend. Circle one name and make a list of scents you associate with that person. *My father: Old Spice aftershave, Scope mouthwash, leather gloves, gasoline, freshly cut grass, vitamins, ginger snaps, the* New York Times. Now choose one scent and write two Mother Pages. *Whenever my father was not in his office, he was seated on the family room couch squinting at the pages of the* New York Times, *the pads of his fingers and thumbs black with fresh ink.* Tomorrow you can write about a scent you associate with another person on your list. As a variation, try the same exercise with a place or a time in your life.

↪ *Making Scents of Motherhood.* In a basket or box, begin a collection of Mother Scents—scented products you associate with motherhood. For ideas, poke around your laundry room and basement, look underneath the kitchen sink and inside the shower stall, open your medicine cabinet, spice drawer, and liquor closet—wherever you store food and condiments, laundry soap and cleaning supplies, medications and cosmetics. Each day this week, choose one item from your collection. Begin by closing your eyes and inhaling deeply. What associations come up? What memories arise? Then open your Mother's Notebook and ride the sense memory as far back as it takes you—to the day before yesterday, to a time when your children were younger, or to your own childhood.

INSPIRATIONS

I never knew real passion until I had my first child. The smell that emanated from the deep recesses of her neck literally intoxicated me. I would lean over that crib and bury my face in her neck and inhale her smell until my back gave out or I began to hyperventilate. I don't wonder how it is that wild animal mothers can always identify the smell of their own offspring, differentiating them from the smells of all seemingly identical babies. The smell of your own offspring is more real and potent than any other sensory experience. (DENA SHOTTENKIRK)

What is it about smells that lingers in our subconscious, comforting and giving joy, making real what would otherwise be wooden and wordy? I'm not sure. But I do know this: Every lesson that I remember from my childhood, from my mother, has a smell at its center. (CHITRA DIVAKARUNI)

WRITING MOTHER'S HELPER

Writing with Your Nose:
A Collection of Mother Scents

Many common household products have distinctive smells with rich associations of motherhood. Use the list below to begin your collection of Mother Scents.

Johnson's baby shampoo	Old Spice aftershave
Johnson's baby powder	cut grass
Balmex	gasoline
baby wipes	rubber cement
A & D ointment	mothballs
Coppertone sunscreen	vanilla extract
Off! insect repellent	cinnamon
Cutex nail polish remover	cloves
Listerine mouthwash	marshmallows
iodine	peanut butter
Bactine antiseptic	rum or whiskey or wine
Robitussin cough syrup	Bazooka bubble gum
Vicks VapoRub	Pine-Sol
rubbing alcohol	Tide detergent
Axe deodorant	Clorox bleach

SAMPLE MOTHER PAGE

Vicks VapoRub
by Alice T. Whittelsey

A deceptively small, colorless liquid blob that packs a wallop as I lean in for a sniff—engaging more than my sense of smell, opening up sinuses and bronchial tubes, lungs, just about everything from my head down to my toes, and a memory.

It's fifty years ago, and I'm sucking in the fumes from the vaporizer at my bedside, greedy for relief from the tightness that threatens to squeeze the last bit of breath out of me. The moist medicated vapor calms my panic, or maybe it's my mother's presence that soothes me, as she hovers nearby till I drift back to sleep. The vaporizer gurgles its lullaby.

Bronchitis and asthma were my constant companions as a child every winter. Being sick wasn't all bad. Besides missing school and capturing mom's attention, the best perk was receiving visits from Miss Jones, the principal of Friends' school, who made a house call every few days to bring me some books. My favorites were from a series of huge bound volumes of an early 1900s magazine for children, called St. Nicholas. Each volume held a year's worth of issues, with spell-binding stories, poetry, fantastic illustrations. I devoured St. Nicholas in ecstatic bites, surfacing only briefly between volumes to breathe in the restorative mist from my vaporizer.

26

Good Enough

Mr. Oswald, my son's seventh-grade English teacher, had left two cryptic messages on my voice mail before he finally reached me on the third try. "Did Miles tell you what happened?" he wanted to know. No, Miles had not.

At the end of the school day, Mr. Oswald had collected an impromptu essay before Miles had had time to finish writing. After the bell rang, the teacher locked the door, as was his habit, and went to the main office to collect his mail. When he returned to the classroom fifteen minutes later, he found Miles hunched over the front desk, pen in hand. A janitor had let Miles into the room to retrieve a book he claimed to have left behind. As Mr. Oswald recounted these events to me, I was reminded of telephone calls from other teachers years past: from Mrs. Macri, his fourth-grade teacher, concerned that Miles was laboring over every assignment and so not completing any on time; from Mrs. Taylor, his second-grade teacher, appalled by the eraser shavings that mounded on his table every day; from Mrs. Leininger, his kindergarten teacher, worried that Miles was gripping his pencil too tightly and forming his letters too slowly.

"Not every assignment needs to be perfect," Mr. Oswald was saying. "Miles needs to know when his work is good enough. Otherwise, he'll make himself sick or do something stupid, like this."

Notwithstanding my passing impulse to strangle the man, I knew that he was right, of course. As writers, we, too, can learn something from his advice. I know an editor who, like Mr. Oswald, tells her writers, "It just has to be good enough." Nevertheless, many of them agonize over first drafts until the manuscripts are long overdue. "There will be a second draft," the editor keeps telling them, "and a third." Neither the English teacher nor the editor is condoning mediocrity. They are cautioning against perfectionism, for perfectionism is like a ball and chain that drags the writer down, slows her down sometimes to a stop so that she ends up like Miles, with a pile of eraser shavings on her desk and no pen marks on her page.

The same thing can happen to mothers. As Judith Warner explains in her book *Perfect Madness: Motherhood in the Age of Anxiety,* there is nothing a woman today won't buy or do in her quest to become a perfect mother. Then we hate ourselves for falling short. Think of all the times you agonize over decisions (the choice of preschool, the selection of pediatrician), second-guess your choices (day care instead of home care, private school over public), and beat yourself up for your shortcomings (for losing your temper, missing parent-visiting day, or unwittingly sending your child to school with a fever). The fact is that we should give ourselves a break, not a beating. Just as we reassure our children in the face of failure that they did their best, we should tell ourselves that, as mothers, we are good enough. No excuses. No apologies.

If only I could heed my own words. For sixteen years and eleven months, I never once forgot to pick up my daughter—not from school, not from town, not after a dance class or music lesson. That is, until one Tuesday night last October. Colette had stayed home from school all day with a bad cold. Usually I'm a good mother when it comes to caring for sick children, but that particular Tuesday I was writing on deadline, putting the finishing touches on a book proposal in preparation for a meeting with a literary agent. I may have suggested that Colette heat up a cup of Lipton Ring-O-Noodle soup. I may have told her to take two Tylenol. Bottom line, I left her to fend for herself. After dinner (take-out Chinese), Colette remembered that she had scheduled a session with Mr. Vojack, her math tutor. Too late to cancel. Besides, she had a math test on Thursday. I dropped Colette at Mr. Vojack's split-level home on Busteed Drive at 7:03, something to take note of because, being a mathematician, he runs his sessions by the clock, always starting and ending precisely on time.

I was in a panic to get back to my desk, but I obeyed the speed limit, having been pulled over on Erie Avenue once before for pushing forty in a 25 mph zone. According to my calculations, I would have fifty minutes alone at home to finish the proposal. I rebooted my computer, pulled up the document, selected Print Preview, and scrolled through the pages, skimming for consistency, checking for redundancy, correcting as I went, then printing out ten sheets at a time because otherwise my printer goes berserk, spitting out pages at odd angles with their edges chewed or torn. I was well into my work, poised to hit the print key for pages forty to fifty, when the telephone rang. Annoyed, I glanced at the clock: 8:23. *Who could be calling at this hour?* I didn't recognize the number on the caller ID, so I went back to work without answering the phone. On the fourth ring, I picked up. "Mom?" *Oh my God!* "I'm just leaving, honey," I said. "Wait inside." As I raced down Erie Avenue, the speedometer pinned at fifty, I decided that in spite of all the years of evidence to the contrary, I was on this day a Bad Mother.

Susan Cheever did not title her memoir of motherhood *The Perfect Parent;* she called it *As Good as I Could Be.* In nearly two hundred pages, never once does she apologize for raising her children through multiple divorces, frequent moves, disrupted routines, financial crises, alcoholism, eating disorders, the unreliability of an absent father, and the unavailability of a working mother. Instead, she marvels that she was able to raise such "wonderful children in difficult times," as the subtitle of her book reads. Reminiscent of psychologist Bruno Bettelheim's definitive text on child-rearing, *A Good Enough Parent,* Cheever's memoir reminds us that good enough lives in the real world, with strep throat, hangovers, and homework. Good enough celebrates us mothers as imperfect, with stretch marks and blemishes and bruises. If we can come to accept imperfection in ourselves, then maybe we can begin to accept imperfection in our children.

Telling a perfectionist to embrace imperfection, however, is like telling an insomniac to go to sleep or an anxious person to relax. It's not that simple. On days when I'm filled with self-loathing, my acupuncturist tells me to close my eyes and smile to myself. The session after that Tuesday in October, she told me to sit up and hug myself. If that sounds too weird, just practice telling yourself over and over, as a mother and a writer, that good is good enough, and in time you will begin to believe it. In time, your set of expectations—both for yourself and for your children—will be replaced by a state of expectancy.

INVITATIONS

↬ *Bedtime Prayers.* Every night before bed, tell yourself three things you feel good about. Encourage your children to do the same. Then write them down in your Mother's Notebook. *I telephoned Aunt Estelle at the hospital and we chatted for twenty minutes. I picked up a deli lunch from Wilkes and dropped it off at the middle school as a surprise for my son. I canceled my dentist appointment and instead wrote for an hour.* The three items do not have to be significant or honorable, nor do they need to be productive. In fact, better if they're not. You can feel good about having lunch with a friend or curling up with a book on a rainy afternoon. By learning to celebrate the small things, we honor the big things that make us human.

✧ *Good Mother, Bad Mother.* On two Mother Pages, write down all the different ways you slip up or screw up as a mother. Or choose one particularly outrageous or inexcusable offense to focus on. As you write, you will most likely begin to see the comedy in the tragedy. Just as we must give ourselves permission to write badly in order to write well, we must forgive ourselves for being "bad" mothers on our way to becoming good mothers.

INSPIRATIONS

Gently remind yourself that life is okay the way it is, right now. In the absence of your judgment, everything would be fine. As you begin to eliminate your need for perfection in all areas of your life, you'll begin to discover the perfection in life itself. (RICHARD CARLSON)

Perfectionism is not a quest for the best. It is a pursuit of the worst in ourselves, the part that tells us that nothing we do will ever be good enough—that we should try again. (JULIA CAMERON)

I should not use that wretched and vile phrase "bad mother." At the very least, I should give myself a break; I should allow that, if nothing else, I am good enough. (AYELET WALDMAN)

27

THEN AND NOW

Growing up, I remember my mother loved to watch old movies starring Cary Grant, Grace Kelly, and Katharine Hepburn. The moment one of her favorite actors appeared on the screen of our fifteen-inch, black-and-white television, she would exclaim, "Look how young he was then!" What she meant was "Look how old we are now!" Nowadays, when I walk down Ridgewood Avenue on my way to the post office or dry cleaner's, I can't help but gape at the young mothers pushing strollers with toddlers in tow. They look so pretty. They look so fit. They look so *young*. Then I remember that, fifteen years ago, I was a young mother like them.

As each of us walks through our days, we retrace footsteps buried layers below, unconsciously comparing the way things are now to the way they were then. I am sitting in Dr. Yankus's office, where Miles has come for his regular checkups since he was three months old. The waiting room is eerily empty, just one other mother with her daughter, perhaps eight, clutching her stomach. On the floor is an assortment of red and yellow Little Tikes toys: a fire engine, a dump truck, a school bus. On the table is a basket of early readers and picture books: *The Cat in the Hat, All about Scabs, I'm a Big Kid Now*. On the wall is a rack of pamphlets with advice on toilet training, sleep problems, and car seats. Where once the waiting room was stocked with novelties and distractions for my entire family, now not one toy, not one book, not one pamphlet, is of any interest to me or to my children.

For the past three years, since Miles turned twelve, I have no longer been allowed in the examination room for his annual physical. I was so insulted at first that I nearly changed pediatricians. Now, as the mother of a fifteen-year-old boy, I think it's a good thing. After the exam, I meet privately with Dr. Yankus in his tiny corner office, where he tells me more information than I care to know. As we chat, I hear an infant cry and a mother coo in a room across the hall, and I remember the way Miles used to shriek and I used to shrivel every time the nurse whipped out her needle with live viruses of measles, mumps, and rubella. Miles lopes past the open door in his size-ten shoes, grunts a monosyllable, and ducks out of the office. Already in the ninth grade, my baby is nearly full grown and half-gone.

Virginia Woolf says that when we write about our lives, the present necessarily colors the past because it is the "*I* now" who remembers the "*I* then." For this final chapter of Part Two, I invite you to return with your notebook to places you frequented when your children were younger or before they were born: an office, a petting zoo, a toy store, the elementary school. On one page, you will write down whatever you remember about the way things were *then*; on another page, you will write down whatever you see in front of you *now*. As you compare your memories of the past with your perceptions of the present, don't be surprised to discover that your children are not the only ones who have grown. You, too, have changed with the years. Although we can never go home again, as Thomas Wolfe claims, visiting old haunts can help us understand how we got from *there* to *here*.

INVITATION

↬ *Then and Now.* For this Invitation, I will ask you to write about a place from two perspectives: *then* and *now*. If possible, try to pay a visit before sitting down to write. If not, you can always write from memory. Begin by generating a list of places you used to frequent when your children were younger or before they were born. Choose one destination you would like to revisit, if not in reality then in your imagination. On one page of your Mother's Notebook, write down everything you remember about the way things were then—five, ten, or twenty years ago. What time of year did you visit? What did you pack for the outing? What was your daughter's favorite activity? Did your son throw a temper tantrum whenever it was time to go home? On another page of your notebook, write down whatever you see in front of you now. Begin by describing the people. What are the mothers wearing? How do the children behave? Then take a look at the facilities. Are they dilapidated or have they been updated? What has changed? What has remained the same? See the Writing Mother's Helper that follows for a list of places to revisit. You don't have to leave your house, though, to compare the way things were then to the way they are now. You can choose any room—your son's bedroom, your daughter's bathroom, the kitchen or basement or attic—and write from the perspective of *then* and *now*.

INSPIRATIONS

The past is much affected by the present moment. What I write today I should not write in a year's time.
(VIRGINIA WOOLF)

Every time I go back to Brownsville it is as if I had never been away. . . . It is over ten years since I left. . . . Yet as I walk those familiarly choked streets at dusk and see the old women sitting in front of the tenements, past and present become each other's faces; I am back where I began. (ALFRED KAZIN)

WRITING MOTHER'S HELPER

Then and Now: Places to Revisit

Certain places instantly bring me back to a time when my children were younger: the Bronx Zoo, Toys "R" Us, Van Saun Park, McDonald's, the Bead Shop, Abma's Farm, the Museum of Natural History, Master Kim's Karate, Baron's School of Ballet. All I need to do is sit on a bench, peer through a window, or wander the hallways and I am flooded with memories—at once lulled by the sameness and taken aback by the change. Use the suggestions below to generate your own list of places to revisit. Then grab your Mother's Notebook and pen and set out to write about *then* and *now.*

playground	summer camp
park	toy store
ball field	novelty stores (baseball
dance or art studio	cards, beads, needlecraft)
children's museum	shoe store
zoo	barbershop
pubic library	fast food restaurant
bookstore	ice cream parlor
diaper aisle at	doctor's or dentist's
the supermarket	office
classroom or auditorium	pet shop
at school	maternity wing or
day-care center	adoption center

PART THREE

Writing Motherhood for Life

I fell in love with my husband under a midnight moon in June at the point on the map where Washington, Oregon, and Idaho intersect. My brother introduced us, wrote me a letter about his Berkeley roommate, talked me into flying from New York to San Francisco, then drove me nearly a thousand miles, many of them on back roads, to meet Mark the summer he was fighting fires in the Umatilla Forest. For five delirious days, I adored this lanky California boy who stashed a pile of handwritten poems under his mattress, roasted his own green coffee beans, and smiled out of the corner of his mouth. On the eve of my departure, he rowed me in a wooden boat to the middle of a nearby pond, the moon high, the virgin timber mirrored in the still water. He pulled in the oars, took my hands in his, and said, with a fierceness that almost frightened me, "I'm not interested in infatuation; I'm looking for love."

Writing is a lot like love. Students come to my classes bursting with stories to tell. The minute they put pen to paper, they are smitten, as much with the dream of writing as with the discovery that they *can* write. Words pour out onto the page. Sometimes they amuse us. Sometimes they surprise us. We giggle. We gasp. But in time the infatuation fades. Now students have to work harder. They burrow around for things to write about. They question and criticize what they write. They decide, finally, that they *can't* write. They begin to feel like a lover on the morning after, disappointed or embarrassed or bored.

Twenty-eight years after I met my husband, the infatuation has long since faded. Every day I have to remind myself to say kind words, to fix his coffee light with two teaspoons of sugar, to kiss him when he leaves for work in the morning. But hardly a day goes by when, for a moment, I don't remember what it was like to be nineteen years old in a rowboat with my new love, even if now he suffers from arthritis and I have bags slung like hammocks under my eyes.

I cannot tell you that writing will get easier with time. But I can promise that, like love, it will get better. If you want to write, if you *really* want to write, you must keep at it no matter what, you must make yourself write the morning after, the morning after that, and every morning from now on. You already know that writing can save your life. Now I will show you how to make writing a *way* of life.

INSPIRATIONS

> *To be a writer, it's necessary to have a passionate love affair with words. To say words we love is like kissing; we can feel the pleasure all over our body.* (GEORGIA HEARD)

> *My love for the alphabet, which endures, grew out of reciting it but, before that, out of seeing the letters on the page. In my own story books, before I could read them for myself, I fell in love with various winding, enchanted-looking initials drawn by Walter Crane at the heads of fairy tales.* (EUDORA WELTY)

> *Writing a book is like rearing children—willpower has very little to do with it. If you have a little baby crying in the middle of the night, and if you depend only on willpower to get you out of bed to feed the baby, that baby will starve. You do it out of love. Willpower is a weak idea; love is strong.*
> (ANNIE DILLARD)

Coming out of the Notebook

Halfway through a college degree program at a music conservatory, I quit playing the cello. Never mind that I had put in upward of 6,610 hours on the fingerboard since the fourth grade. In the end, I quit playing the cello because I was afraid to come out of the practice room much the same way that a homosexual may be afraid to come out of the closet. I nearly made the same mistake with writing. From the time my children were little, I wrote quietly, almost secretly, in my notebook every day. As my children grew older, I tried my hand at short stories, I started an adolescent novel, I submitted a few articles for publication. For months, maybe longer, I dreamed of writing the book *Writing Motherhood*. Then one day an article appeared in the local newspaper that I had intended to write—mused about writing for nearly a year—and I knew that if I didn't write this book now, I never would. It was time for me to come out of the notebook.

Submitting pages for publication is only one of many ways to come out of the notebook. You can take a writing class, or teach one. You can join a writing group, or start one. You can read aloud entries from your notebook, to family or friends or total strangers. You can host a reading and invite other mothers who write. You can copy down favorite passages and give them away as gifts. You can transcribe select pages onto your computer and e-mail them or blog them. You can begin a Writing Mother's Portfolio, a collection of revisionary drafts, from raw writings to finished pieces. If, after a time, you don't find some way to come out of the notebook, your pages will grow mildewed and moldy, like a basement that has neither light nor air. Here I will take you through the first steps of coming out of the notebook.

INSPIRATIONS

Don't let [your work] just pile up in notebooks. Let it out.
(NATALIE GOLDBERG)

As I reach out to create the writing communities I need, I have one rule: I do not share my writing in process with anyone who does not make me want to write.
(DONALD MURRAY)

Writing is a social act, an act of communication both intellectual and emotional. It is also, at its best, an affirmation—a way of joining the human race.
(WALLACE STEGNER)

A Sabbatical:
Playing Hooky

The Tuesday my son played hooky from school coincidentally fell during the week I played hooky from writing. There were differences, however. His stolen absence was planned and granted with parental consent; mine happened with no forethought. He looked forward to his day off with glee; I looked back on my week with guilt. He made every minute count; I wasted hours. With today's ramped-up lifestyles, everybody needs a personal day now and then, but we must first give ourselves permission to power down.

When my children were little, I became so concerned about the lack of downtime that I was prompted to write an article for the *Ridgewood News* titled "Is Your Family Overscheduled?" The question, of course, is rhetorical. I mean, is there a family you know that *isn't* overscheduled? I included in the article a fun and friendly checklist as a barometer of busyness: *Do you need to schedule playdates for your children at least two weeks in advance? Do you spend more time in your car than you do in your kitchen? Does your family frequent McDonald's more than twice a week? Is your calendar color-coded?* Evidently, I was not alone in my concerns. Not long after the article appeared, my town announced its first annual Ridgewood Family Night, familiarly known as Ready, Set, Relax! On the last Monday in March, teachers are not allowed to assign homework and coaches are not allowed to schedule practices so that families can spend some quiet time at home together.

Because I am not one who likes to be told when to do something and when to do nothing, in place of Family Night I have instituted an alternative tradition, one I am hesitant to put into print for fear the truancy officer will come knocking on my door. Let me say first that I am a huge believer in education. I am a teacher. Nonetheless, a few times a year, I allow my children to play hooky from school (some people like to call it a mental health day, but with members of my family on Prozac and lithium, I prefer to think of it as playing hooky). Sometimes they use the day off to sleep late, watch television, and catch up on homework. Other times we plan an outing, like the Tuesday Miles and I drove to New York City, watched a movie from the nose-bleed section of a theater in Times Square, then splurged on Michael Jordan basketball shoes at the Sports Authority next door. I got the idea for playing hooky from an essay by Sandi Kahn Shelton, who confesses to having showed up unannounced at her daughter's middle school from time to time, signing the girl out of class, then taking her somewhere—anywhere—out to lunch, to the mall, to the beach. Shelton calls these escapes "rescue raids," not because they saved her daughter from a test or assignment but because they restored the intimacy in their relationship.

I have since applied the practice to writing, except instead of playing hooky I take a sabbatical. I always knew that universities grant eligible professors time off every so many years for study, rest, or travel. But I only just learned that the word *sabbatical*, defined as relating to the Sabbath or any period of rest that recurs in regular cycles, derives from the ancient Jews, who were by law required to let their lands and vineyards remain fallow every seven years. Whether we are talking about teaching or farming, everyone agrees that fertility almost always follows a fallow period. The same is true for writing.

Before you reread your notebook, as I will ask you to do next, give yourself permission to take a sabbatical from *Writing*

Motherhood—a day, a week, even a month, of no writing. You've been working hard, sporadically if not steadily, and you could probably use some time off. Your mind will still be working, gathering material, filing it away, but your writing muscles need to rest and rebuild. You will also want some elbow room in order to gracefully transition from writer to editor, from creator to critic, if you choose to follow the 10 Easy Steps for revising your Mother Pages, as outlined on page 265. While we can never read our own writing with complete objectivity, time and distance give us greater perspective. Equally important, just as you return home after a night out or a week away feeling recharged and renewed, so you will return from your sabbatical eager to roll up your sleeves and get back to *Writing Motherhood*.

INSPIRATIONS

> *You've done a lot of work and you need a period of time (how much or how little depends on the individual writer) to rest. Your mind and imagination—two things which are related, but not really the same—have to recycle themselves.*
> (STEPHEN KING)

> *Writers have fallow times too. The problem is, when I can't write, I panic; I often think of these times as a problem, a waste. But I keep telling myself that these times are an organic part of the writing process.* (GEORGIA HEARD)

The Game of Dibble:
Rereading Your Mother's Notebook

I am rummaging through old notebooks in search of a Mother Page I once wrote on wholeness. I need it for a chapter I am writing, but I can't find it. Half a dozen notebooks lie propped open on the floor; fifteen or twenty more are stacked in piles at my knees and elbows. I am overwhelmed by the mass of material I have collected in my writing life. Most of it I may as well throw out, along with my stained sweaters and shrunken T's. But some of it is worth keeping. How do I salvage the valuables from the junk heap?

Whenever I reread old notebooks, I am reminded of Dibble, a favorite childhood game we played every summer at the Skyview Pool. *Pool* is a misnomer, *mud hole* more accurate, for it was dug out of a clearing in the woods by eager young mothers and fathers with borrowed shovels and a hired backhoe and is overhung to this day with deciduous scrub and scrawny oaks that litter the mossy brown surface with leaves and strands of pollen. A rooted dirt path leads to the deep end, where there are twin docks: one, with a diving board that was later dismantled when the Health Department expressed concern that someone could hit his head on the muck at the bottom; the other, the site for the game we called Dibble. To start the game, the Dibbler jumped off the dock fisting a four-inch stick. Once underwater and out of sight, he swam as far and as deep as he could before releasing the stick and darting out of the way. Meanwhile, the Seekers crouched on the dock in hushed immobility, toes hanging, eyes scanning, ready to pounce the second the stick surfaced—which it usually did just when you considered it lost and always in the least expected place.

I have come to believe that a similar phenomenon happens with writing. In old notebooks, I stumble upon words that unexpectedly reappear in my writing again and again, sometimes whole lines and passages I don't remember having written before. Over the years, I have repeatedly written about my mother, my brother, and growing up in Skyview Acres. These subjects keep resurfacing in my Mother's Notebook the way a dog keeps sniffing at your heels. Eventually, I must turn around and say "Sit!" so I can give the animal the attention it wants.

Now that you have taken a sabbatical from *Writing Motherhood,* I invite you to revisit your Mother's Notebook. Just follow the steps outlined in the Writing Mother's Helper that follows. As you reenter your notebook and read over your pages, remember the game of Dibble. Trust that the really important material—the good stuff—will resurface without your having to dive down to fetch it, if not this time, then when you need it. I know this the way I know that each of us has within us the reserves and the resources to deal with whatever arises in our lives as mothers. All we need to do is be patient and watch for the stick to surface.

Inspirations

When I reread my notebooks it never fails to remind me that I have a life, that I felt and thought and saw. It is very reaffirming, because sometimes writing seems useless and a waste of time. Suddenly you are sitting in your chair fascinated by your own mundane life. That's the great value of art—making the ordinary extraordinary. We awaken ourselves to the life we are living. (Natalie Goldberg)

Rereading your practice notebooks after a period of time is like taking a trip to a place that is at once familiar and yet somehow different, like revisiting an old neighborhood.
(JUDY REEVES)

WRITING MOTHER'S HELPER

Rereading Your Mother's Notebook: How to Play the Game of Dibble

In describing the 7 Building Blocks of *Writing Motherhood*, I promised that no matter what happens you can always come home to the Mother Pages. Now, as you sit down to revisit your Mother's Notebook, pretend you are a guest in someone else's home: be gentle, be kind, be courteous. Reading over your notebook takes compassion, but it also takes planning. You will need some supplies, and you will need a stretch of time. If possible, read over your notebook in two or three sittings, ideally within the span of a week, so that you can recognize the arc of your journey and appreciate how far you have come.

Before You Reread Your Mother's Notebook . . .

- Set aside a block of time when you can be alone and uninterrupted. In addition to your notebook, you will need a few highlighters or colored pens and a pad of small Post-its. Turn off the telephone, make a cup of tea, sit down in a soft chair, and have a soft heart.
- Fire your internal critic. This is not a time to judge yourself but rather a time to practice self-acceptance. Be curious, not critical.
- Hire a cheerleader. As you read, think of an imaginary friend who can sit on your shoulder and whisper positive feedback into your ear. Remember that your notebook includes *all* your writing—

good and bad, inspired and boring, experimental and routine. Taken together, your Mother Pages chart your journey through *Writing Motherhood,* and like all journeys this one is undoubtedly up and down.

As You Reread Your Mother's Notebook . . .

- Notice which subjects you keep revisiting, which sticks keep resurfacing. These want attention. Jot them down on a page in your notebook titled "Dibble."
- Highlight or underline words and sentences that move you, surprise you, embarrass you. These can be used as starting points for new writing. Add them to your list of writing starts.
- Tag favorite pages with Post-its. These you may later decide to transcribe onto your computer.

After You Reread Your Mother's Notebook . . .

- Type up five or more entries from your notebook. Don't edit them. For now, just copy down the Mother Pages as you wrote them. And don't judge them. Some of the pages will be fine as they are; others you may want to revise.
- Print out your selected entries and store them in a folder or binder that will serve as your Writing Mother's Portfolio—a collection of "exploratory drafts" or works in progress. Ideally, your folder will have a few pockets so you can track each piece from raw copy to final draft.

Revision:
Reseeing Your Mother Pages

For many of you, *Writing Motherhood* is all about process—the daily doing. Like a number of my students, you probably get cranky the days you don't write your Mother Pages. For some of you, though, *Writing Motherhood* may also be about product—the end result. You want to have something to show for your efforts. *Here it is. See what I've done.* Shortly before I began work on this book, I grew impatient with the seemingly endless, seemingly pointless process of writing my Mother Pages. I told myself that I knew all about process. As a cellist, I had practiced six hours a day. As an undergraduate, I had studied six hours a day. Now as a writer, I write every day. "Fuck the process," I wrote in my Mother's Notebook in December 2002. "Give me some product."

I know this is about as unevolved a statement as anyone could make—as un-Zen as claiming that I'd rather dwell on the past or worry about the future than live in the moment. I also know that every writer insists that getting published is not what it's cracked up to be. Still, I told myself, there must be some place midway between the rough beginnings in my notebook and the unruffled finality of the printed page.

Whether or not you are interested in submitting for publication, there are plenty of good reasons to revise your writing. For one, revising helps you hone your craft. As you work and rework a piece of writing, you naturally become more skilled as a writer.

For another, revising brings great satisfaction. Not only is it rewarding to watch your writing improve, but it is also reaffirming to hold a finished document in your hand. Most important, though, revising brings clarity. As you write and rewrite a draft, your writing gets sharper and clearer as you come closer to saying what you really mean to say. In this way, revising lets us see things we didn't see before. Thus the most literal definition of the word—to revise is to envision again—points to its most lofty purpose.

Although you may get lucky on occasion, writing rarely comes out right the first time. More often it takes several go-rounds before we arrive at a satisfactory place. I like to think of these successive revisions as "exploratory drafts" on the road from a first to a final copy—a journey you can track in different pockets of your Writing Mother's Portfolio. Keep in mind, however, that the goal of revision is not to create the best piece of writing but rather to make each subsequent draft just a little bit better than the one before. This will help you keep your internal critic in check as you switch from writer to editor and back to writer again.

Notwithstanding the title of William Stafford's classic book on writing, *You Must Revise Your Life,* we don't get many opportunities in our lives to redo or restate something we did or said. If you think of revision, then, as a second chance, you will agree with Toni Morrison, who says that the best part of writing—"the most delicious part"—is *re*writing.

INSPIRATIONS

The best part [of writing], the absolutely most delicious part, is finishing it and then doing it over. That's the thrill of a lifetime for me: if I can just get done with that first phase and then have infinite time to fix it and change it. I rewrite a lot, over and over again, so that it looks like I never did. I try to make it look like I never touched it, and that takes a lot of time and a lot of sweat. (TONI MORRISON)

Writing is hard work. A clear sentence is no accident. Very few sentences come out right the first time, or the third. (WILLIAM ZINSSER)

When we revise our writing and do a good job of it, we see it anew, and from a different perspective. We become our own reader, and we become critical and questioning. (RUTH VINZ)

WRITING MOTHER'S HELPER

8 Reasons to Revise Your Writing

Whether or not you decide to submit pages for publication, consider these reasons to revise your writing:

1. **Craftsmanship**—As you work and rework a piece of writing, you naturally become more skilled as a writer.
2. **Clarity**—Your writing gets sharper and clearer as you come closer to saying what you really mean to say.
3. **Vision and insight**—Revising lets you see things you didn't see before, giving you insight into your subject and yourself.
4. **Gratification**—Not only is it rewarding to watch your writing improve, but it is also reaffirming to hold a finished document in your hand.
5. **Feedback**—While you may be reluctant to share the rough pages of your Mother's Notebook, you will be more inclined to

read aloud a draft in revision. Positive feedback helps neutralize negative self-talk.

6. **Validation**—With feedback comes recognition, and with recognition comes validation.
7. **Communication**—Even though writing is a private act, the written word is meant to be heard. Revised drafts can be filed in your Writing Mother's Portfolio, ready to be read aloud, e-mailed to friends, or submitted for publication.
8. **Release**—In revising a draft, you work through an idea over and over until finally you let it go.

WRITING MOTHER'S HELPER

New Visions of Revision:
From First Draft to Final Copy in 10 Easy Steps

Many books on writing offer in-depth coverage of editing—from first draft to final copy (see Appendix II for a list of books I recommend). Consider this a crash course. Except for the first and last few steps, which show you how to begin and when to be done, you don't need to shepherd every piece of writing through all ten steps. Just pick one or two that seem relevant to your particular draft. If you revise on the computer, you might want to use Microsoft Word's Track Changes feature in the menu of tools. I prefer to revise on a hard copy, with an assortment of colored pens and pencils, highlighters and Post-its. Either way, be sure to save your first draft as well as each exploratory draft along the way. If you belong to a group of Writing Mothers, you can use the 10 Easy Steps to workshop your writing in twos or threes.

As you revise your draft, repeatedly ask yourself these two guiding questions: *What works?* and *What needs work?* In other words, don't just look for what's wrong; identify what's right—and build on that. You may sometimes need to cut material, even passages you especially love, but other times you will have the opportunity to generate new material. Approach revision the same way you approach writing—with the understanding that there is no right way and the assurance that you will learn how to do it by doing it.

1. **Put it away.** Often we are too close to our writing to see it objectively. After reading over your notebook and typing up select entries, file them away in your Writing Mother's Portfolio. Wait a while—a day, a week, even a month—before choosing a piece to revise. Time and distance will give you greater perspective.

2. **See it again.** When you are ready to resume work, reread your draft as though you were seeing it for the first time. What do you like? What questions do you have? What did you learn from "re-seeing" your writing?

3. **Let your text talk.** If possible, read your draft out loud rather than silently. Reading out loud lets your ear be the editor. The text will tell you where to cut and where to add, when to speed up and when to slow down. Learn to listen to your own writing.

4. **Clarify your meaning.** According to literary legend, John Steinbeck summed up every novel he wrote (yes, even the six-hundred-pagers) on a three-by-five index card. After you read over your draft, ask yourself, *What is this story about?* On an index card, jot down five possible answers. Keep them short. You can read your draft to friends and ask them to do the same, then compare notes. Your first task in revising a story is to make sure its meaning(s) is clear. Did you say what you really meant to say?

5. **Fortify your structure.** Ernest Hemingway claimed that writing is about architecture, not interior design, by which he meant, I believe, that writing must be supported by a sound structure. Wall hangings won't stay up if the walls fall down. On a piece of paper, sketch a blueprint of your draft. How is the material organized? Where does the story begin? What

happens in the middle? How does it end? Is there a moment of tension or a turning point? You will be amazed how often a viable structure emerges organically as you write, but sometimes you may discover that your beginning, say, is buried somewhere in the middle.

6. **Test for authenticity.** Pat Schneider, in her book *Writing Alone and with Others,* credited the poet Margaret Robison as saying that "the only purpose of revision is to get more deeply to the truth." Have you told the truth, the whole truth, and nothing but the truth? Have you said everything that needs to be said about your subject? Where have you backed away from something important? What have you talked around, hinted at, or skipped over altogether? Tap the walls of your draft for hollow places. Once you have identified a hole in your story, simply open your notebook and fill in the gap.

7. **Change perspective.** John Irving, after spending six years writing the draft of a first-person novel, decided to rewrite the entire manuscript in the third person. As an experiment, see what happens if you write about yourself in the third person, using *she* instead of *I.* Writing in the third person lends objectivity and insight to the otherwise narrow perspective of personal narrative. As another way to play with perspective, try rewriting your draft in the present tense, even if you are recounting (as you probably are) an event that took place in the past. Narratives written in the present tense seem to unfold as we read them.

8. **Go for economy.** Mark Twain, in a postscript to a friend, repuledly apologized for having written such a long letter, explaining that he hadn't had time to write a short one. Now that you know what your draft is about and have said everything there is to say on the subject, ask yourself, *What is essential to my story, and what is not?* Examine your draft both at the macro level (are there unnecessary tangents and long, windy descriptions?) and at the micro level (do you really need all those adjectives and adverbs?). Make every word count. For fun, try cutting your draft in half. You can always reinstate the original, but you might discover that the condensed version is more

powerful. To ease the pain of cutting, store the deletions in a computer folder called "Junk Pile."

9. **Do the housekeeping.** Proofreading your draft is the least important activity of revision but a necessary last step in writing. Once you have rewritten your draft to your satisfaction, it is time to clean up the surfaces: word choice, spelling, punctuation, grammar, and the like. Consult grammar handbooks, usage manuals, a dictionary, and a thesaurus.

10. **Know when to quit.** Hemingway rewrote his stories more than thirty times before considering them done. But like overcooking, there is such a thing as too much revision. If you find yourself bored to death or sick and tired of a draft, it is probably time to stop revising. Only the writer knows when to quit.

Ways to Share Your Mother Pages:
Going Public

Some of my students keep their Mother's Notebook under lock and key for fear that someone else might read it. Others stop short of burning old notebooks in case they die suddenly, tragically, without having time to dispose of their personal papers. Most of us are mortified at the thought of exposing the sludge of our soul.

While I agree that the Mother's Notebook should be safeguarded as a private record, not paraded as a public document, I have seen pages go bad because they are never aired or shared. Even if you are writing for yourself alone, try to read aloud passages from your Mother's Notebook now and then, if not for critique then to hear the breath and bone of your words. If, on the other hand, you crave publicity, know that going public is not limited to submitting for publication. As you will see here, there are many ways to share your Mother Pages.

READ THEM ALOUD

Reading aloud after you write is as important as breathing out after you breathe in. Your voice may quake, your heart may pound, your cheeks may turn red, but after you read aloud your writing, you will feel relieved, perhaps even elated. If you belong to a group of Writing Mothers, you will have plenty of opportunities to share your Mother Pages. If not, you will have to make a point of find-ing the right time and the right audience. In my experience, the best time to read aloud a page from my Mother's Notebook is immediately after writing it, before the ink has had a chance to dry and my mind to judge. The right audience, though, depends on the writing. Sometimes I choose to read aloud a selection to the person I wrote about—my son, my mother, my father. Other times I choose someone who will understand what I have written. The afternoon I wrote the pages that became the chapter called "Moth-ering Our Mothers," I read them aloud on the telephone to my sis-ter Rena. She cried as she listened, which was precisely the feedback I needed at the moment—an emotional response. This brings me to the next point. Before reading aloud your pages, con-sider telling the listener how you want him or her to respond, choosing from among the suggestions in the Writing Mother's Helper that follows. In this way, your listener will understand what you want, and you will get what you need—the encouragement and affirmation to continue writing. For more ideas on ways to read aloud your writing, see "How to Start and Run a Group of Writing Mothers" on page 277.

GIVE THEM AWAY

From time to time, one of my students will read aloud a page that practically jumps out of her notebook—about a friend who saved her, a daughter who came through a frighteningly trying time, a mother whom she has finally forgiven. The rest of us unanimously insist that she copy down the page and give it away to the friend, the daughter, or the mother. Some of my students have given away their Mother Pages as gifts on birthdays and anniversaries, or as cards on Valentine's Day, Mother's Day, or Father's Day. Sometimes putting the words in print rather than saying them out loud is both more meaningful and more lasting.

Post Them Online

The easiest way to share your Mother Pages online is to e-mail them to friends and family. If you are more ambitious, you might consider posting your own mommy blog—an online version of the Mother's Notebook. Or you could join one of the many collectives of mothers who blog. For those of you who want to take the next step and submit pages for publication online, *Writer's Market Companion* is a good source for sites and links, as are a number of the resources listed in the next section. For more ideas on how to share your Mother Pages online, see "Ways to Connect in Cyberspace" on page 289.

Publish Them

Along with the recent popularity of book memoirs of motherhood, more and more magazines and newspapers are printing the personal side of parenthood. Over the years, I have managed to publish articles that offer one parent's perspective (*mine!*) on everything from instant messaging to aging out of elementary school, articles that began in the pages of my Mother's Notebook. If you have already transcribed some entries onto your computer and filed the drafts in your Writing Mother's Portfolio, you may be ready to begin submitting them for publication. I suggest you start small, as I did, with a school newsletter or town circular before submitting to the big-city newspapers and consumer magazines. In *Writer's Market* and *LMP* (*Literary Market Place*) you will find listings of publications that print articles about parenthood. Other resources include the Web sites www.authorlink.com and www.mediabistro.com. You may also want to subscribe to one of the many journals for writers, such as *Writer's Digest, The Writer, Poets & Writers,* and *Publishers Weekly.* Before you submit your writing, however, be sure to familiarize yourself with the style and content of each publication and carefully read the submission guidelines. Otherwise, as Stephen King says, you will be shooting darts in the dark. And if you think you will perish if you don't publish, you might consider *self*-publishing, an increasingly viable option for first-time authors.

INSPIRATIONS

It is important to read aloud what you write. . . . It is part of the writing process, like bending down to touch your toes and then standing up again. (NATALIE GOLDBERG)

We urge you to read your work out loud, whether you're alone or writing with others, so you can hear the music of your writing. (TODD WALTON AND MINDY TOOMAY)

Writing that has just come from the pen of a writer should not be critiqued by other people. A piece of writing, newly born, is as fragile and raw as a newborn baby, and should be treated as respectfully, as tenderly. (PAT SCHNEIDER)

With good writing, I think the most profound response is finally a sigh, or a gasp, or holy silence. (TIM O'BRIEN)

WRITING MOTHER'S HELPER

5 Ways to Respond to Readalouds

Only two people in the whole world respond exactly the way I need them to respond every time I read aloud my writing—no matter what, they make me feel like the next Anne Lamott: Deborah Chiel, my writing partner since we met at a workshop in Taos, New Mexico, five years ago; and Terry Lilienthal, wise woman and my dear friend going on four decades. Because Deborah now has a five-year-old and Terry just rounded eighty, I am on occasion obliged to read my writing to someone else, in which case I have learned that everyone is happier if I tell the person ahead of time exactly how I want him or her to respond. As a result, critique never disintegrates into criticism, and I walk away feeling bolstered up rather than beaten down. Whether you are reading to one person or to a group, be specific in your wants and needs; tell them if you like a hard touch or a light one, if you have a kink in your lower back or in your neck and shoulders. Here are five different ways a listener can respond to your writing:

1. **Emotional response.** The selection you are reading is especially close to your heart, and you want the listener to respond emotionally. Before you read, ask him or her to answer these questions: *How does it make you feel? What emotions come up?*
2. **Associative response.** Here again you are looking for a human response. You would like to know whether the listener relates to what you have written, if your personal story carries a universal truth. Before you read, ask him or her to answer these questions: *What does it make you think of? What experiences in your own life come to mind?*
3. **Affirmative response.** You are feeling particularly vulnerable at the moment and want only encouragement and affirmation. Ask your listener to respond to these directives: *Tell me three things you like. Tell me one thing you learned. Tell me one thing you would* not *change.*

4. **Evaluative response.** You feel confident in your writing, and you value this person's judgment. Make sure he understands, however, that you are looking for *critique* (constructive evaluation), not *criticism* (destructive condemnation). You may want him to answer a specific question about the selection: *Do you think this works in the third person? Does it end too abruptly?* Or you could ask her to respond to these more general questions: *What works? What needs work? What do you want to know more about? Does anything confuse you? Tell me one thing you would change.*

5. **Receptive response.** You are interested less in hearing what someone else has to say than you are in being heard. Think of this reading as a gift; you are offering the listener a glimpse into your soul, and you want him or her to respond in kind. There are two ways to elicit a receptive response to your writing. First, you can ask the listener simply to recall from memory a few lines and phrases from your text. By giving back the words you wrote, a listener naturally points to the hot spots— places in your writing that are electric or alive. Second, you can tell the listener that you want no response, except perhaps a chuckle or a head nod. More than recall, silence sends the message that you are being heard without judgment. A silent response is especially effective in large groups, where critical discussion can so easily overtake the readings.

Connections and Collaborations— Finding Other Writing Mothers

Barring summer vacations, snow days, and strep throat, once almost every week for the past four years I have driven across the George Washington Bridge and down the West Side Highway to the Cosi café on Seventy-sixth Street and Broadway for a meeting with my writing group. To call it a group is an exaggeration. There are two of us: Deborah and I. At our first meeting in the fall of 2002, a little over a year after we had met at a writing workshop, we talked about why we had come and what we hoped to gain from writing together. Based on our conversation, we drafted a mission statement and agreed on a daily schedule. Over the years, we have become increasingly lax, joking that we graduated from Writing Group 101. As a result, I must admit that on occasion we barely open our notebooks. Some weeks we don't manage to meet at all. But whenever we do write together, my writing is almost always more alive than when I write at home alone—in part, because it is suffused with the talk from neighboring tables, the clatter of the take-out counter, and the froth of the espresso machine; in part, because when I write across from Deborah, I am reminded that I am not alone. This much I know: had it not been for my writing group, I may never have written this book.

If you read the acknowledgment pages of a random sampling

of books, you will see that few writers go it alone. Although writing requires solitude, most writers are not solitary. In the same way that mothers have depended on other mothers for as long as women have been birthing children, writers have sought out other writers since we first put pen to paper. From coffeehouses to Internet cafés, from writing classes to artists' colonies, writers have come together to listen to and learn from one another through the ages. Today the popularity of coauthorship and the proliferation of anthologies suggest that collaboration and community are now considered essential components of the writing process. In this section of the book, I urge you to reach out to other Writing Mothers, either in person or online. Find a group of mothers who share your dream to write, and you will discover women who speak your language. You will find your kind.

INSPIRATIONS

Finally I had joined up with my tribe. I was not alone in that Wilderness of Uselessness. From then on I leaned on and learned from other mothers, those of the Friday morning playgroup and others they led me to. I learned by listening to their stories and telling mine. (GAYLE BOSS)

Writing can be a lonely endeavor, much of the work must be done in solitude. However, too much solitude—or too much conversation with people who do not write, and too little with those who do—can lead to depression and despair. (PAT SCHNEIDER)

The old idea of the writer as solo artist is as outdated as the belief that you can't make jam out of jalapeños. Writers can and do write in community. And they write good stuff. (JUDY REEVES)

How to Start and Run a Group of Writing Mothers

A group of Writing Mothers functions like any other writing group. The difference is that all its members are mothers who want to write about motherhood. A number of excellent books on the market today, notably *Writing Alone, Writing Together* by Judy Reeves and *Writing Alone and with Others* by Pat Schneider, cover every facet of starting and running a writing group—from the fears that keep you from joining to the signs that tell you when to move on. So that you don't feel overwhelmed, I will give you just enough information to help you get started. You can consult other sources later on as you need answers to specific questions.

There are lots of different ways to organize a group of Writing Mothers, but there is one common denominator. At the heart of every group must be unwavering trust. Notice that the words *trust* and *truth* are only one letter apart. For members to tell the truth on paper, they must trust one another in person. You may want to begin your group with an activity I use in my classes, called the Trust Game. Ask members to stand in a close circle, shoulder to shoulder, hands held in front of their bodies as if ready to catch a ball. Invite someone to volunteer to stand in the middle of the circle. With her hands crossed over her chest and her eyes closed, she can begin shifting her weight forward and back, side to side. As she starts to fall off-balance, the other members will catch her and gently pass her from one to the next around or across the circle. The feeling of near danger and sure safety is the same feeling she will have when, after writing along-side other members, she prepares to read aloud her pages. She must trust that the group will hold her up. No matter what, they will not let her down.

Because you will want every member to feel safe, your group may want to honor the same three commandments I insist on in my classes:

- **Confidentiality**—Whatever arises in this room stays in this room.
- **Receptivity**—We will listen to one another with our full attention and without criticism or judgment.
- **Privacy**—Every member reserves the right to remain silent.

Although everyone will be invited to read aloud her writing, no one will be forced to. When it is her turn to share, a member is always free to say, "I pass."

My most recent class of Writing Mothers decided to continue meeting on their own after the last session had ended. I receive their group e-mails regularly, with postings of upcoming meet-ings, apologies from individuals who have missed a week, and plans for writing retreats at one member's beach house or another's mountain cabin. Of all the years I have taught *Writing Motherhood,* this class was among my most enthusiastic. Now the group has taken on a life all its own. Based on my observations of their experience, and on my own experience as a leader and member of many writing groups, I offer you the suggestions below as you begin to think about starting or joining a group of Writing Mothers.

You do not need to read any further, however, to get started. All you need is one other person, an available space, and a regu-lar time, and you can begin getting together with another mother to write. Or you can do what one of my students, Jill, plans to do: Simply tell a few friends that every Tuesday, say, from ten-thirty until noon, you will be at your kitchen table writing, and anyone is welcome to join you.

IF YOU START IT . . . THEY WILL COME

As so many of my students have already found, writing groups naturally emerge from writing classes. Consider signing up for a writing class at a community school or area college, or take a one-day workshop at a nearby center for holistic learning. Before the end, be sure to exchange e-mail addresses or phone numbers with members who have expressed an interest in continuing to meet. If you decide to start a group from scratch, it's probably best to begin with people you know. A best friend, however, is not always the best choice, unless you feel confident that you can resist the temptation to chat. Think of mothers you've met and admired in playgroups, in Mommy & Me classes, in book clubs, on volunteer committees, and through work. They can, in turn, recommend other mothers who may be interested in joining. The parents' association of your local school is another good source for spreading the word, in PTA meetings or in the parent newsletter. You can also scout prospective members in places where writers and literary mothers hang out: at author readings, at book signings, in bookstores, and in libraries. Usually it takes only one person to initiate, and the rest will come.

THE IDEAL NUMBER

The group that emerged from my last class of *Writing Motherhood* totals twelve, a large number for writing groups but manageable in this case because the women were already comfortable with one another from class. At the other end of the spectrum is my writing group, consisting of only Deborah and me. The downside is that when one of us, or one of our children, is sick,

we can't meet. Eight is probably the ideal number—large enough
to be dynamic yet small enough to feel safe. Whatever its size, try
to include in your group mothers of all ages and stages, as well as
writers of varying styles and abilities.

TIME AND PLACE

Before you get too far, you might want to talk about logistics. *How
often will your group meet?* While once a week is optimal, every
other week, or even once a month, may be more realistic. *When
will you meet?* Decide whether it would be more convenient to
meet during the day, when your children are in school, or after
work. *How long will you meet?* Two hours is ideal, an hour and a
half minimum. *Where will you meet?* My most recent group of
Writing Mothers rotates houses to share the burden of hosting.
Another group that started from one of my classes meets at a
branch of the public library. Deborah and I continue to meet in
coffee shops and restaurants. Try to find a place where you can sit
in a circle, since circles foster a sense of intimacy and equality.
That said, members should feel free to move away from the circle
if they require more elbow room to write. Although some groups
successfully operate on a drop-in basis, whereby members come
when they can, your group will have a much better chance of lasting if people are punctual and regular in their attendance.

THE FIRST MEETING

Once your group has agreed on logistics, use the first meeting to
explore these other questions:

- *What is the purpose of your group?* Ask members to write down
  their own reasons for joining, then consider how the group can

best meet those collective goals. Together, draft a mission statement that spells out the purpose of your group, and copy it down in your Mother's Notebook. Be sure to include in the mission statement the three commandments—confidentiality, receptivity, and privacy—or any other values you believe are important to the interaction of the group. Reread your mission statement from time to time, and when necessary, revise it.

- *Should you name your group?* I think you should. A name creates cohesiveness at the same time that it sums up the group's purpose.

- *What if more people want to join?* You may want to decide on a maximum number of members and stick to it. As some people move on, others can join. In most groups, new members are referred by existing members. To make sure someone new is compatible with the group, you can suggest a trial period.

- *How will you run the group?* To begin, use *Writing Motherhood* as your blueprint. You can proceed chapter by chapter, or you can choose those chapters that interest you from week to week. Several activities described in the section "Games Writers Play" on page 295 are ideal for writing groups. My most recent group of Writing Mothers chooses two or three writing starts each time from those listed in Appendix I. After a while, your group should feel free to set out on its own. In the "Daily Schedule" that follows, I give you more specific ideas about how to run each meeting.

- *How will you respond to one another's writing?* Reading your writing aloud can be scary, even to experienced writers. Look over the "5 Ways to Respond to Readalouds" on page 273. I suggest you begin with the receptive response, since this is both the safest and most affirming, but over time you can experiment with others. Decide whether you want to respond only to writing generated during your meetings or also to writing done outside the group.

- *Who's in charge?* In group settings, leaders naturally emerge, but in writing groups everyone must have a voice. Although members will probably not assume equal responsibility for the management of the group, it's a good idea to rotate other leadership roles. In my most recent Writing Mothers group, for example, two women seem to have taken on the managerial task of sending out e-mails to poll members and schedule meetings. But other women take turns hosting, leading the meeting, selecting writing starts, and watching the clock.

- *How can you keep the group going?* As with any relationship, healthy groups manage to stay together through ups and downs, difficulties and disagreements. How? By having periodic check-ups and routine physicals. Once or twice a year, revisit some of the same questions you considered on your first meeting. Give members an opportunity to air grievances, make requests, explore options. By taking the pulse of your group now and then, you will keep its heartbeat strong.

The Daily Schedule

If your group follows a set schedule, your writing sessions will not so easily digress into social hour, a temptation for us all. Try beginning and ending your meetings the same way every time. You can open the meeting with an inspirational reading—a poem or passage from a book, the group's mission statement, or a set of affirmations. Or you can light a candle and allow a moment of silence to help members settle down. After the opening circle, allot so many minutes to writing; forty-five minutes would allow you to complete three writing starts. Then decide how much time you should devote to sharing your pages; it takes approximately three minutes to read aloud one fifteen-minute writing. You may want to set aside the last fifteen or twenty minutes as an open forum—for a question-and-answer session, discussion of writing (or mothering) issues, information exchange, notification of upcoming events, book recommendations, general announcements, as well as complaints, congratulations, and commiserations. For your closing circle, you can invite each member to state a personal goal for the week, or you can allow a final moment of silence before blowing out the candle.

A Year-End Reading

I like to host a year-end reading, called Mothers' Voices, before my classes break for summer vacation. Some years, I have held the reading in my home; more recently, in a spacious performing arts studio in town. Students read aloud a few pages from their Mother's Notebook or, for those who have begun revising their pages, a selection from their Writing Mother's Portfolio. More formal than the weekly readalouds, Mothers' Voices gives us the opportunity to honor one another's writing in a serious, supportive way. Consider organizing a year-end reading, especially if your group has been writing together for many months. To underscore the importance of the event, hold the reading at a new venue and invite family and friends. Instead of sitting in a circle, arrange the chairs in a semicircle or in rows, with a single chair or podium facing the audience. Determine in advance the content and order of readings (you can circulate a sign-up sheet the week before), and reserve all commentary until everyone has finished reading. While I discourage food and drink during regular weekly meetings, for the year-end event you may want to serve wine and cheese or tea and cookies afterward.

Beyond the Group

The most successful groups break the boundaries of the weekly meetings with forays into the outside world. Deborah and I, for example, try to plan a few field trips throughout the year—to a bookstore, an author reading, a writing workshop, or another literary event. If your group is game, you can also schedule a daylong or overnight writing retreat once a year. Perhaps someone in your group has a weekend or summer house she is willing to offer. Such shared experiences will bring renewed energy to your regular meetings, as they have to mine.

INSPIRATIONS

I don't know how to express the almost ecstatic experience that rather frequently happens when people write together and affirm one another's new work. There are so few places in our normal social lives where we are privileged to meet one another so vulnerably—to laugh and cry and laugh again. (PAT SCHNEIDER)

In writing groups, we bear witness to each other's efforts, we learn from one another, and spark each other's creativity. We share camaraderie and create community. (JUDY REEVES)

There's nothing like knowing a group meeting is coming up to get you writing. It's a deadline, in a way, but a nonthreatening one. (ELIZABETH BERG)

WRITING MOTHER'S HELPER

8 Reasons to Join a Group of Writing Mothers

You may be content to write on your own for months, even years, but you will eventually need the support of a community of writers. As you begin to think about joining a group, consider these compelling reasons to write with other mothers:

1. **Community**—Both writing and mothering are lonely endeavors. By joining a community of mothers who write, you will connect with women who share your interests and ideals. In a group of Writing Mothers, you will find kindred spirits who speak your language.

2. **Support**—In a group, you will be taken seriously as a mother who writes and a writer who mothers; you will not have to explain or excuse your writing. What's more, as you read aloud your Mother Pages, you can trust that the group will listen with compassion and interest.

3. **Structure**—Few of us have the confidence or the commitment to write on our own. We need a set time and place to show up to write. As a member of a writing group, you will have not only the structure of the weekly meetings but also the impetus to write between meetings. Joining a group of Writing Mothers can make the difference between continuing and quitting.

4. **Craft**—Without your knowing it, you will naturally develop your craft as you listen to other mothers read aloud their writing. This is why it is best to welcome members of different styles and abilities. Sometimes you can learn more from the beginning writer, who is unschooled and experimental, than you can from the polished writer who prefers to play it safe.

5. **Courage**—As you listen to other mothers take risks and break taboos on paper, you, too, will be become more honest and more courageous as a writer.

6. **Faith**—Already worn down by external pressures and internal

criticism, we mothers can easily talk ourselves *out* of writing. On our own, we quickly lose confidence and conviction. Groups help us keep the faith.

7. **Information**—During readalouds, you will learn from other members both about writing and about mothering. But you may want to set aside a few minutes each week for a formal information exchange, when members can share news of upcoming events, tips on publishing, and other helpful information. Each member can give freely in her area of expertise.

8. **Cooperation**—In a world undermined by *one-ups-momship,* it is liberating to belong to a circle of mothers in which everyone is on an equal footing. A well-run group of Writing Mothers discourages competition and fosters cooperation.

WRITING MOTHER'S HELPER

6 Pitfalls of Writing Groups— and How to Avoid Them

Most writing groups are not run by trained leaders, so members must take it upon themselves to address problems as they arise. Here are six solutions to the most common problems of writing groups:

1. **One person dominates.** Without a professional to lead your group, an aggressive personality can easily take over. This is the person who is first to read aloud her writing, and first to comment on someone else's writing. Once she starts talking, she doesn't know when to stop. The solution is to rotate the leader each week, so that over time every member will have an opportunity to take charge. The job of the leader is to open and close the meeting and to navigate the group through the

daily schedule while managing interpersonal dynamics as best she can.

2. **One person defers.** If in her personal life a member is accustomed to tending to everyone else's needs before considering her own, as many mothers are, then it might be difficult for her to negotiate time for herself in a writing group. Her inclination to defer may translate into a disinclination to read aloud her writing. She may also not feel free to contribute to group discussion. The success of a group depends on the equal participation of all members, regardless of their ability as writers or experience as mothers. Even so, no one should feel pressured to contribute in a way that does not feel safe to her. When the time seems right, the leader can gently ask this person, *Would you like to read today?* or *Is there anything you would like to add?*

3. **Attendance is spotty.** Nothing will kill a group more quickly than members who are on-again, off-again. Anyone who wants to join your group must commit to showing up regularly. If, in spite of her best intentions, one member repeatedly misses because a child is sick, a toilet overflows, or her mother is in the hospital, then perhaps this is not the right time for her to belong to a writing group.

4. **Someone always arrives late or leaves early.** If you wait for everyone to arrive before getting started, members will have no incentive to be punctual. The most effective meetings are run by the clock. They begin and end precisely on time. Those who arrive late will get the message; those who must leave early should do so on tiptoe. Ritualistic openings and closings make it easier for the leader to begin and end on time.

5. **Our writing time is giving way to social hour.** As groups gel and friendships evolve, it becomes harder and harder to stay on task. There is so much to talk about! Now more than ever, you need to follow your daily schedule. You may want to assign a timekeeper to help the leader watch the clock.

6. **The group is losing focus.** If you find yourselves spending more time talking and less time writing, your group may be

losing sight of its purpose. Reread the mission statement from time to time. You may need to redraft it as your individual and group goals change. As in any relationship, the key to a lasting group is its ability to adapt as its members evolve.

WRITING MOTHER'S HELPER

Sample Mission Statement for a Group of Writing Mothers

Four years after we first met as a writing group, Deborah and I made several changes: when and where we meet, as well as how we conduct each session. What has *not* changed, however, is our purpose—the reasons that first brought us together to write. Use our mission statement to help you clarify your group's purpose:

Writing Mothers is a community of NYC-area mothers who support one another in living the writing life. Our purpose is:

- *to write together in weekly meetings that inspire us to continue writing on our own;*
- *to explore and celebrate our writing voices in readalouds, during which we listen to one another's writing with compassion and without criticism;*
- *to help one another meet our personal goals as writers—both our weekly objectives and our long-term dreams; and*
- *to encourage one another to attend writing events outside of the group.*

Note: Our group is intended to be a support and inspiration, not a responsibility or guilt trip.

Ways to Connect in Cyberspace

Both for the modern mother who is more inclined to text-message than to telephone and for the traditional mother who still feels like an alien in cyberspace, the Internet is today's equivalent of the park bench. At any time of the day or night, while your baby is napping or when your child is home sick from school, you can confess, commiserate, and collude with other mothers online. Web sites offer forums for mothers to share their hair-pulling, heart-wrenching experiences raising children. So-called mommy blogs, online diaries transmitted by shell-shocked mothers from the trenches of parenthood, give the blow-by-blow accounts of our compatriots. And search engines grant mothers instant information on every subject from hiccups to head banging. Even if you consider yourself old, you don't have to be old-fashioned. Plenty of grandmothers in my classes e-mail their grandchildren and surf the Web. You may want to begin by visiting the *Writing Motherhood* Web site (www.writingmotherhood.com). Then you can consider these other ways to connect with mothers down the block, across the country, and around the world.

SEND AN E-MAIL

Sometimes we do our best writing in e-mails. Spontaneous, candid, and conversational, electronic messages capture an immediacy that other forms of writing fail to achieve. When we write an e-mail, we write in the moment, without forethought or reflection, and the next moment we get instant feedback. I recommend that you save or print favorite e-mails and store them in a computer file or paper folder. One of my students hopes to self-publish a series of e-mails she sent over the years to her grandchildren. Another recently asked me to read a string of e-correspondence written a few years ago by girlfriends struggling to adjust to new motherhood. Although e-mailing can generate some good writing, its greatest appeal is the flexibility it affords us to communicate with other mothers on our own terms and according to our own schedule.

START OR JOIN A LOOP

If you find yourself carrying on several e-conversations at once, either by e-mail or instant message, you may know enough women to start a loop of mothers who write. The purpose of a loop is not to promote online discussion or exchange, as you will find in a chat room and on a message board, but rather to encourage members to write independently in their notebooks daily. Lots of writers belong to online writing loops, many of which organically emerge from classes and workshops. (I joined one through a workshop taught by Natalie Goldberg, for instance.) Some of these, especially the large ones, are managed through free services like Yahoo! Groups, which make it simple to archive messages, share photos, coordinate events, poll members, and create links.

It is easy enough to administer a loop on your own, however. Through the address-book feature of AOL and other servers, you can generate a list of e-mail addresses and assign the group a name. In this way, you can send the same message to as many people as you wish with just one click of the button. As host, you would provide a daily or weekly Invitation in the form of a writing start, along with an Inspiration or quote by a well-known writer or mother. I suggest you rotate the role of host to share responsibility for administering the loop. While you may want to e-mail one another the pages you write, knowing that other mothers are using the same writing start each day is usually enough to keep most members in the loop.

POST A BLOG

That you have opened this book and read this far tells me that you may be someone who prefers to remain on earth rather than travel through cyberspace. Still, blogs—or Web logs—can be a great way to find a readership for your writing. Mothers, long isolated and alone, were among the first group to infiltrate the blogosphere. Today thousands of mothers post daily entries in online diaries, and tens of thousands more sign on each day to read and respond to the around-the-clock accounts of life on the home front. Mothers blog for a variety of reasons: to document their lives, to stay in touch with friends and family, to connect with other mothers. Some women claim their online diaries have saved them—from rage, depression, and boredom. Others hope their blog will lead to a book deal.

To help you decide whether blogging is for you, read a sampling of blogs to get an idea of the possibilities and pitfalls. Ask friends for the Web addresses of their favorite postings, or visit one of the many online collectives of women and mothers who blog. (BlogHer, DotMoms, DiaryLand, and Blogging Mommies are good sites to browse.) If you decide you are ready to get started, any of the collectives will point you in the right direction, either by hosting your blog or by linking you to a blog builder. Free platforms are offered through Yahoo!, Google, and MSN, but you can get more sophisticated features through boutique servers such as BlogHer, Six Apart, and WordPress, in some cases for a small fee.

Because blogs make public what literary tradition has long considered private—the confessional pages of a diary or journal—consider whether you would be inspired or inhibited by an audience reading over your shoulder as you write. And keep in mind that writing a blog is not the same as writing in a notebook. A blog may give voice to your writing, but your notebook will help you find your voice and develop your craft as a writer.

SURF THE WEB

To get your feet wet, you might want to check out the Web sites of books and authors you love. Most domain names derive from the author's first and last name (www.annaquindlen.com) or from the title of the book (www.penonfire.com). There you will find information about the author, news of upcoming workshops and appearances, reviews and excerpts of books, along with links to other sites. Some author Web sites feature blogs and e-mail loops as well.

If you are interested in joining an online community, check out one of the larger Web sites that cater to women and mothers, such as www.iVillage.com, www.salon.com, www.urbanbaby.com, and www.babycenter.com. With so many connections and so much daily traffic, these sites can seem like Grand Central Station to mothers commuting through cyberspace, but it won't take long before you feel like a seasoned traveler. In addition to providing information and advice, these sites offer lots of opportunities for interaction. You can ask questions and get answers in theme-based message boards; carry on conversations in topic-specific chat rooms; read and write blogs; sign up for e-classes; and subscribe or submit to online publications.

CHECK OUT THE E-STANDS

If you are a fan of a consumer magazine for writers or mothers, visit its Web site, which is more interactive than the paper counterpart, with opportunities to join boards, post blogs, and submit stories for publication. Along with the mainstream magazines, look for the smaller publications you won't find on most newsstands—both the literary journals and the elite magazines that treat motherhood as literature. *Brain, Child,* for example, not only publishes essays and fiction by well-known authors but also features stories from readers in a column called "Backtalk." *Mothering,* which relies heavily on submissions from readers, publishes parent-authored essays and poems and hosts an online writing group for mothers. And *Literary Mama,* started by a group of writers in the San Francisco Bay Area, claims to be the first literary magazine devoted solely to writing about motherhood. In addition to publishing high-quality fiction and nonfiction, poetry and profiles, the site hosts a blog and an e-zine with dispatches and updates delivered directly to your e-mailbox.

INSPIRATIONS

Whenever I send an e-mail to another mother at 1 in the morning and I get an e-mail right back, I always feel like I want to cry because it feels so good to know I'm not alone. This is a hard job. As isolated and exhausted as you may feel, knowing that 25 other women on your block are doing the same thing, I think, is comforting. (KATE MOSES)

We quickly learned that women who were starved for companionship and intelligent conversation would be online reading it wherever they could—while breast-feeding or in the middle of the night, when they were awake with hot flashes. Now, of course, the Internet has become a major source of information and communication for mothers. (Camille Peri)

For many mothers, reading and writing blogs is a great way to feel less isolated and to learn from the experiences of women you might not otherwise meet. They may be different from you in lots of ways and yet you find more common ground than you expect. (Julie Moos)

Games Writers Play

The minute writing begins to feel like another chore on our list, we mothers, who already feel overworked and underappreciated, will be the first to put down our pens. The following games can help restore the joy of writing. Most of the games can be played alone, but they generate more laughter and spark more surprise when played with a partner or in a group of Writing Mothers. I suggest you read over the directions ahead of time so you will be sure to have the necessary supplies. For most of the games, you will want to keep a stopwatch on hand. Remember, you can be serious about your writing without taking yourself too seriously.

CIRCLE WRITING (FOR GROUPS ONLY)

For this game, you will need a stack of paper, preferably lined, and a sampling of first lines borrowed from published novels, short stories, and essays or taken from one another's notebooks. (See "Unforgettable First Lines" on page 112 for a list to get you started.) Sit in a circle and advise players to write legibly but quickly. The game will lose momentum if individuals take too long to complete each go-round. Each player begins by copying down a borrowed first line at the top of a sheet of paper. When everyone is ready, pass the papers one person to the right. Each player silently reads the sentence at the top of the page, then adds a second sentence to the story. After a few minutes, pass the papers to the right again. Continue around the circle until the papers return to their original writers (if your group is small, you may want to make several go-rounds). Take turns reading aloud the collaborations. Be prepared to laugh.

PARTNER WRITING

Partner writing is a variation of circle writing. All you need is one other person, but the game can be played in groups, too, with alternating partners each time you play. Follow the instructions outlined above, except instead of passing the papers in a circle you will exchange them with a partner ten times. As a variation, allow more time for each go-round. Instead of limiting yourselves to one sentence, try writing as many as two or three, even a whole paragraph, before exchanging papers. If you are doing partner writing within a group, be sure to read aloud the collaborations to everyone.

ALPHASSOCIATION

For this game, you will free-associate to letters of the alphabet, proceeding sequentially from *A* to *Z* or randomly choosing a letter each time you play. Let's say you picked the letter *G*. On a blank page in your Mother's Notebook, write down *G is for . . .* and begin listing words that begin with the letter *G*. *G is for great, G is for gasoline, G is for graduation, G is for grown-up, G is for grandma, G is for glass.* When you hit on a G-word that resonates, follow the memories and associations wherever they lead you. *The street came to me through a prism of glass bottles, in shades of rose, amber, and jade, that stood in staggering sizes along the windowsill of my mother's kitchen.* Write for fifteen minutes. Then choose another letter. You can play the game twenty-six times!

DICTIONARY

This game lets you thumb through the dictionary without having to read it cover to cover, as some writers claim to have done at least once in their lifetime. Open your dictionary to any page (say, 1,184 of *Webster's Ninth*) and choose the first word that catches your attention. You may like the way the word looks or sounds (*supersonic*); you may find it evocative or controversial (*superstition*); or you may be curious to know what it means (*supinate*). Don't bother to read the definition, though. Just copy down the word on a page in your Mother's Notebook and use it as a writing start. Write down anything that comes to mind, or everything you know about the word. If you are playing the game in a group of Writing Mothers, pass the dictionary around the circle until each player has chosen her word. To add an element of surprise, have each player choose a word for the person to her right and so on around the circle.

THE THESAURUS GAME

A variation of Dictionary, this game makes use of the numerical system for grouping related words in a standard thesaurus. To play the game, pick a number from 1 to 1,000. Now locate the word that correlates with that number in your thesaurus: *889 Hopelessness, 62 Disorder, 537 Memory, 997 Sobriety, 352 Weight.* You may choose the lead word or any of the related words listed within the grouping. (*Burden,* for example, is among the words listed as a synonym for *weight.*) Copy down the word on a page in your Mother's Notebook and use it as a writing start. Write for fifteen minutes. If you play the game in a group, take turns picking the number and selecting the word.

The Writer's Palette

Words to the writer are like colors to the painter; there are so many shades of meaning. This game, while fun to play, will train you to be more precise in your choice of words. Choose a primary color—say, *red*—and, taking turns around the circle, generate a list of words that connote the color red: *garnet, ruby, rose, burgundy, crimson, maroon, scarlet, vermilion, rust, cherry, cinnamon,* and so on. Now write for fifteen minutes about the color red—an object, a memory, an association. The only stipulation is that you can't use the word *red* in your writing. Read aloud your pages, then play the game again, this time choosing a different color from the Writer's Palette.

Loaded Words

So-called *loaded words* carry connotations beyond their dictionary definitions; they mean different things to different people. Examples include swear words, racial slurs, social taboos, or words with religious, political, or sexual innuendos (*fuck, retard, incest, masturbation, redneck*). You know a word is loaded if it musters up controversy, incites an argument, or produces a physiological reaction. In casual conversation, we politely talk around loaded words, which is one reason why they make such explosive writing starts. Ask each player to jot down a loaded word on a piece of paper and fold it in half twice. Place the folded notes in a basket and pass the basket around the circle. Each player blindly chooses a note, silently reads the loaded word, then uses it as a writing start. Write for fifteen minutes. Return the folded notes to the basket and repeat the game three times before reading aloud your writing.

GRAB BAG OF WRITING STARTS

Props, or three-dimensional prompts, inspire us to enlist all our senses. When we write about an object, we can look at it, touch it, smell it, taste it, and listen to it. What's more, an object holds a different story for every person who holds that object in her hands. To play the game, you will need to collect a variety of props and hide them in a grab bag. The objects can be chosen randomly from your house and yard, or they can loosely be related by theme (motherhood, childhood, sex, travel, food). The following objects relate to the theme of motherhood: a kitchen timer, a yo-yo, a box of Band-Aids, baby wipes, a report card, a retainer case, a package of macaroni and cheese, *Goodnight Moon*, birthday candles, a Barbie doll, a training bra, a thermometer. If you are playing the game in a group, pass the grab bag around the circle and have each player choose an object without looking. The element of surprise is key. Also, try to refrain from conversation so you can channel the energy onto the page. Then give yourselves fifteen minutes to write. Return the objects to the grab bag and play the game again. Take turns assembling a collection, or have each player bring in two or three objects to add to the Grab Bag of Writing Starts.

WRITING OFF THE PAGE

This game invites you to use the written word as inspiration for your own writing. If you are writing in someone's home, in a library, or even in a café, you will have access to plenty of published materials. Otherwise, be sure to bring along a stack of books, magazines, and newspapers. To play the game, choose a word, phrase, or line from a publication and use it as a writing start. Any word that jumps off the page for any reason makes a good writing start: the title of a book, the first line of a novel or short story, a verse from a poem, a headline from a newspaper or magazine, an item on a menu, a place-name on a map, lyrics from a song, instructions in a cookbook, ingredients on a can, directions to a board game. Copy down the word or phrase on a page in your Mother's Notebook and write for fifteen minutes. If you are writing with a partner or in a group, take turns lifting words off the page.

WRITING OFF THE WALL

A variation of Writing off the Page, this game lets you broaden your search by scavenging for words in the real world. As you go through your day, scour walls for interesting words and phrases and copy them down on a page in your Mother's Notebook. You will find words everywhere: on storefronts, office buildings, bulletin boards, posters, flyers, banners, flags, billboards, buses, trucks, even road signs. Don't overlook the graffiti on subway cars and in bathroom stalls. To play the game, either alone or with others, choose one of the words or phrases from your list and use it as a writing start. If anyone asks what you are doing, tell them you are Writing off the Wall.

WRITING OFF THE CALENDAR

As mothers, our days are dictated by the calendar, so why not use national holidays and school schedules as inspiration for writing? Halloween, Thanksgiving, Hanukkah and Christmas, Passover and Easter, Labor Day and Memorial Day, Valentine's Day and Mother's Day, birthdays and anniversaries—all the holidays are filled with stories. To play the game, look at the calendar and choose a holiday that resonates with memories and associations, or one that is fast approaching. Alone or in a group, generate a list of things you associate with that holiday. For Halloween, your list might look like this: *candy corn, costumes, face paint, pumpkins, ghost stories, skeletons, spiderwebs, haunted houses, trick or treat, cabbage night.* For birthdays, it might look like this: *invitations, party favors, balloons, birthday cakes, add-a-pearl necklaces, sweet sixteen, gift wrap, presents, thank-you cards.* Now choose one item on your list and turn it into a writing start: *Write about her first Halloween costume. Carving pumpkins. Give me a memory of trick-or-treating. Who are your ghosts? Write about his favorite birthday cake. Her first birthday. Turning twelve. Who didn't come to the party?* Write for fifteen minutes. Repeat three times. Because holidays are festive occasions, if you are writing in a group, you may want to create atmosphere with decorations, music, gifts, or food.

INSPIRATIONS

A little fun can go a long way toward making your work feel more like play. We forget that the imagination-at-play is at the heart of all good work. (JULIA CAMERON)

Taking your writing seriously doesn't mean giving up the fun of it. Playing with words—squeezing out the sound of them, arranging them on the page in nonsensical visual dollops—is a delightful way to get some fun back into your work.
(JUDY REEVES)

Afterword

Your Mother's Notebook
Will Keep You Afloat

I started work on *Writing Motherhood* in the spring of 2003. To begin, I was mad with ideas, sketching feverishly on the backs of cardio schedules at the gym and in the margins of take-out menus at deli counters and Chinese restaurants. I filled two and a half notebooks in three months. Then one day I stopped, breathless, unsure how to proceed. So I did what my eighth-grade English teacher had taught me to do. I wrote an outline. But the 8½-by-11-inch paper could not contain the mess of my imagination, so I drove one morning to Staples and purchased a three-panel presentation board—black foam core—along with Post-its in assorted neon colors. Summer arrived and still the board remained mostly blank—except for major headings such as Introduction, Part One, Part Two, Part Three. More worrisome, I had not yet begun the long trek from the rough pages of my notebook to the neat copy of my computer. As the weeks passed, I began to feel at once hunted by the book and haunted by the fear that it would never get written. I couldn't sleep. I couldn't eat. When my writing group reconvened in September after summer break, I slumped across the table and said, "If I don't write this book, I am going to die."

Not long after, I found a pea-sized lump in my right breast. I

Afterword

was sitting in bed, peeling off a stretch camisole, when the meaty heel of my right hand brushed past a pointy sharpness where before there had been only gelatinous fat. I knew. I knew even before I went to see Dr. Leipzig, who sent me to Dr. Levy, who referred me to Dr. Cody.

At first, I could not write. My therapist kept telling me that illness is an important chapter of *Writing Motherhood*. Mothers get sick. But I was afraid that if I wrote the words down, the events happening to me would be real. Then I could not *not* write. I wrote in waiting rooms, in doctors' offices, at the foot of my children's beds while they slept. I wrote down what the doctors told me, and I wrote down what I planned to tell my children. From diagnosis through treatment and recovery, *Writing Motherhood* was a lifeline. My Mother's Notebook kept me afloat.

The next September, I arrived for the first fall meeting of my writing group with the beginnings of a manuscript under my arm. Remembering what I had said twelve months before, I sat tall and said, "If I write this book, I will live." My yoga teacher tells me that no one is so powerful as to be the cause or the cure of illness. I do not mean to imply such omnipotence. Rather, I want to say that, for me, choosing to write is evidence of choosing to live.

Appendix I

NO END TO WRITING STARTS:
A LIST TO KEEP YOU GOING

As you near the end of *Writing Motherhood*, you may feel anxious about setting out on your own. Where once you were eager to know how to get started, now you want to know how to keep going. Here is a list of ninety-nine writing starts that will keep you writing for weeks to come. Some of the writing starts ask you to answer a question: *What room in your house is off-limits?* Some give a command or directive: *Write about a favorite or fearsome teacher.* Others suggest a general topic to write about: *brown-bag lunches, snow days, a bad babysitter.* Still others provide a phrase that will jump-start your first sentence: *On the day you were born . . . If I knew then what I know now. . . .* Most of the writing starts will inspire you to write about your experiences as a mother, but don't be surprised if some days you find yourself writing about *your* mother, *your* childhood, *your* memories. Motherhood has an uncanny way of bringing each of us back home, face-to-face with the bare bones of our past. All you need to do is grab a writing start and start writing—two Mother Pages every day.

1. Tell me everything you know about motherhood.
2. Write about maternity clothes.
3. On the day you were born . . .

4. The color pink or blue.

5. My mother never told me . . .

6. My father always said . . .

7. Give me a memory of the tooth fairy.

8. Baby teeth.

9. What do you have to say about television?

10. Write down the recipe for a meal you cook regularly.

11. What is your child's favorite food?

12. Dinnertime at my house is . . .

13. What is your policy on fast food (or junk food)?

14. A visit to the doctor or dentist.

15. Best friends.

16. What did you pack for your last trip?

17. Tell me everything you remember about an airplane ride.

18. When I think of coming home from vacation . . .

19. Write about a time you moved.

20. Give me a memory of sleepaway camp.

21. Name labels.

22. Write about being homesick.

23. These are the things I fear most. . . .

24. What does your child want to be when he or she grows up?

25. Write about something you still have from childhood.

26. Hand-me-downs.

27. A bad babysitter.

28. Describe a time you watched your child through a window.

29. Write about holding hands.

30. Training wheels.

31. Footsteps.

32. Tell me the directions to your child's school.

33. Write about a route you drive daily.

34. Car seats (or seat belts).

35. I am thinking of the first (or last) day of school. . . .

36. Write down everything you remember about back-to-school night.

37. Write about a homework assignment.
38. Recount a parent-teacher conference.
39. Crossing guards.
40. Tell me everything you know about the school cafeteria.
41. Brown-bag lunches.
42. School photos.
43. Give me a memory of gym class.
44. Write about a time your child got detention.
45. Write about a favorite (or fearsome) teacher.
46. The school principal.
47. Report cards.
48. What do you know about school lockers?
49. Snow days.
50. Holiday cards.
51. Give me a memory of a birthday party.
52. Make-believe.
53. Board games.
54. Tell me about a bad habit.
55. Write about the mother next door.
56. I remember her (or his) first haircut. . . .
57. A telephone call.
58. Describe a scary movie.
59. Nightmares.
60. Write about bedtime.
61. In the middle of the night . . .
62. Nursery rhymes.
63. A favorite picture book.
64. What did you find in his or her pocket?
65. If I knew then what I know now . . .
66. Sleepovers.
67. Write about winning or losing a game.
68. Music (or dance) lessons.
69. Brothers and sisters.
70. Tell me everything you know about teenagers.

71. Write about shaving.
72. What do you have to say about pierced ears?
73. Recount an argument or fight.
74. Driving lessons.
75. Write about a household appliance.
76. Dirty laundry.
77. What room in your house is off-limits?
78. Unmade beds.
79. Write about a rule you enforce.
80. Table manners.
81. Write about a lie someone told.
82. Tell me everything you know about breasts.
83. Before I became a mother . . .
84. After he became a father . . .
85. Write about the last time you had sex.
86. Birth control.
87. The bathroom scale.
88. The first time she got her period . . .
89. The last time you saw him naked . . .
90. Training bras.
91. On not having a son (or daughter).
92. Write about a high fever.
93. Give me a memory of potty training.
94. Stepmothers.
95. Describe the first time you met your mother-in-law.
96. When I think of my mother, I think of her . . .
97. Write about a grandparent.
98. I don't want my children to know . . .
99. These are the things I will never forget. . . .

Appendix II

A WRITING MOTHER'S LIBRARY: RECOMMENDED READING

I end every session of *Writing Motherhood* with a celebration of our writing. One by one, students come forward to read aloud pages from their Mother's Notebook. Some laugh or cry as they read; a few hyperventilate; one or two turn beet red. Afterward, everyone feels exhilarated, exhausted—and hungry. I cannot send my students out into the world without nourishment, any more than I can send my children off to school without breakfast. So we eat. And while we eat, we share *booktales,* passing around treasured books like hors d'oeuvres on a tray. As a final offering, I give you a list of the books that sit on the shelves next to my desk, those that have been most significant to my development as a writer over the years. You are already familiar with many of them, as I have referred to these titles and quoted these authors again and again throughout my book. May they nourish you, as they have nourished me, on your continuing journey through *Writing Motherhood.*

BOOKS ON WRITING

Your local bookstore most likely stocks a variety of classic books on the craft of writing. The titles listed here combine inspirational wisdom with practical guidance on how to write from the text of your own life.

Aronie, Nancy Slonim. 1998. *Writing from the Heart: Tapping the Power of Your Inner Voice.* New York: Hyperion.

Cameron, Julia. 1992. *The Artist's Way: A Spiritual Path to Higher Creativity.* New York: Putnam Books.

Dillard, Annie. 1990. *The Writing Life.* New York: HarperPerennial.

Goldberg, Natalie. 2000. *Thunder and Lightning: Cracking Open the Writer's Craft.* New York: Bantam Books.

————. 1990. *Wild Mind: Living the Writer's Life.* New York: Bantam Books.

————. 1986. *Writing Down the Bones: Freeing the Writer Within.* Boston: Shambhala.

Heard, Georgia. 1995. *Writing Toward Home: Tales and Lessons to Find Your Way.* Portsmouth, NH: Heinemann.

King, Stephen. 2000. *On Writing: A Memoir of the Craft.* New York: Scribner.

Lamott, Anne. 1994. *Bird by Bird: Some Instructions on Writing and Life.* New York: Anchor Books.

Lauber, Lynn. 2004. *Listen to Me: Writing Life into Meaning.* New York: Norton.

Murray, Donald. 1984. *Write to Learn.* Fort Worth: Holt, Reinhart and Winston.

Reeves, Judy. 1999. *A Writer's Book of Days: A Spirited Companion and Lively Muse for the Writing Life.* Novato, CA: New World Library.

————. 2002. *Writing Alone, Writing Together: A Guide for Writers and Writing Groups.* Novato, CA: New World Library.

Romano, Tom. 1995. *Writing with Passion: Life Stories, Multiple Genres.* Portsmouth, NH: Heinemann.

Roorbach, Bill. 1998. *Writing Life Stories: How to Make Memories into Memoirs, Ideas into Essays, and Life into Literature.* Cincinnati: Story Press.

Schneider, Pat. 2003. *Writing Alone and with Others.* New York: Oxford University Press.

Zinsser, William, ed. 1987. *Inventing the Truth: The Art and Craft of Memoir.* Boston: Houghton Mifflin.

BOOKS ON MOTHERHOOD

The following books and anthologies provide models of how to write about motherhood. Whether they are told in fiction or in memoir, by a single author or as a part of a collection, the stories and essays explore every facet of motherhood—from birthing and raising our children to remembering and mourning our mothers.

Cahill, Susan, and Shirley Abbott, eds. 1988. *Mothers: Memories, Dreams and Reflections by Literary Daughters.* New York: Meridian Books.

Cheever, Susan. 2001. *As Good as I Could Be: A Memoir of Raising Wonderful Children in Difficult Times.* New York: Simon & Schuster.

Davey, Moyra, ed. 2001. *Mother Reader: Essential Writings on Motherhood.* New York: Seven Stories Press.

Kenison, Katrina. 2000. *Mitten Strings for God: Reflections for Mothers in a Hurry.* New York: Warner Books.

Kenison, Katrina, and Kathleen Hirsch, eds. 1996. *Mothers: Twenty Stories of Contemporary Motherhood.* New York: North Point Press.

Lamott, Anne. 1994. *Operating Instructions: A Journal of My Son's First Year.* New York: Fawcett Columbine.

————. 1999. *Traveling Mercies: Some Thoughts on Faith.* New York: Anchor Books.

Leibovich, Lori, ed. 2006. *Maybe Baby: 28 Writers Tell the Truth about Skepticism, Infertility, Baby Lust, Childlessness, Ambivalence, and How They Made the Biggest Decision of Their Lives.* New York: HarperCollins.

Acknowledgments

My children and I have an agreement: I get to write about them now; they get to write about me later. Still, I am eternally grateful to my children for being the source of my inspiration and the subject of my stories. Thank you, Colette, for coming to me as an old soul; your wisdom and compassion far outpace your years—you enrich my life. And thank you, Miles, for your sensitivity and boundless enthusiasm; you light up my days.

Tracy Brown, my agent, has miraculously foreseen every step along the path from proposal to publication. Thank you, Tracy, for your initial enthusiasm and ongoing assurance. Samantha Martin, my editor, somehow always knows when to press and when to let up. Thank you, Sam, for your keen encouragement and quiet counsel. Jamie Moss, my good friend and book publicist, has given so generously of her expertise. Thank you, Jamie, for so tactfully and tirelessly spreading the word.

I want to thank all of my teachers—too numerous to name—and all of the authors whose words appear in my book. I also want to thank all of my students—you know who you are. Over the years, you have taught me more than I could ever hope to teach you.

I thank Terry Lilienthal, wise woman and dear friend, who opened her house and her heart to the writing of this book. I thank Pamela Hill Epps, my lifelong friend and soul mate. Pam, we will grow old together. I thank my friend and co-mother Dana

Hopper. Thank you, Dana, for all that you do every day, and for reading my manuscript pages so lovingly and thoughtfully. I thank my healers—Rachel Gertner and Lynne Sacher—and my doctors—Shari Leipzig, Anne Moore, Hiram Cody, and Patricia Hicks—for keeping me healthy in body and spirit. I am also indebted to Kathy Brenner for her faith and friendship, and for placing that phone call. And Deborah Chiel—where do I start? You are my writing partner, unofficial editor, publishing coach, and true friend. Not a day goes by when I don't give thanks for the summer you and I found each other in Taos.

I am filled with gratitude for my parents, Sumner and Shirley Matison, for always listening to me, trusting me, encouraging me to do whatever it was I dreamed of doing. Thank you, Dad, for your wisdom and wit and gentle way. And thank you, Mom, for your big heart, open arms, and intuitive knowing. I am the mother I am because of you. I thank my dear aunt, Estelle Rogers, who has been a second mother to me since the day I was born. Thank you, Estelle, for pointing me down the path of creativity. I thank my sister, Rena Matison Greenblatt, for her loyalty and love, and, most recently, for being a partner in parenting our parents. And I offer a prayer to my brother, Jason Matison, who is smiling now, I know.

Finally, how can I begin to thank my husband, Mark, for his constant support and unwavering love? For years, Mark has given me the space to write without expectation—never doubting, always believing. He has nurtured the writer in me with the same devotion with which he has fathered our two children. If I had it to do over again, Mark, I would choose you.

About the Author

Lisa Garrigues is an award-winning writer and an experienced educator. She has taught English at the middle and high school levels, in public and independent schools. In addition to teaching *Writing Motherhood,* she leads a variety of workshops in memoir and personal narrative. She has an undergraduate degree from the University of California at Berkeley and a master's in education from Teachers College, Columbia University. Ms. Garrigues lives in Ridgewood, New Jersey, with her husband and two children.